# ONE ON THE GROUND

# ONE ON THE GROUND

The Story of One Family Before, During, and After
Continental Flight 3407 Crashed Into Their Home

## Karen Wielinski

LIBRASTREAM

BUFFALO, NEW YORK

Rights and Permissions: john@librastream.com

www.OneOnTheGround.com

Hardcover ISBN: 978-1-68061-006-2
Trade Paperback ISBN: 978-1-68061-007-9
Ebook ISBN: 978-1-68061-008-6

Cover Design and Interior Layout by Leslie Taylor
Buffalo Creative Group | buffalocreativegroup.com

Cataloging-in-Publication Data

Names:      Wielinski, Karen, author.

Title:      One on the ground : the story of one family before, during, and after Continental Flight 3407 crashed into their home / Karen Wielinski.

Description:      Buffalo, New York : Librastream, [2017]

Identifiers:      ISBN: 978-1-68061-006-2 (hardcover) | 978-1-68061-007-9 (trade paperback) | 978-1-68061-008-6 (ebook) | LCCN: 2016960132

Subjects:      LCSH: Wielinski, Doug, 1947-2009--Death and burial. | Aircraft accidents--New York (State)--Clarence Center--Personal narratives. | Aircraft accident victims' families--New York (State)--Clarence Center--Personal narratives. | Husbands--Death--Personal narratives. | Aircraft accidents--Human factors. | Air pilots--Training of--United States--Standards. | Aeronautics, Commercial--United States--Safety measures--Standards. | Liability for aircraft accidents--United States. | Continental Airlines--Trials, litigation, etc. | Colgan Air--Trials, litigation, etc.

Classification:      LCC: TL553.525.N7 W54 2017 | DDC: 363.12/409747--dc23

LIBRASTREAM
BUFFALO, NEW YORK

First Edition
Printed in the United States of America

# DEDICATION

To the greatest gifts Doug gave me:
Kim, Lori, Jessica, and Jill.

# TABLE OF CONTENTS

## PART TWO — The 3407 Families

## PART THREE — 6038 Long Street

## PART FOUR — The Trial

## PART FIVE — Aftermath

Acknowledgements

About the Author

The Douglas C. Wielinski Memorial Scholarship Fund

# FOREWORD

It was a dark and stormy night. No, I'm serious. It WAS a dark and stormy night in January of 2011 when I met Karen. The occasion was the first night of my Creative Writing Workshop's winter session, a gathering of writers I have held since 1984. As it happened on that particular Tuesday night, and had happened on so many wintry Tuesdays before, a hardy group of writers came in from the squall, stomping snow from boots and shucking coats and hats before settling into chairs around the table in the library. A few were my regulars, some of whom had been writing with me for many years. A couple, however, were brand new, folks I was pretty sure I had never met. So I thought we would do well to share some brief introductions and answer that obvious question: What brings you out of a warm house into the cold and snow to attend a writing workshop?

One by one they told their stories—about dreams of writing novels, poems, children's stories, memoirs or family histories that might, one day, make treasured gifts for children, grandchildren or descendants unborn. Purely by chance, the last person to introduce herself was a stranger to me, although her last name, Wielinski, did seem somehow familiar. At her turn, she paused nervously, took a deep breath and began.

"You've all heard of Flight 3407," she said. "Well, that was my house the plane crashed into, and that was my husband who was killed."

You can imagine the painful, awkward, unsettling silence that fell over the room.

As the instructor—really I'm more of a host than an instructor—it would fall to me to offer something appropriate at that point, to put everyone at ease. I doubt I managed that. What I do remember is that Karen picked up the ball and ran with it from there.

"After that happened," she continued, "and after many hours with counselors and therapists and after many tears, I decided that I had two choices: I could fold my tent and decide that my life was over, or I could pick myself up and carry on. I've decided to carry on." Karen went on to say that writing had, in the past, provided some comfort to her, and since she needed a way to keep herself busy, the writing class might be just the thing, especially since she would be with people who did not know her and had no preconceived notions of what she must be experiencing. She had no way of knowing that she had just sown the seeds of what would become this book. She had no way of knowing that the amorphous writing prompts I suggested in those early days would help her mine her memory for the jewels that give the book its fullness and perspective. It was probably a surprise to her, but not to us who had been hearing her weekly manuscripts, that she would eventually set a daunting task for herself to make a book that would tell her story, Doug's story, and her family's story.

As you will see in the pages that await you beyond this Foreword, Karen has succeeded beyond her wildest dreams in telling her story. In the years since 2011, she has worked tirelessly—heroically, you could say—to get her story down on paper. She has become a mainstay in my classes, turning rough drafts into polished chapters of this book, using my arbitrary and relentless deadlines as motivation. Her tasks were many: to relive every second of the tragedy, to give us a window into life in the Wielinski household before that awful day, and to share the process of picking up the pieces and rearranging them into a new life. Through all this, she has grown as a writer and shown the incomparable value of writing as a way to understand life. And she has given a special voice to the Flight 3407 families.

While you will find unbearable sadness in this book, through Karen's eyes you'll find as well, humor, humanity, and the confidence that comes from believing that better days lie ahead. She deserves your congratulations.

*Rick Ohler,*
*East Aurora, NY*
*2017*

P.S. At the conclusion of that first class in January of 2011, I suggested, as had become our routine, that we should adjourn to a local watering hole to talk about writing in a less glaring light while we sipped a little glass of cheer. I certainly would have understood if Karen had declined. But without hesitation, Karen said, "I'm in. I'd love to go." There was the spirit that would drive this book. Five years and one published book later, Karen and I and a fellowship of writers are still gathering to write and are celebrating with a little glass of cheer afterword.

# PREFACE

The day after Flight 3407 crashed into our home on Long Street in Clarence Center, New York, I sat in a hotel suite and watched a news crawl race across the bottom of the television screen—The crash of Continental Flight 3407 resulted in the loss of everyone aboard the plane and one on the ground. That "one on the ground" was my husband Doug. Although I knew it was not intentional, that phrase always made me feel like Doug was an afterthought.

We made ourselves available to the press on a limited basis immediately following the tragedy. We did not know how to express the grief and terror we felt. It seemed too personal to share but, as time went on, I knew I had to make Doug more than an afterthought. How could I accomplish that goal?

The answer began with a need to keep myself busy. I moved thirty minutes south from Clarence Center to the small village of East Aurora, New York. Scanning the classes available through the community education program, I found a creative writing class. I dabbled in writing throughout the years, sent a few articles to magazines (rejected), and found some fulfillment when I started a school newsletter and wrote articles on activities at my daughters' Ohio elementary school in the town's *Loveland Herald*.

I updated an essay I wrote about my Grandma Schwab back in the late 1980s, and nervously attended my first session of Rick Ohler's creative writing class in January of 2011. The nervousness I felt came from a variety of sources: not knowing anyone, concern about how my piece would be accepted, and knowing I would need to explain who I was and my connection to the crash.

It was the start of a new life as a writer. Rick and my fellow classmates offered the encouragement I needed to test my abilities as a writer. At that time, Rick would suggest prompts to stir our imaginations. I would shake my head and wonder what in the world I could possibly compose about "Sharing a Passion," "Land of Make Believe," or "Edge of the Undertow." But, my deepest emotions soon found a voice—I wrote about Doug and the life we shared with our daughters: Kim, Lori, Jessica, and Jill. The essays reflected the terrors unleashed following the crash, and the people who became a part of my new life. I shared memories of the life Doug and I began first in Eden, New York in 1979, then Cincinnati, Ohio beginning in 1983, and our return to Western New York in 1997. Writing became therapeutic—a means of releasing the sorrow, anger, and fear caused by the loss of Doug, our home, and our life as a family. I also discovered the joy that can still remain after tragedy, and the benefits I derived from accepting the friendship and comfort of others touched by the crash.

Not only did I receive support from Rick Ohler and the writing group to pursue this quest, but my writing journey received an unexpected ally when Erik Brady, a sports writer with *USA Today*, entered my life in 2011. Erik also wanted to make Doug more than "one on the ground," and he succeeded when Doug's story appeared on the front page of USA Today on July 29, 2011. Doug became a real entity—a husband, father, friend, and sports collector to thousands of readers. Erik started this revelation, and I was encouraged to continue the story.

In 2012, an ember began burning in my mind to assemble a book that would encompass Doug's importance to our family, and the trial that tried to minimize the need for him in our lives. I revealed the crazy path our lives took in that first year following the crash, my involvement with the residents of Long Street and the Memorial created there, and the impact the families of those lost on Flight 3407 had on my life.

The book is broken down into five parts:

**PART ONE — February 2009 to February 2010:** A journal of what we encountered each month, followed by stories pertinent to each month—past or present.

**PART TWO — The 3407 Families:** My acceptance of their friendship and the fight for airline safety.

**PART THREE — 6038 Long Street:** My involvement in the completion of the Memorial and connection with the Long Street residents.

**PART FOUR — The Trial:** Events leading up to the trial and emotions swirling around the legal process.

**PART FIVE — Aftermath:** Our life today.

The date at the end of each essay indicates the original date it was written.

A quote from Kahlil Gibran expresses my feelings on how this book was completed:

*"In friendship or in love, the two side-by-side raise hands together to find what one cannot reach alone."*

*~ Kahlil Gibran*

As you read this story, I hope the love I had for Doug and the happiness we shared as a family will resonate through its pages. I hope it will demonstrate the courage and strength of the 3407 families—ordinary people who have become extraordinary as they fight for one level of safety for all aircraft. They, and those they lost, are remarkable people.

If you are facing tragedy, may our story offer you the possibility of survival, endurance, and continued love.

# REACTION

It felt as if a fist had rammed into my chest.

I sat with my attorneys, Phil and Anne Rimmler, in their office. We were there to review a new animation of the crash of Flight 3407. It had been developed for plaintiffs' use if any of the 3407 cases went to trial. Back in May of 2009, video animation was created when the National Transportation Safety Board revealed its original findings on the cause of the tragedy. I had also heard the audio from the cockpit several times in the past. I thought I was prepared to view this new reenactment.

We watched the events of Flight 3407 unfurl on the computer screen as it began its fateful journey from Newark, New Jersey to Buffalo, New York. Weather had caused a backup at Newark. I imagine that agitated passengers called those waiting in Buffalo to voice their frustration, and no doubt there were sighs of relief when the aircraft finally lifted into the night sky.

Flight time from Newark to Buffalo was fifty minutes. This animation included a timer at the top of the screen indicating "seconds until the crash." As the animation continued, we kept up conversation. I wasn't constantly watching the screen, but my eyes would gravitate toward that timer. As each second ticked off my heart beat faster.

The audio wasn't new. What has now been referred to as "nonessential conversation" transpired between the pilot and co-pilot as they approached the landing. Once again, I heard the co-pilot talking about how she had never been in an icing situation and that she wasn't sure how she would handle that scenario. When I first heard that audio released in the original investigative report, I desperately wanted to shout: *Wake up, you could be in that position right now!*

Sixty seconds remained... closer and closer... My heart beat faster and faster. I sat at the edge of my chair and leaned toward the computer screen.

A vision flashed in my mind: on the ground, Doug, Jill and I were oblivious to what was about to occur, but by now we would have paused. "What is that?" we would have wondered.

My eyes glued to the screen, I heard the pilot and co-pilot's screams and a desperate "Christ!" And then the blow was delivered.

My hand covered the gasp that escaped from my mouth as I fell back into the chair, sobbing. My hands shook. Phil passed tissues. Anne patted my shoulder.

What transpired on that screen was nothing new. I had seen and heard it all before. Why had my reaction been so strong?

I quickly realized why. This was the first time I had seen the animation combined with the audio transmission. The timer ticking down the seconds also was unnerving. I knew how this would end, yet my anticipation intensified with each second. The biggest difference? Now the passengers were more than just names. I knew their stories. I knew the pain their families carried. I knew the aftermath of the crash of Flight 3407.

My reaction and thoughts about the trail of emotion left by the crash stayed with me for many hours after I left the law office.

# PART ONE

## FEBRUARY 2009 TO FEBRUARY 2010

# February 2009

*"We are all subject to the fates. But we must act as if we are not, or die of despair."*

~ *Philip Pullman, The Golden Compass*

**Thursday, February 12, 2009**

The ground was soft and wet, covered with a combination of paper and wallboard. I had socks on, no shoes, and Jill had nothing on her feet. We kept to the right going towards our neighbor's house, saw that the way toward Long Street was blocked, and ran to the back of their yard. We raced along the gate around their pool, continued beside trees and fences of other houses, until we ended up on Clarence Center Road.

Considering what I have learned since the crash, I am so thankful that we ran to the right of our house. If we had gone to the left, I am afraid we would have seen images that would have haunted us forever.

I have no idea how much time elapsed between when the plane crashed and Jill and I escaped. We were told there were several explosions after the crash. We never heard them.

At Clarence Center Road, we ran toward Long Street, where I hoped we could find our neighbors.

I knew none of the people standing in a driveway on Long Street near the corner. Jill collapsed on the ground. "That is our house," I screamed. "Can someone please help my daughter." That moment was captured by one of the bystanders and appeared on You Tube. You cannot see Jill or me, but you can hear my frantic voice begging for help. It is chilling.

Out of nowhere a neighbor I knew, Paul Beiter, appeared. I

will never forget the look on his face.

"What are you doing here?" he asked in disbelief.

"I don't know where Doug is," I screamed. Paul guided us into his house. It was such a relief to see him and other neighbors I knew. Looking at the blaze of what once was our home, no one could believe we were standing there.

Again, I asked them to get some medical help for Jill. She and I sat on their stairs. As I looked out the door to the street, I saw a stretcher. Was someone on it? I experienced a small amount of hope. "Is that Doug on the stretcher?"

Paul went out to check. "No one is on the stretcher," he reported.

My daughter Kim usually got home from visiting her fiancé Jeff around 11:00, but I was terrified that she might have arrived early and been near the house when the plane crashed. I kept asking Paul's wife Michele to look and see if Kim's car was parked in front of the house. She assured me that it was not. I needed to know that Kim was OK and looked in the phone book for Jeff's family's phone number. I was in such a state that I could not remember how he spelled his last name. Michele gave me her cell phone to call Kim's cell. Later I learned that Kim did not answer that call because she did not recognize the number.

A paramedic finally arrived at the Beiters'. He checked Jill and me out. I do not recall when I became aware of throbbing pain in my left shoulder. As a precaution, he placed a brace around my neck.

My mouth felt like a desert. "Could I please have a glass of water?"

"No, not until you are examined in the hospital."

You're kidding, I thought. The minute he left, I asked Michele for at least an ice cube to suck on.

The three young Beiter girls were huddled together in a corner of the living room, but sprang into action and found shoes for Jill and me.

Michele later told me she had gathered her family when she realized she could feel the heat from the inferno across the street through her living room window. I would also learn that Paul had been looking out his kitchen window when the plane crashed and had witnessed debris flying across the street into his neighbor's yard.

The paramedics returned and said that Long Street was blocked. Jill and I would have to walk down to the Clarence Center Fire Station and wait for an ambulance. Kathy McGreevy—our neighbor Joe McGreevy's mother—turned up at the Beiters'. "Would you like me to go with you?" she asked.

Kathy was an acquaintance. I did not know her well. Her daughter had played basketball with Jill, and I occasionally saw her when I was walking. I appreciated her support, and she stayed with us for several hours.

Looking back, I sometimes feel that no one really knew what to do with Jill and me. Less than an hour after crawling out of our destroyed home, there we were casually walking down Long Street, following a paramedic, and stepping over fire hoses and snow piles in borrowed shoes.

I did look at our home before walking down the street. The front of the house was still visible, but would not win any fight to remain erect. Flames wove their way through the window and door as they soared high. It all seemed surreal.

The ambulance was still enroute, so we waited inside the fire station. Finally, our ride to the hospital arrived. As we were getting settled my friend Kathy McGinley suddenly appeared at the back of the ambulance. We tried to speak and a paramedic demanded that she leave.

"Listen" I shouted. "My husband is probably dead, my house is destroyed, and I want to talk to my friend!"

We were given a few moments and she would later meet us at the hospital.

Because of icy road conditions the ride to Millard Fillmore Suburban Hospital seemed to take forever.

We were greeted at the emergency room by a sea of silent doctors and nurses. They were waiting to treat survivors. None would arrive.

At first Jill and I had to go into separate examining rooms. My left shoulder was very sore and it was difficult to lift my arm. As I was wheeled to the x-ray area, I could see television reports of the crash.

"Turn that off!" someone shouted.

Finally I connected with Jeff's mom. "Is Kim with you?" I asked the second I heard her voice. Her assurance that Kim was safe with Jeff in Clarence Center relieved some of my anxiety.

FBI agents talked to Jill and me separately. Eventually we were allowed in one room.

Many people were calling the hospital trying to talk to us, including Jess' boyfriend and my niece. I realized then that I could not wait until the morning to call my out-of-town daughters Jess and Lori. How would I tell them what had happened? Jill told me she would call, but I knew that I was the one who had to make these heartbreaking calls.

Jess was with her boyfriend and Lori was with Chris. I was thankful that their boyfriends were there. CNN News reports had already showed them what was happening on Long Street. What did I say to them? I do not recall the exact words: "A plane crashed into the house. We don't know where Dad is. Kim, Jill, and I are OK. Are you all right?"

The two Kathys stayed with Jill and me until Doug's brother and his wife, Eddie and Maureen, arrived. Again, how do you explain what seems so impossible?

I have no idea when I finally talked to Kim—probably around two am. Although I had been told she was OK, I could not rest until I spoke with her. She was back at Jeff's house. "Please stay there with him until morning," I said.

Representatives from the American Red Cross visited, and gave us Target vouchers, and told us we would be taken to the Residence Suites where we could stay until we had other lodgings. We were told to call them for any support we would need. The hospital gave us a set of scrubs, toothbrushes, and toothpaste. I was given a sling to support my shoulder. "It doesn't seem to be broken, one of the medical people told me, Eddie and Maureen drove us to the hotel.

I think Jill and I just needed to be by ourselves. We clung wordlessly to each other on the bed. Jill slept a bit, but I couldn't. The realization that Doug was gone and the uncertainty of what would follow kept me awake.

*What would become of us?*

### Friday, February 13, 2009

Toward dawn I decided to take a shower. As I let the pulsating water hit my body, I thought of a movie, *Best Friends*, that had been shot in Buffalo. Goldie Hawn and Burt Reynolds were in it. In one scene, Goldie tried to drown her sorrows in a shower. Strange that I would think of it then, but that was what I wanted to do. Wash away all the pain—mental and physical.

I felt sequestered. What was happening? I turned the television on. A crawl under pictures of the blazing scene said that 49 people on the plane and one person on the ground were killed. There was no mention of Jill, Kim, or me.

Family, friends, and co-workers would be concerned and wonder what happened to us. The best way to update them would probably be through the media. Maureen's sister, Barbara Burns, was a reporter for WBEN radio. I could ask Maureen for her number. I knew Barbara so talking to her would be easier than with another reporter.

Jill asked me to turn the television off.

I went to the phone and called work—crazy. I felt I had to let my boss know I would not be coming in, but no one answered. The school had closed because of the crash. I found my boss' home number, and reached his son.

"My mom and dad are out looking for you," he said.

"We're at the Residence Suites," I told him.

Eddie and Maureen returned to get a list of what we needed. We gave them sizes for tops, jeans, shoes, and underwear—basics to tide us over until we could shop for replacements.

We needed money. Sometime during the morning I called HSBC bank to see what was needed to obtain a new debit card.

The young man I reached—in India, I believe—was very helpful and shocked to learn of the crash.

"I will have to look that up on the internet," he said.

We were told there was food, coffee, and tea in the lobby. I had no appetite.

The hospital called. An apologetic doctor told me that my x-rays had been reviewed, and I did have a broken collar bone. At least that explained the shoulder pain. "Keep your arm in the sling," the doctor said.

There was a tearful reunion as Kim and Jeff arrived. Kim shared her emotional journey, telling how she had met roadblocks on the way home and was diverted to a development north of Long Street. From there she saw a huge plume of smoke.

## Kim's Story

*The smoke was visible even though it was dark. I remember hitting the brakes in the middle of the street. When I tried calling Mom's, Jill's, and Dad's cell phones, a message indicated the numbers were not in service. I had never felt such gripping fear. I have no idea how I turned right onto Goodrich Road where I parked my car. I jumped out, leaving my purse behind. I can't even remember if I turned the car off.*

*I saw two boys heading toward Long Street and I asked if I could join them. When I reached the corner of Maple and Long Street, I stared in horror. The smoke appeared to be rising from our home.*

*"My house, my house!" I screamed.*

*One of the boys alerted a sheriff standing nearby. He tried to find a neighbor who could help me. One neighbor, whom we did not know well, refused to let me in. Looking back, I guess I can understand why they'd be put off by a hysterical woman on their doorstep. Luckily, another did, and kindly helped me call Jeff. The state I was in, I couldn't even manage to push the buttons on the phone.*

*The woman held my hand and tried to reassure me. She and her husband literally held me up and walked me down to Maple towards Goodrich Road. We got in their car and drove to the Clarence Center Elementary School to wait for Jeff. When he arrived, we drove to another home near the school. A man was trying to call different hospitals to get more information. Jeff and I sat in the living room. The television was showing a view from Long Street. There was the brick house to the left and our house was not there. The garage with the basketball hoop was the only thing standing.*

*I started getting phone call after phone call from friends and Lori and Jess. They had heard about the accident and wanted details. All the phone calls and questions were overwhelming. I didn't even know what was going on myself.*

*I felt some relief when I found out that Mom had talked to Jeff's mom, and later when she called me from the hospital, but I definitely was in a state of shock.*

*During the night Jeff and I held each other and cried. I know I was hysterical and hardly slept at all. When I woke up Jeff forced me to take a shower because I smelled like smoke.*

We had all experienced a night of terror, but how difficult it must have been for Kim to handle all that uncertainty.

I did reach Barbara Burns, who asked if she could record our conversation. I agreed. Our call was brief. I quickly told her about how Jill and I had somehow escaped. Later attorneys would instruct me not to discuss those details because of the lawsuits that would be filed. I am glad that I talked to Barbara before that restriction became a part of my life. Lawsuits take years. I am sure I might be asked someday, "How can you remember your feelings at that time?" What I say today is exactly what I told Barbara the day after the crash; my original reaction is on the record.

Eddie and Maureen returned from the mission to Target. The Red Cross vouchers, they had discovered, had to be used completely during one visit. What a task it must have been for them to determine all those little day-to-day items we use—things we take for granted that are somehow always at our fingertips. We now had a variety of clothes, shoes, boots, hygiene supplies, towels, cleaning supplies, and other everyday things.

My boss, John Ptak, and his wife, Ann, arrived. Their faces could not mask their shock. More hugs, tears, and the retelling of the horror of the night before. My relationship with Dr. Ptak had always been businesslike. After the crash he went out of his way to help me and the girls. He became a friend in the process.

Doug's other brother, Billy, was in Florida. He thought it would be dangerous for Lori and Jess to drive to Buffalo in such an obviously emotional state. He called Continental Airlines to see if they could provide air transportation. Because Doug's name was not on the 3407 flight manifest, however, they told Billy that free air fare was not available. This did not sit well with him. When he went to the airport for his own flight back to Buffalo, he confronted Continental representatives and voiced his displeasure. They gave Billy transportation without charge.

Lori, Jess, and their boyfriends drove all night.

Lori and Chris arrived first.

As I hugged Lori, she told me that she and Chris were ready to postpone their upcoming wedding planned for August 1. But I was adamant that their wedding would still take place as planned. Doug would want it that way. We needed some joy among all the sadness we faced.

## LORI'S STORY

*It had not been a typical weekday night in Bellevue, Kentucky where I live. Instead of heading home after work, I joined a group of friends for dinner and a movie,* He's Just Not That into You.

*I was tired after a long day of work and an evening with friends. As soon as I got home, I was ready to go to bed around ten o'clock. Almost immediately after getting into bed, my phone rang. I noticed it was Kim. I decided not to answer and simply call her in the morning. When it rang again, an uneasy feeling clenched in the pit of my stomach. Why was she calling again? I answered this time, and she told me a plane had crashed on Long Street. I imagined a small plane crashing in the empty lots behind our house, but she said that it had struck a house. She told me to turn on CNN, which was covering the crash, and assured me she would call me back when she heard any further news from Mom, Jill, or Dad. Like Kim, I tried calling everyone's cell phones without success.*

*Chris and I turned on the bedroom TV to CNN. I could not believe what I was seeing—a fiery scene on Long Street. I felt sick to my stomach and my mind wandered through different scenarios of what was going on. Chris tried to re-assure me that we needed more information and we had to stay calm. We moved to the television in the living room. CNN said that the plane had landed on a house farther down Long Street. I just didn't know what to believe.*

*Finally, I connected with Kim again. She was near the crash site and had heard from others that Mom and Jill had been seen walking outside before the crash. It made no sense. Why would they be walking at that hour?*

*My phone kept ringing. Friends called. Aunt Barbara called. Everyone wanted to know if I had more information than what CNN was reporting.*

*There was some relief when Mom called and assured me that she and Jill were okay. "Lori, the plane fell on our house," Mom said. "Jill and I were in the house. The ceiling fell on top of me." I was in disbelief. Although I heard her words my mind could not comprehend the reality of what she said.*

*Mom's voice wavered, yet still sounded strong—the sound of a mother trying to be strong for her daughters.*

*Although she told me Dad had not been located yet, I clung to the hope that he would magically show up and everything would be OK.*

*Shortly after that, Uncle Billy called me. Chris took the call and went to an upstairs hallway to talk while I sat in the bathroom and waited for more news. Chris came back and I could tell from the tears in his eyes that the news was not good. "He didn't make it."*

*I collapsed into Chris' arms and fell to the floor. I felt limp. I didn't want this to be real. I couldn't imagine never seeing Dad ever again. Chris held me tight and comforted me. He told me that Uncle Billy was trying to get us a flight to Buffalo, but there was no way I was going to get on a plane at that point. I threw a bunch of stuff into a suitcase, not thinking about it, just doing it.*

*As I was finishing up, Jess called. She was getting ready to drive to Buffalo, too. "Do you know anything about Dad yet?" she asked.*

*She hadn't heard the news. I simply said, "Uncle Billy just called, Jess. He didn't make it. He's gone."*

*We both cried. I assured her that we would be OK, trying to be a strong older sister, but I felt nothing close to OK at that moment. Shortly after talking with Jess, Chris and I were ready to go. We stepped out the front door to leave. It was still the middle of the night. We were exhausted and distressed, but we had to get to Buffalo. I looked up at the dark sky and over to our house. It felt like a really bad dream—things didn't seem real. I had a feeling of overwhelming anxiety and I felt beside myself. It was a feeling I could not escape.*

*Chris and I drove for a bit, but as daylight hit we had to stop at a rest area to sleep. We were exhausted. Ginger, our dog, was calmly curled up in my lap. I think she could sense my pain. More friends called and texted as they realized that my family lived on Long Street. It was so painful to share the news with each person who contacted us. I didn't know what to think, and I didn't know what would happen once we were reunited in Buffalo.*

*My anxiety continued to build. We approached Columbus, Ohio. We lived in Cincinnati for 14 years. Whenever we made the trip to Buffalo, Dad would always point out a lighthouse on top of a church as the expressway took us through downtown Columbus. There was a statue of a man with a fishing pole outside the lighthouse. Dad would always say, "Look there's the man in the lighthouse. He must get so tired always standing there." I sadly got ready to see this familiar site. As we passed by I looked up, only to see that the man had fallen to his side. I couldn't believe my eyes. I like to think it was a sign from Dad. I like to think he was letting us know that things were never going to be the same, but he would always be with us.*

Jess arrived later in the morning. Jess hugged me tight. "It feels so strange to see you without Dad," she said. "You two were always together."

Later, she shared her agonizing story with me.

## JESS' STORY

*I was having a quiet Thursday at my apartment in Highland Hills, New York. I was watching* The Office. *I noticed that one of the characters was wearing the same shirt Mom and Dad had given me for Christmas. I texted Jill and asked her to tell Mom. I regret now that I did not call. I would have been able to talk to Dad one last time.*

*By 10:00 p.m. I was in bed reading* The Maltese Falcon. *That reminded me of Dad because Humphrey Bogart was one of his favorites and he loved that movie.*

Around 10:45 I turned out the light and offered my evening prayer that Mom, Dad, and my sisters would be safe and have a good day tomorrow. Right at that moment my friend Nicole called. "Have you talked to your family tonight?" she asked.

I was confused by the question, but it soon became clear why she was calling. A plane had crashed near Long Street. I hung up the phone and began trying to reach Mom. I called the house phone and got a horrible beeping noise. I tried to assure myself that the plane could have crashed a few streets over into some lines and that the phones were just disconnected.

Then I tried Jill's, Kim's, and Mom's cell phones. They rang but went directly to voicemail. I began to panic and called my boyfriend, crying hysterically. I told him that I needed him to come to my apartment.

I finally reached Kim, who was returning from Jeff's. She was only a few short blocks from Long Street. She had no idea what was going on, but there was smoke. She could not see where it was coming from.

My boyfriend had started to investigate online. I refused to look because I didn't want to see a picture that would confirm it was our house. I couldn't believe it was our house. All the stories online kept changing their information. First they said an old man lived in the house that was hit. Then they said it was a house with an old man and a baby. Both of those stories reassured me that it wasn't our house and everyone was OK.

My friends kept calling me to see if I was OK, and if I had heard any news. Looking back, I think they knew what was really going on, but they didn't want to hurt me. They wanted to leave me with some hope.

We ended up calling the police station in Clarence, and they referred us to the town hall. The town hall referred us to the hospital.

*I talked to Kim again, but she was in shock and did not have a clear picture of what was going on. I was desperate for information. I called my friend Takla, whose friend Jayce lived in the house behind ours. I was able to get his cell phone number. He was now living in Rochester and had no idea what was going on, but he gave me his parents' number. I was too emotional to talk to them, but my boyfriend called and explained who he was and asked Jayce's mother what she could see from her house. She said there was a lot of smoke and it was difficult to see. Could she see our green and white house? She said yes. This gave me hope that everything was OK, but I would later realize that she had seen another green and white house two doors down from 6038.*

*I called Kim to pass on this information, but she had terrible news for me. The plane had hit our house. Someone saw Mom and Jill and they were OK. She was not sure about Dad's fate. Kim had not talked to either Mom or Jill, so I continued to fear that I had lost them all. I was finally able to contact my Mom and she confirmed that it appeared Dad had not survived. I was relieved that Mom and Jill had survived, but sick that Dad had not. When I hung up, I felt physically sick and went into the bathroom and threw up.*

*I did not sleep at all before we left for Buffalo. Lori ended up calling me a little after 4:00 a.m. I remember talking with her and telling her maybe Dad got out too, but just wasn't with Mom and Jill.*

*"Jess, Dad did not get out," Lori said. I think that was when I finally believed it.*

*I remember opening my closet and thinking I had to pack something to wear to Dad's funeral. This made me cry even harder. Everything seemed so surreal.*

*It was a horrible six-hour drive to Buffalo. I drove most of the way because I had to keep my mind busy. Mom called when we were still about three hours away in Binghamton. She said her collar bone was broken and Jill had some bruises. I could not believe that they both got out of the house with only those injuries. I thought Mom was protecting me and did not want to tell me something worse, like someone lost an arm or leg. I had to see them both to believe they were both OK.*

The rest of that day was a blur.

The hotel staff moved us to a larger suite. This one included a loft area with a bed, two couches that opened up into beds, two bathrooms, and a kitchen area.

My friend Sue Muchow brought cell phones donated by AT&T. She became our courier and picked up prescriptions, got contact lenses, and brought food and a box full of office supplies. We made phone calls to my sister, cousins, and out-of-town friends, always accompanied by tears.

Every possible media source seemed to know where we were. The majority of calls came to Jess or her boyfriend's cell phones, perhaps because of their proximity to New York City. Calls coming to the hotel's office were carefully screened, and no one was given direct access to us. Even Governor Patterson's office called with condolences.

"The Governor would like to personally meet you," we were told, but I knew if he came so would a contingent of the media. I was not ready for that.

Flowers arrived from a CBS Producer of *The Early Show*.

"Anything we can help you with at any time! I am soooo sorry for your loss."

Scott Levin, from local television station WGRZ called several times. He had been a neighbor of ours in East Amherst. He was on vacation in Florida, and once while talking with him I could hear Disney music in the background. Our conversations were general, and I was cautious about what information I gave him. It seemed the sensible thing to do until I secured legal representation.

An on-line petition had been started in an effort for us to

receive an *Extreme Home Makeover*. Although we did not initiate or accept that offer, we did appreciate the consideration they extended to us.

Billy and Doug's other brother, Jackie, and their wives stopped to offer their help. From that point on Billy would become a much-needed source of financial and legal guidance. Many of the girls' friends arrived to give support.

We learned that Takla, a high school friend of Jess, had lost a cousin on Flight 3407. Family members had been taken to the Indigo Hotel in Amherst, where a command center was set-up for the FBI, National Transportation Safety Board (NTSB), and airline officials. Takla came and kept us updated on those developments. Billy also kept abreast of that situation.

Lori's friends Holly and Dave were especially helpful. Holly and Lori brought me a planner to keep me organized. They sorted through boxes of donated items that were already pouring in. They helped me construct a list of things I needed to do: call insurance companies, stockbrokers, banks, and credit card companies; obtain new legal documents such as wills, birth certificates, licenses, passports, social security cards—all destroyed in the house. Get in touch with people who had called: Doug's boss and the director of human resources, state police officers, Monsignor Leising from Nativity Church, and many others. We also made a list of important numbers: The Erie County Crisis Center, disaster coordinator, Continental reps, American Red Cross personnel. These lists seemed endless.

Friends from work brought food donated by the local Dash's Market. I tried to eat soup, but just could not seem to stomach anything.

Jill's boyfriend Dan arrived from Fort Bragg in North Carolina.

One by one relatives and friends departed. The Sabres were playing that night, and we decided to watch the game. We all were thinking about the game Jill and Doug had gone to the day before the crash.

At one point, Jill's expression became anxious.

"What is it?" I asked. She pointed to the clock. It read 10:20. Had it been only twenty-four hours since our lives had changed so drastically?

We settled down for what we hoped would be some rest. Later, I heard Jess crying and I went to her. "I keep thinking about Dad being burned," she sobbed.

I tried to reassure her that he would have died instantly, and hopefully had not suffered. We all prayed that was true.

We were so exhausted that sleep did finally come, but I awoke before dawn. I got up and sat in a chair. I knew I had to eat something; a few spoonfuls of soup had been my only nourishment. What could I keep down? Even a small piece of coffee cake seemed hard to swallow.

### Saturday, February 14, 2009

Valentine's Day. Well, that would never be the same. Lori's Chris tried to spread some cheer by bringing us a bouquet of white roses.

I learned about the other victims of Flight 3407. *The Buffalo News* included short biographies of the passengers. They were no

*Karen & Doug*

longer just names, but real people, with families and lives cut short.

I can still picture myself standing in the suite and opening the paper. I had to catch my breath as I looked at a picture of Doug and me. It had been taken during the Christmas holidays and we were standing in the Long Street family room. How odd to see our image staring back at me, and how my heart skipped a beat seeing my Doug in that blue mock-turtleneck sweater that always complemented his grey hair. I had to set the paper aside.

Over the next few days a steady stream of friends and relatives arrived: my sister Barb and her husband Bill, Jill's friends from Brockport, Jess' Clarence friends. "It's like spring break," Billy said. "I have to step over all the kids."

At one point, I was so overwhelmed with the buzz of activity that I sought solace in a bathroom. Sitting on the toilet, I cradled my head with one hand (the other confined to the sling), and just cried in an attempt to release pent-up emotion.

My cousin Jan called. Aunt Agnes was recuperating in a nursing home after surgery and Jan had found it hard to break the news about the crash. Getting on the line, Aunt Agnes tearfully offered the use of her home for as long as we needed. I was happy—and relieved—to accept.

So far we had avoided the "headquarters" at the Indigo Hotel, but then we were summoned. The coroner wanted to talk with us.

A swarm of people milled around the lobby. Security was tight, and we were required to sign in and receive photo badges. My picture showed a serious woman. I told the girls I looked like a lioness ready to protect her cubs. We were taken upstairs where the girls, their guys, and I were seated around a table facing the coroner. Although Doug's brothers had also been asked to come, they were escorted to a separate room.

I have forgotten the coroner's name, but she was one of several who were attempting to identify the remains. She made us feel at ease. We knew why we were there—to provide details—that would enable Doug to be identified. It actually felt good to talk about Doug. We shared his physical characteristics: recent dental and gum work, broken bones and surgeries—all sports related—mustache and the curls down the back of his neck. I always encouraged him to have the hairstylist leave those longer every time he went for a haircut.

Although it was the physical aspects she needed, she let us share his personal side with her, too—what he meant to us, and even humorous anecdotes. Before we left, the girls had to scrape their gums with a wooden stick for DNA samples.

Other NTSB associates who worked on retrieving items from the crash site talked with us.

"How can you do such a grueling and painful job," we asked.

"We do it for the families."

I even asked them, "Have you come across any remains of a cat?"

They had not, they said, but would keep that in mind. (Spots was later identified).

A representative from Continental Airlines was also introduced to us. She would be our liaison. She told us that she would assist in any way she could.

We did not encounter any media or the other family members during that first visit to the Indigo.

That weekend we drove to Billy's home for a dinner with Doug's extended family. The drive was a nostalgic journey as we passed spots I associated with Doug: Duff's, where we went after all those Friday night baseball games at the beginning of our relationship; a plaza parking lot at Maple and Sheridan where I had to meet Doug once to give him something he needed for work; the medical building where Doug went for his physical when we were moving back to Buffalo; the UB campus—so many of Jess' volleyball tournaments were held there—and we often went to their July 4th fireworks display. Doug would pack a small cooler with drinks and snacks.

At Billy's it hit me hard. I was now alone, the widowed aunt. I hated that realization, that feeling of loss and loneliness. It left a knot in my stomach, also not helped by the fact that I still could not seem to eat anything.

### Sunday, February 15, 2009

The Sunday after the crash I was introduced to another aspect of this tragedy—the legal side. The law firm opened its office doors that Sunday so the attorneys could hear my story. They seemed compassionate, and I even detected tears at one point. I could work with these people.

### Monday, February 16, 2009

On Monday my sister drove Jill and me to our general physician. His office was always crowded and usually meant long waits. We had called ahead to see if we could immediately be put in an examining room—we did not want to endure the stares of those who might recognize us. Luckily, they complied. The exam was routine, and I was given the name of a physical therapist for my shoulder.

I also stopped by work and was greeted by many sympathetic co-workers. Many had endured the grueling task of screening calls from the media in the days following the crash. The school superintendent, Dr. Tom Coseo, took me into his office to discuss the possibility of a memorial service for Doug being held in perhaps the high school gym or auditorium. The support I received from the school district was tremendous, and the memorial service was scheduled for Saturday, February 21st at the middle school.

When we returned to the suite, we packed the cars and moved to Aunt Agnes' house. Her home was a warm and comforting change from the hotel suite. Floral designs covered many surfaces. Being surrounded by her familiar things, reminders of my family's past, introduced some peace into our crazy lives. A definite bonding experience was growing among the nine of us, as the girls, their guys, and I spent the next few weeks sharing this space.

Although I had heard Jill describe her experience the night of the crash, I was amazed one evening when she shared additional details. I had assumed the force of the crash had dropped the upstairs bedroom floor to ground level. That was not the case.

## JILL'S STORY

*I was home on a break from SUNY Brockport. My studies were finished and I was excited about starting an internship at the Pinehurst Golf Resort in North Carolina in March. Earlier in the evening I had spent time at my boyfriend Dan's house.*

*I had been watching* Private Practice *on a television in Kim's front bedroom. During a commercial, I went down to the family room and chatted with Mom and Dad. We talked about school and my upcoming internship. There had been a number of different internship opportunities. I had called Dad several times to get his thoughts on what direction I should take. He offered suggestions, but left the final decision up to me. I knew, though, that the thought of possibly playing golf at Pinehurst seemed like a good selling point to Dad.*

*I went back upstairs to Kim's room to catch the rest of the program. It wasn't long before I heard the familiar sound of a plane overhead. We lived near the airport and were used to hearing the planes. Something was different, though, very different. The noise grew incredibly loud— deafening actually.*

*The next thing I knew, I remember looking at the floor and seeing that it was almost slanted. The force of the crash had knocked me off the bed. As my mind cleared from the initial shock, I knew I had to get out. I saw flames already blocking the front windows. Pure panic started when I realized if I didn't find another way out I would burn to death. I frantically felt my way along the walls until I came to an opening. I now believe I either emerged from the upstairs bathroom window or the crawl space in the hall ceiling. I was barefoot. I eased my way down to the ground on something slippery—more than likely the plane wing. Access to the front of the house was blocked, so I made my way to the backyard. I saw my mom popping out of a space at the back of the house. I ran over to her.*

It was mind-boggling to me that she had to work her way down from the wreckage to ground level. Again, a sickening feeling grabbed hold of me as I realized how close I had come to losing her.

**Wednesday, February 18, 2009**
The other families had been taken to the Long Street site shortly

after the crash. We waited until the Wednesday after the accident. The site had already been cleared of debris. One plane engine remained. As we approached, all work ceased and the workers and law enforcement officers lined up in a show of respect. It was an impressive sight. Had our home actually been on this piece of land? The front and back concrete steps were still visible, as was a small portion of the blue cistern wall in the basement—evidence that, yes, it had. We circled together, held hands, said a prayer, and wept. As we left I shook the hands of those workers and officers near us, and thanked them for all their efforts and support.

Some of the things I needed to do seemed bizarre—like calling the utility companies to close our accounts.

A woman from the gas company said, "Oh they'll just go and read the meter."

"There is nothing left to read," I replied.

"Well, will you be rebuilding?"

I know it was a logical question, but after all the emotional events of the past few days, it was more than I could handle. I passed the phone to Jess' boyfriend. "Tell her we are not going to rebuild!" I managed to say between sobs.

### Thursday, February 19, 2009

The school lent us two laptops. The use of my left hand was limited, so I typed everything with one hand—all in lower case. One of the first emails I sent went to a friend from Atlanta who was in town for a brief visit.

```
i was starting to send you an email this morning
and then got the call from the medical examiner
saying doug had been identified—never could finish
your email...think of us tonight around 10:20...
hanging in there...good and bad moments.
```

The call from the medical examiner came one week after the crash. It confirmed what we basically knew, but the official announcement still jolted me. I had to lay the phone down and pause a moment to compose myself.

"What was the cause of death? Did he suffer?"

"Just as we are telling all the families, blunt force — no smoke in lungs."

Now that Doug's remains had been identified, we decided to still have the memorial service at the middle school that Saturday, but we would also have a wake on Sunday and the funeral mass on Monday. People were coming from out of town for the memorial service, so hopefully they could stay for the funeral mass too.

### Friday, February 20, 2009

When reciting "For better or for worse" in my marriage vows, I am sure I never considered what became my next task, picking out a casket and burial plot. Billy went to the funeral home with me. We were escorted to the basement, where lines of caskets waited for review. The first one I was shown had copper accents. I didn't care what it cost (the airline would be paying the bill) and it was the perfect choice. Part of Doug's work involved copper applications. That copper casket made the process less painful. He would have approved.

I did not hesitate when it came to deciding on the cemetery either. Doug and I had once taken a tour of the Clarence Fillmore Cemetery. He liked that many of the Clarence founders were buried there. He also discovered the tombstone of a young man killed in Vietnam who had been in the same regiment as Doug. The young man had been killed just prior to the time Doug was sent there.

"I know there is probably no chance, but what if somehow I was sent to replace him?" Doug had wondered.

Next I had to choose a plot. Billy and I explored the available open areas. How do you make such a decision when a blanket of snow covers the ground? I chose a site partially concealed by bushes—private, yet easy to find. Again, the airline would be footing the bill, so yes, maintain flowers in a pot forever!

Even as I had to make monumental choices, day-to-day decisions also had to be made. The girls and guys decided to make a trip to the grocery store. I let them go by themselves—I needed some time alone. It was probably the first time I had been alone since the accident. They were concerned and, quite frankly, so was I. I passed the test, and I did not fall to pieces.

Their experience at Wegman's was pretty amazing. One of the managers told them they could fill as many carts as they pleased—no charge. They took advantage of this kindness and arrived back at the house with not only a good supply of groceries, but pots and pans, dishes, cleaning supplies, and almost everything else needed to set up housekeeping again. It was another example of the generosity of the community.

Our liaison from the airline wasn't so terrific. In fact, she added to the stress of the upcoming memorial. The only word I can think of is badgering. She insisted that the girls go shopping for new clothes. My friend Kathy Southard finally took them. Outfitting four girls is a time-consuming process, and it was a stress-filled event. The girls would have to call the liaison for approval of any purchase, so there was no way to hide their connection to Flight 3407. They returned emotionally drained, each with a new set of black clothing.

### Saturday, February 21, 2009

We arrived early at the middle school and were escorted to the library to meet family members and a few friends. I was especially anxious about connecting with Doug's good friend. His name is Jim Maciejewski, but most people call him Macie. It was a bittersweet reunion—good to embrace the man who had been Doug's friend since grade school, but heartbreaking to see his pain.

It was overwhelming to walk into the auditorium and see it filled with people who wanted to support us and celebrate Doug's life. I later learned that more people watched the memorial service from classrooms.

A large portrait of Doug, taken during one of his high school lectures about his Vietnam experiences, had been placed at the foot of the stage, along with a historical display he had worked on with the town historian. Doug had come across old postcards and combined them with photos he'd taken of the current buildings. It had been quite an undertaking. Seeing both the portrait and the board brought tears to my eyes. *How would I get through this?*

The music, provided by the Clarence High School Chorale music teacher, Louis Shafer, and his wife, Christine (who had been the girls' guidance counselor), was beautiful and haunting. Monsignor Frederick Leising, our Pastor at Nativity of the Blessed Virgin Mary, gave a poignant homily.

The girls and I wanted to share some remembrances of Doug with those assembled. We knew emotionally we would not be able to read them. Jill's good friend, Annmarie Dean, read Jill's reflection, and Lori's Chris read the others.

I was so proud and impressed with the beautiful words my girls had composed about their dad.

Kim saw Doug as someone in constant "motion throughout every aspect of his life: family, friends, work, house projects, memorabilia collecting, history, sports. The list goes on and on." Kim was not especially athletic, but she remembered a "volleyball game where he saw an athletic side of me that he had never seen before." His recognition of her that day remained a happy memory. She recalled his morning treks to the Clarence Flea Market and the excitement of the "good finds" from the morning. "My life has forever been changed, but I have his strength to get me through," she said.

Of all the girls, Lori has followed in her dad's footsteps. "My dad was my role model and always will be. I always wanted to grow up and be just like him, which is why I got into business and marketing. During the last conversation with my dad, I told him about my recent success at my new job. I know he was proud of me, and he said, 'Just keep doing what you're doing.'"

Lori included a wonderful story in her remembrance: "Once when Dad went to Germany, he said he would bring us girls back a nice German boy. He came home with a wallet-size photo of 'Dieter.' He said Dieter was a nice boy and was excited to meet us. Of course we all believed him, when actually he had just stumbled upon the photo on the ground."

Lori found a meaningful way to put this tragedy into perspective: "My Dad was always into history—most recently the history of Clarence and those who lived here in the past—and he shared their stories with others. Now everyone will pass on the story of his life, as he will forever be a part of history."

Jess recalled how Doug "always remembered every detail, no matter how small." Doug and I had visited Jess one time. While we were driving, a Billy Joel song came on. Jess mentioned how she had been trying to win tickets to a sold-out concert at Shea Stadium. A few weeks later Doug sent tickets to Jess. "Whenever I thought about my wedding day, I always pictured Dad and me dancing to a Billy Joel song."

Jill said her dad was involved in every aspect of their lives. "He was always there for us."

I was especially touched with how she viewed the relationship that Doug and I had: "He loved my mom so much. Every day I could see it by the way he looked at and treated her. I knew she was the love of his life."

She concluded her remembrance by saying, "I hope to take what he has taught me and move forward to this next chapter in my life. I want him to know that I will always be his little girl who misses and loves him more each day."

My own words summed up my life with him: "Doug had a heart of gold. He was one of the good guys, a great, loving father to his girls and the best person for me to share my life with. We had many things in common and enough differences to make life interesting. I could still look at him after more than 30 years and feel that special thrill I felt back when I first watched that curly-haired catcher. The pain is great, but the memories are greater and the love will remain."

After the memorial service, we went to the cafeteria area to greet those who had attended. Jess, Jill, and I made a quick restroom stop, and by the time we returned the cafeteria was packed with people. I lost track of the time, and completely lost sight of the girls. There was no organization. I was surrounded by a constant flow of family and friends. Included in this group were cousins I had not seen in years, and old neighbors and friends from Loveland, Ohio who made the journey just for the memorial.

How many times can I say, "overwhelmed, but so grateful?"

The cafeteria has two sides, separated by the serving area. I later learned that the girls were "working" that other side.

My co-workers in the school district office had also arranged for finger foods to feed this huge group—most donated by the community. Such an outpouring of support was astonishing.

At the end of the day, we were exhausted, but still had the wake and funeral mass ahead of us. We began to question whether a wake was actually necessary, when so many people had attended the memorial service. Those doubts quickly vanished, though, as we faced a steady stream of well-wishers at the Sunday wake.

### Sunday, February 22, 2009

The girls, their guys, and I stood to the left of the closed casket. As the day progressed, I gravitated away from the girls—advancing more and more toward this parade of people before they reached us.

The girls, laughingly, told me, "Pretty soon you will be meeting them in the parking lot."

I felt the need to reach out to them—acknowledge them and show my appreciation for their support—people from all facets of our lives: co-workers, school friends, neighbors, and family. I basically was on my feet from four to nine p.m. Many remained and mingled for quite a long time.

The practice of filling boards with pictures of a loved one's life is a wonderful way to memorialize them. Sadly, we did not have the means to provide such a pictorial—only a few pictures remained to celebrate our existence as a family—and I do not know why I did not think to ask Doug's brothers to bring pictures of his youth.

Kindness continued to be extended to our family and to those who had made the journey from Cincinnati where we had lived for almost fifteen years. Kim's friends, Renee and Liz, extended their stay so they could attend the funeral mass. Our old neighbors, the Southards, and my boss, Dr. Ptak, opened their homes to these visitors.

**Monday, February 23, 2009**

The blur of weekend activities culminated with the funeral mass on Monday. All nine of us scrambled to coordinate showers and bathroom time, press a shirt or two, wolf down a bit of breakfast, and assemble at the funeral home for the procession to the church.

We soulfully followed Doug's casket to the front of the church and were surprised by five celebrants. Along with Monsignor Leising, there were representatives from Niagara University, where Doug had earned his Master's degree; Father Yetter from St. Mary's in Swormville; and Father Edward Schroeder, who had officiated at our wedding almost 30 years before.

I took comfort from Monsignor Leising's words. He reminded us that Doug would always be part of our circle of life.

Jim Macie delivered the eulogy. He explained how he and Doug had met in third grade and developed a lasting relationship, fueled by their love of athletics and sports collecting—over fifty years of friendship.

As communion was distributed a continual line of participants passed by and I realized just how many people had attended the mass.

It was a cold morning, and a blanket of snow covered the cemetery. A canopy sheltered the grave site where Doug's flag-draped coffin had been placed. After a military salute, that flag was solemnly folded and presented to us.

The cold temperature, along with the emotion of this final goodbye, chilled our hearts and souls.

We had laid a loved one to rest. Now, we wanted to celebrate Doug's life in a way he would have approved—lunch at Brennan's. I had asked my boss, Dr. Ptak, to arrange a gathering there. Close to one hundred guests came together, and we stood and raised our glasses to a man who loved and lived life to the fullest.

Life without Doug had officially begun.

**Tuesday, February 24 to Saturday, February 28, 2009**

We continued with preparations for Lori's wedding. There were appointments with the baker to taste cake samples. We visited two florists. A moment of light-headedness hit me as we discussed floral arrangements. I had just buried my husband and now I was planning a wedding without him. It seemed crazy, but necessary, to concentrate on a future happy event.

Jess' twenty-fourth birthday was on February 26. Linda Lou, my fellow co-worker at WXRL Radio, arranged to secure the back room at Frank's Grille in Lancaster for an unplanned birthday celebration. Lori and I had bought a bright birthday plate and small cake topped with a candle. It was good to gather the family for a happy occasion.

Jess, Lori, and their boyfriends left for the drive back to their homes. Everyday life—whatever that would bring—continued.

As February came to a close, I reflected on the *Prayer of St. Francis of Assisi*, an excerpt of which we had included in the memorial service program:

> Lord, make me an instrument of thy peace.
> Where there is hatred, let me sow love;
> Where there is injury, pardon;
> Where there is doubt, faith;
> Where there is despair, hope;
> Where there is darkness, light;
> Where there is sadness, joy.
>
> Grant that I may not so much seek
> To be consoled as to console,
> To be understood as to understand,
> To be loved as to love;
> For it is in giving that we receive;
> It is in pardoning that we are pardoned;
> It is in dying that we are born to eternal life.

These were words so appropriate for the curve fate had thrown our way.

*4/27/13*

## DAILY BREAD

What sustains us? What feeds our desire to carry on? What helps us through adversity?

After the crash we received hundreds of cards and letters that nourished our hearts.

We began to look forward to trips to the post office and school, eager to get the white totes that held the cards and letters bearing heartfelt messages of condolence and support. They came addressed in a variety of ways: to "The Wielinski Family, General Delivery, Clarence, NY" or "For the Wielinski Family c/o the Clarence High School", or "c/o the Clarence Community & School Credit Union."

They came from California, Indiana, Michigan, Ohio, Pennsylvania, Colorado, Florida, Maryland, North Carolina, every part of New York, and even Bristol, England. Many were from friends and family. Some were from people we hadn't seen in years.

What a surprise it was to find one from my Brownie leader, Miss Maryann, whom I probably hadn't seen since I was eight or nine. Considering my own age, she must be in her 80s now. She had connected me with the tragedy after reading an article in the Buffalo News, which referred to my maiden name, Schoenwetter, and the fact that I had attended St. Mary of Sorrows school. Later, I was able to find her phone number and called to thank her for her well wishes. I never could have imagined that I would talk to her again.

Another note came from a man I had worked with at National Gypsum over thirty years ago. He told me that his sister lived in Clarence Center, and that her brother-in-law was a Long Street neighbor who lived a few doors from us.

The daughter of one of my mother's old pinochle club friends contacted us. She went to high school with the sister of one of the plane victims, I later learned.

Kim Fox, my sister's sister-in-law, shared her own personal loss: "The horror you must have experienced. It's so unbelievable that Bill and Barbara both have sisters who lost their husbands in airplane accidents. (Her husband had died in the crash of a small plane.) Even after four and a half years, it still seems unbelievable to me at times. I can assure you that I understand the loss of Doug…the rest I can't understand because your experience is so different from mine. A wise friend who lost her son ten years ago…told me that if one doesn't grieve, grief will wait for that person. Please don't second guess your feelings…some may tell you after a few months to just get over it and get on with your life. Those are the people who don't understand what you're going through because they've never been there."

Sister Pat Russo, one of my high school teachers, attended the memorial service and funeral mass for Doug. She described these as "inspiring and uplifting services, as we were introduced to a man with strong family and community values. I learned a lot about your Doug, and only wish that I had gotten to know him better."

Many of these wishes came with monetary donations in amounts ranging from five dollars to more than $1,500. The Clarence/East Amherst Moms Club sent an assortment of gift cards. The employees at Luvata, where Doug worked, held a gate collection. Donations came from churches, school districts, businesses, veterans, teachers, students, those in the military, and even Little League teams.

One family sent us bracelets made by a girl who had died in 2008. She had made the bracelets during her illness with beads that spelled words of encouragement. Wearing those bracelets after she had died had helped her loved ones cope with her passing. They hoped we would also feel that comfort.

Three of my cousins, Suzy, Amy, and Stacey, sent me a charm bracelet. "We have started your bracelet for you with the beautiful circle heart bead. May this bead be a reminder to you of all the love you have in your life—the love you and Doug shared, the love of your children, the love of family and friends, and ultimately, the love of God."

A Clarence High School teacher, Ron Kotlik, wrote: "Doug was truly a kind and generous man. His participation in the history classes at Clarence and UB was a terrific experience for the students. The way Doug prepared for those lectures, including his fantastic Power Point presentations and handouts was truly appreciated by all. His willingness to come to UB on his own time and even read the material for class demonstrated his kindness for others."

From fellow employees:

"I worked with Doug at Luvata and admired him for his love of family."

"Doug would share bits of news of his family with me…he was so proud of his family. I know he was looking forward to the next stage in the girls' lives…the weddings!"

"From 1998 to 2000 I had the great privilege of working with Doug. He was a steady, reliable leader and friend whom I shall miss."

"It was a pleasure to work with Doug in my days in the accounting department and as the receptionist. I remember many days talking with you while you waited in the lobby until Doug finished his work for the day. (Doug broke his leg playing hockey and couldn't drive for six months!)

"I remember the last time I saw Doug running after lunch. He had a huge smile as usual and stopped to talk about his new job in New York and how happy his family was to move back home and be around the extended family again."

Bill Eulberg worked with Doug in Cincinnati. His letter was especially touching. "I had not communicated…for a couple of years and vowed this Christmas I needed to change that. Little did I know that communiqué would be hastened by his death. Jan & I were always impressed with him taking the girls to the German language school … His hockey prowess was fascinating to me.

"He was a great person to work with, and I always enjoyed his company when we traveled. I also enjoyed hearing about the Buffalo contingent that would travel to Cincinnati for the Bills games. Some of those revelers were lost for days at a time. He sent me a Green Bay Packer Christmas tree ornament. That Santa has enjoyed a prominent position on the tree since he arrived. When he was hung on the tree this year, I felt the incentive to get in touch with Doug. I regret that did not occur. The prominence of Packer Santa will be amplified in the years to come."

An Ohio friend's daughter told us, "I remember Doug was so nice to take his time to let me interview him for a school project." Somehow children know how to put heartfelt sympathy into words. My cousin's eight- year-old daughter made a construction paper card covered with hearts, wishing us a "Happy Valentine's Day," and saying, "I feel so sorry for you. I hope you feel better."

So many condolences came from people we did not know. "Like you, we are ages 57 & 61 and our life together means everything," one couple wrote. "We can only sympathize with your emptiness."

"Your husband was a customer of ours at the bank. We had many nice talks and he always spoke so kindly and lovingly about you and your girls."

"I attended School 43 with Doug and spoke with him at the reunion in 2004. What I remember is how proud he was of his family and the photo he passed around for everyone to see—what a beautiful family. I am so stunned at what happened."

Another father whose daughter and Jill played on the same premier soccer team and competed against each other in high school sports warmly wrote: "I did not know that Doug was a Vietnam veteran, that he played baseball, that one of his passions was collecting sports memorabilia. I always looked forward to seeing Doug. Some parents took these sports contests too seriously. Not Doug. Win or lose, he was invariably gracious and sportsmanlike, a wonderful role model for his daughters. Of course, he wanted Jill's team to win, and of course he wanted her to do well, but Doug respected the other team and its players."

I am not exaggerating when I say we received hundreds of cards and letters. Who would ever suspect that there were so many different sympathy card designs? How all the notes buoyed our spirits. Is it any wonder that we couldn't wait to dive into these messages of support? I still have them.

In the beginning, we started spread sheets listing the names and addresses of those who sent these special condolences. Somewhere along the way, the volume multiplied to such an extent that we were unable to keep the record up to date.

I gave myself a goal—to personally thank all those who supported us with a monetary gift. This goal has been hard to reach. It is a slow task, but I feel the need to pick up a pen and take the time to let people know what their kind remarks meant—and still mean—to me. Emotions get in the way, and I work in spurts until my heart can bear no more. I have written more than 600 personal thank you notes.

Say what you will about emailing, tweeting, or texting—the personal handwritten note still carries quite an impact, one that provided my girls and me our daily bread, nourishment we greatly needed to face another day. I would gladly receive more.

*8/14/11*

# MARCH 2009

*"Our world as we know it has changed and those changes require that we in turn adjust to a new "normal."*

*~ Author Unknown*

During the weeks after the accident, I had felt sequestered, venturing out into the real world on a limited basis. Going out depended on the generosity of others. We had no car, and I couldn't drive anyway because of my injury.

My boss called West Herr Automotive and they gave us a car at no charge. Finally, the sling on my arm came off, and my mobility increased.

It was time to face reality and try to learn how to fit into this new life.

While my Aunt Agnes had opened her home to us, I needed to find Kim, Jill, and me a more permanent place to live. Although I would have preferred a house, I knew an apartment would be a more logical choice. I needed time to decide where we would live. The search began, and we found a duplex on Kraus Road in Clarence Center.

Before we moved in, Jill, Dan, and I travelled to Loveland, Ohio. A memorial mass had been scheduled for Doug at our former parish, St. Columban. Kim had just returned to her teaching job and would not join us. We would spend St. Patrick's Day with Lori and Chris, in Bellevue, Kentucky directly across the river from downtown Cincinnati.

It would be the first holiday without Doug, and memories flooded back. I thought about finding ourselves among St. Patrick's Day revelers in Toronto where my love of Guinness beer began, or the time we enjoyed the performance of a bagpiper in Brennan's Bar. The aching void was deepening.

While trying to lend a helping hand, I almost added to our chaos. I decided to take Ginger, Chris and Lori's dog, for a morning walk. Instead of clipping the leash to a sturdy part of her collar, I attached it to her tag ring. Once out the door, she started to run. The leash pulled free. The street traffic was busy. If she gets hit by a car they'll never forgive me, I thought as I chased after Ginger. She ran a few doors down and headed toward a neighbor's fenced yard. It took falling to my knees and crawling in the mud, but I caught up to her and avoided tragedy.

The morning of the memorial mass, I suddenly noticed circle-like flashes of light in my eyes. This had happened once before, and had been identified as an optic migraine. It is a scary sensation and progresses until seeing becomes almost impossible. I didn't want to alarm the girls, but I couldn't help but fear that the stress of the last month had caused something more serious. Maybe it was even a stroke. I asked Lori to call the paramedics. Of course, by the time they arrived, the flashing had stopped. I felt better after being checked out so I turned down a trip to the emergency room.

Old friends, neighbors, and even some relatives attended the memorial mass that evening. How heartwarming to see them. I read the eulogy that I had written for the Clarence memorial. The only discomfort I felt during the service came as the deacon gave his homily. He included remembrances of his wife's death. "How comforting it is to be able to be with our loved ones and say goodbye when they pass." I know he meant well, but that statement felt like a dagger in my heart. There was no chance for us to say "goodbye" to Doug, and he was completely alone. No one else commented on what I thought was inappropriate, so perhaps I was the only one it bothered.

After the memorial mass we enjoyed the warmth of a quiet dinner with some close friends and relatives. This ongoing support continued to be welcome and sustaining

A surprise awaited us the day before we would head back

home. Neighbors of Lori had a litter of kittens. From the start, I insisted that I would not even look at them. I wasn't ready to replace Spots, our old cat who had also perished in the crash.

When I heard that Jill was checking out the kittens, guess who else went over to see them. They certainly were cute. Was I

 actually agreeing to bring this black and white kitten home with us? I could hear Doug's voice in my head. "Are you out of your mind?" he would have been saying.

Yes, Belle officially joined our family that day. She made the eight-hour trek back to my aunt's house

*Belle*

with a lay-over in Columbus, Ohio to visit a friend. How awkward is it to call someone and say, "Do you mind if we bring a kitten along with us?"

That little kitten has become one of my life lines, and there are times when I think some of Doug's spirit lives on in her. She is my shadow, following my every move. She is the warmth that comforts me in the middle of the night. On the times I give in and let the tears flow, she'll often give me a bite. It's as if she's telling me to "snap out of it, and get yourself together," which is something I'm sure Doug would also say.

In the beginning, we had been bombarded by the media. My friend Sue and I joked that the only calls we would consider accepting had to come from Oprah or Obama. While we were in Columbus, Sue called with the news that Oprah's producer had called. "You're kidding," Sue had replied because of our joke.

But this was no joke. I received an email from an Oprah producer asking if I was interested in telling my story to Oprah's viewers and sharing memories of Doug. It was flattering and I was tempted, but the timing just wasn't right. I wasn't ready to face a studio audience along with viewers from across the country. I was still too fragile and could imagine myself falling apart at the seams. Perhaps only fools refuse Oprah, but I did.

Moving day arrived. Jeff's friends brought their trucks to help move the many boxes of things people had donated. We went from having nothing to having too much.

Furniture came from Mort Muchow's barn. Mort was among many new friends who had stepped forward to help. Dan's dad bought us mattresses. We made mad dashes through stores to get missing necessities.

Right after that exhausting move we learned that the location wasn't the wisest choice. We were directly on the flight path into the Buffalo airport. When we were looking at the duplex I remember hearing the real estate agent whispering to the landlord, "This isn't on the flight path, is it?" I heard him reply, "no." That was definitely not true.

Hearing planes pass over was almost unbearable, especially on Thursday nights around 10:15 pm, the day and time of the crash.

Another problem was the open area nearby that seemed to magnify sound. Stormy weather, with gusts of wind, produced unnerving sounds. Was that the wind, or a plane? Such sounds often led to my heart pounding and a panicky feeling of not knowing where to go or what to do to ease the distress. We had planned to stay for a year in the duplex before making any permanent decisions. I realized quickly that I couldn't wait that long to find a new home.

Normalcy was slowly creeping back. The next step would be returning to work. Although I had been to the office for a few hours at a time, my first full day back was March 23, 2009. What a feeling of comfort my cubicle provided. I had stapled to the cubicle wall a greeting card Doug had once sent. "For you, Love…We're good together because we share laughter, dreams, quiet moments, special memories, private jokes…and each other," it proclaimed.

I wondered when I had received the card. Was it for an anniversary or birthday? I could not remember the occasion. Because the sentiment on this card really seemed to capture the essence of our marriage, I had attached it to the cubicle wall. Now it was a comforting reminder of Doug's love.

My curiosity aroused, I pulled the card off the wall. "We're good together because we share love. Happy Easter." Doug's signature evoked a flood of emotion, but it was the date that struck me—March 23, 2008—exactly one year ago. I will never know why I waited until that day to open the card, but I felt Doug was giving his approval to take another step without him.

My job surrounds me with good, caring people. Some of my co-workers decided to throw us a "shower" to help replenish all the household items we needed to start up again. How would someone in my situation survive without a never-ending network of support? I did not register at a home store, as one of the girls suggested, but I did discuss the things that we still needed.

"Some liquor might be nice," I said. One of the guys nearby laughed out loud. "If you were me, wouldn't you be drinking?" I good-naturedly replied. On a Friday evening, we were indeed showered not only with gifts but love and support.

Another work acquaintance had mentioned on a Longaberger consultant website that I collected their baskets and pottery. Actually my "collection" had been quite modest, but what ensued was unbelievable. We started calling it "The Longaberger Relief Project," as box after box of Longaberger products arrived. The number jumped to over thirty. It turns out that the mother of a special young man who works at the school had initiated this windfall. Her son would excitedly deliver each box, snapping my picture with his camera as I opened the boxes. Tammy Longaberger's office also contacted me and sent several pieces of their pottery.

Some very special deliveries came Jill's way, too.

The Buffalo Sabres organization heard that she and Doug had attended a game the night before the crash. They sent her a signed jersey.

Jill's former high school basketball coach, Mark Layer, put together a box of memorabilia commemorating her team's successful 2004-2005 season. Included was the team picture, and photos taken at Senior Night, and a program booklet outlining their success as division and section champs her senior year.

As I looked through the basketball photos, I remembered how disappointed Doug had been that a business trip had prevented him from attending. That was always something he regretted. He wasn't one for missing any of the girls' sporting events. Once, while away on business, he even flew into Jamestown so he would be there for one of Jill's games.

"I loved coaching Jill," the coach replied to my thank you email. "She was terrific in every single way. I do remember the Jamestown game that Doug came to. He loved watching the girls play, and I always enjoyed being able to chat with him about sports... I think of you often."

Kim, Jill, and I attended an informational meeting for the Long Street residents on March 31 at the Clarence Town Hall. It would be the first time since the crash that I had seen some of these neighbors. We hugged, caught up, and remembered that awful night.

What type of questions would be asked about the future of the site? When the official program started, I sat there trying to control my urge to dart from the room and find a spot to sob. Would the pounding of my heart settle down to a normal beat?

Some neighbors that I did not know complained about people driving down the street to look at the site and then turning around in their driveways. This temporary disruption seemed minor compared to what the 3407 families and I had lost. Seriously, I wondered, did it warrant heated discussion?

Some people did want to know what would happen to the site. I was relieved when the town supervisor, Scott Bielewski, handled that inquiry by saying it was still too early and people had to give us time to make decisions.

A local shirt factory had produced T-Shirts depicting a broken heart held together with a bandage, to "heal" the community. Proceeds were used to distribute large baskets of flowers and gift certificates from area retailers to the Long Street and 3407 Families.

The month of March had passed in a flurry of activities, many of which were new to me: financial decisions, stock transfer into estate accounts, therapy for the collar bone injury, and continuing plans for Lori's wedding in August.

Because Lori and Chris were out-of-town, it was up to me to check out a photographer they were considering. A pang of sorrow went through me when I had to tell the photographer that I would be walking Lori down the aisle.

Setup for the tasting at the reception hall also needed to be arranged. That would be another solo evening. Doug's presence would be in spirit only.

The road ahead was difficult and adjusting to a new normal was not going to be easy.

*1/14/12*

## SPOTS

Fish, a turtle named Blinky, and a canary were my only pets growing up. My mother's nerves could not handle any other creature. Doug grew up with dogs, but he had never suggested that we get one. Enter Spots. This stray black and white cat made the rounds of our neighborhood in Loveland, Ohio. I began to feel a bit of pity for this poor stray and started leaving scraps of tuna on the front porch. I was pleased to see that her thin body was filling out.

Lori decided the cat's name should be Spots in recognition of her coloring. As the girls were starting to have more interaction with her, I decided it would be a good idea to take her to the vet for any necessary shots. "She's about seven months old," the vet told us, "and oh, she's going to have kittens." No wonder she was filling out.

Up to this point, Spots had been strictly an outdoor cat. One day my neighbor called and inquired, "Would you like to see your kittens?" Spots had climbed up to the neighbor's still-in-progress porch roof and squeezed into a storage area where she had delivered a litter of four. I carefully moved the kittens to a shed in our backyard. Spots did not approve of this transfer and carried them back up to the storage area, one-by-one. My neighbor had no objections, so they remained in their place of birth until several days later when, again one-by-one, Spots carried the kittens into our garage.

*Spots*

What an adventure and learning experience it was for us to watch the development of those kittens. In the end, three made their way to new homes, and we kept Fuzzy. Unfortunately, following in her mother's footsteps as an outdoor cat, Fuzzy was only seven months old when she died after being hit by a car.

Spots eventually came into the house, but still enjoyed her sojourns into the neighborhood. She joined us when we made the move back to Buffalo.

On the evening of February 12, Spots, then nineteen years old, rested comfortably on the chaise lounge in the living room. The poor old girl was on borrowed time. She had been diagnosed with cancer of the throat a month earlier.

After this death sentence, I felt the need for a second opinion, and scheduled an appointment with another vet. The night before that visit, I held Spots as we sat on the chaise. I was convinced that we would be forced to put her down the next day. I sobbed as I held her, yet couldn't move to reach a tissue lest I disturb her. The awkward situation was sadly comic.

Before leaving for the vet, I called Doug. "Did you say good-bye to Spots?" I asked. He assured me he had. Therefore, he was surprised when I walked back into the house, Spots in my arms.

"I couldn't do it," I said. "They said her heart is good and she was jumping up on tables. She still can enjoy some life."

"You're just putting off the inevitable," Doug said.

"Well, I think she's happy that I spared her for now."

Doug was right. The expiration of those nine lives cats supposedly possess can only be delayed so long. Looking back, ending her life then would have probably been more peaceful than her actual demise.

*1/12/12*

# APRIL 2009

---

*"We all at certain times in our lives find ourselves broken.*
*True strength is found in picking up the pieces."*

~ Jeremy Shingongo

I started "walking among the ruins" in April.

Global BMS, a company specializing in disaster recovery and damage restoration, had the daunting job of collecting, cleaning, and sorting items retrieved from the crash site and the contents of the garage.

I wish I would have been there when their crew entered our garage. Surely, they did not expect to find the space filled wall-to-wall and without any available space for cars. This was a Wielinski fact-of-life. Our garage was for storage. Cars didn't fit.

We had received a letter from Global saying that most of the items had been shipped to their facility in Texas. A small number of things were placed in a storage shed in Clarence Center. Kim, Jill, and I arranged to meet our attorney at the storage facility for our first opportunity to see what had been salvaged.

An eerie feeling came over us as we stepped into what felt like a cavity of remains. A pump and an old water fountain that had been in a covered area next to the garage were there. Doug had searched years for that iron pump. He could always find small pumps, but never a tall one. Finally, about a year before the crash, his search was successful. The old water fountain probably came from a park and arrived at our house one Sunday after his early morning hunt. Both the pump and fountain were part of our flower garden next to the back door on Long Street. Doug had moved them under the covered area for the winter. Both are now in my backyard. They evoke happy memories of Doug and his quests.

Other things from our outside shed and garage included the lawn mower, snow blower, empty metal shelving, ladders, tools, bicycles, and the work bench Doug had built. Two unbelievable items had been found leaning against the wall of the shed: the back door of the house, and one of the sliding doors from the family room. The door of the house was completely intact—not a crack in the glass. The only visible damage, shards of wood by the hinges, was apparently caused when the door was blown from the house. The sliding door also was completely whole. Unimaginable!

Seeing the pump, fountain, and work bench was comforting; seeing the doors, unnerving.

Shortly after that crazy afternoon, the girls and I entered the world of psychology. Kim, Jill, and I would have a group session. As we rushed out the door for the appointment, I fumbled in my purse to find the psychologist's name and address I had scribbled on an envelope. I was unable to locate the envelope. She was not in the phone book but I knew the general area where her office was located. Not wanting to waste time, we headed out. It was obvious that I probably did need a psychologist, as I stopped in several medical buildings on North Bailey, checking lobby directories for her name. What sane person would do that? Unbelievably, I found her right at our appointment time.

This session gave me an opportunity to ask Jill if she was upset with me for not searching for Doug the night of the crash. The question had haunted me. After we were reunited, I had grabbed Jill's arm and told her that because of the fire and my fear of the fuel from the plane exploding, we had to get out of there, and could not look for Doug.

"Making me leave probably saved my life," she said, relieving my anguish.

The session was emotional. If one of us cried, we all cried. That was our last group session before we would all begin regular, individual counseling.

Doug had subscribed to *Sports Collectors Digest*. That publication was still being delivered to me, and I had passed it along to Lori's Chris, who saw an obituary for Doug. The mystery of how it got there was solved when Jim Macie sent an email to advise he had submitted it because "those in the sports hobby would like to know of his passing."

Doug was heavily involved in collecting sports memorabilia. It was not until I accompanied him on a trip to Philadelphia in 1978 that I realized the scope of his hobby.

The fact I actually went with him was quite a step for such a conservative Catholic girl—unmarried and spending a weekend together. I'm sure I told my parents I was going. My mother had two unmarried daughters in their mid-twenties, and her goal for us was marriage. She probably would have agreed to anything that might result in a proposal.

"Karen will stay at her cousin's in Kenneth Square, Pennsylvania," Doug told his mother.

When his mother later learned we had shared a motel room, she told Doug that I was a "foolish girl!"

Great, I wasn't exactly scoring approval points.

My eyes were opened as I realized the immense interest that existed for sports memorabilia. Vendors filled the convention center, and I was amazed at the prices people would pay for this old stuff. I also came to realize the love Doug and Jim had for collecting. It was like watching kids in a candy store. I could see the nervous excitement in their eyes. Where could they look first and whom could they talk to about some new find? The wheeling and dealing—so much to see, so little time. Their excitement would rub off on me, and the thrill of collecting would become a part of my life.

Easter 2009 arrived, as did the girls and most of their guys. We followed tradition: early mass followed by breakfast and then dinner in the early afternoon. This normal routine helped us get through Easter without Doug.

I made a decision during Easter week. The HR department where Doug had worked had told me they would keep his voice mail message until I was ready to listen to it. One afternoon at work, I decided the time had come to hear his voice. I met Ben, from our school Technology department in a conference room where he had set up the equipment to record Doug's message. (It seemed fitting for Ben to assist me. He had helped Doug with the technical aspects of his Vietnam presentations to the students at the high school.) We would do a dry-run first. I sat with my back to Ben, dialed the number, and once again I heard Doug's voice.

"Hi, you've reached Doug Wielinski. I'm in the office today but currently away from my desk. If you'd like to leave a message, please do and I'll try to return your call when I get the opportunity." Such a brief message. All systems checked out, so I called once more and his voice was preserved. I left the conference room, went to the ladies' room, sat in a stall, and cried.

My girls have not yet listened to that recording, but it will be something nice to have for them in the future.

Letters had started arriving from our mortgage company threatening foreclosure on the Long Street house. Imagine! For some reason I had missed a payment. Computers apparently did not have a heart, and did not read papers or watch the nightly news. Isn't it hard to foreclose on something that doesn't exist anymore? Luckily, the insurance company came through and I was able to pay off the mortgage.

Preparations for Lori and Chris' wedding continued. Lori and I, along with Chris and his parents, went to a tasting at a local Country Club, and arrangements were finalized for the bridal shower that would take place in May.

Jill and I had been sharing a car, so I bought a RAV4 thanks to some insurance money and an advance from the airline. It was the first time in my life I had a brand-new car.

I began the quest to get new birth certificates. When we opened our bank account upon returning to the Buffalo area in 1998, a safe deposit box had not been available. We had never looked into getting one later, so all of our important documents—birth certificates, passports, and our marriage certificate —had been in the house on Long Street.

Jessica and Jill had been born in Ohio, so their birth certificates would have to come from Clermont County.

Kathy Hochul and the Erie County Clerk's office had been instrumental in obtaining new passports and drivers' licenses in February. Her office again came to our rescue and suggested we contact the Buffalo mayor's office regarding the remaining birth and marriage certificates we needed. Everyone was very cooperative.

Oprah's people still pursued us. Their taping for the season would end on May 8. If we were interested the segment would have to be taped before that date. Again, I was tempted to say yes, but with Lori's shower taking place on May 9 it seemed impossible. I also asked myself if going to Chicago, facing Oprah, and exposing my family to a national viewing public for an eighteen-minute segment was worth the stress. Once again, my answer was "no, thank you."

Kim, Jill and I drove to the Brockport campus of the State University of New York on a Friday evening to attend Jill's Recreation and Leisure Department dinner. Jill would be one of the seniors honored at the event. Doug, Jill and I had enjoyed the dinner in 2008, and people were still talking about how we had won several bottles of wine in the silent auction. Apparently, it had set a record.

Now, during this evening in 2009, I think we were all a bit on edge as we waited for someone to bring up the subject of the crash. The focus of the night remained on Jill and the seniors. There was no discussion of our tragedy.

Humor continued to work its way into our lives, and it was welcomed. A local teacher had asked my friend, Sue, if I would be interested in clothing that had belonged to his Aunt. When Sue arrived at the duplex, I assumed there would be a few boxes of clothes. Her vehicle was completely filled with boxes and bags. I think this assortment included all the aunt's clothes from the 1960s to her death. From the looks of the clothing, she was a professional woman. Unfortunately, what was stylish in the 1960s wasn't in vogue today.

Sue and I lugged everything inside the duplex and sorted through it. It was an unusually hot April day. I couldn't possibly turn the air conditioning on yet, could I? Windows provided no breeze, and we couldn't put on the ceiling fan—our kitten Belle obviously had experienced some dark encounter with a fan and freaked out whenever it was turned on.

Sweat poured off us, as we laughed our way through the sorting process. At one point, I held up a purple chiffon dress. "I swear this looks like something my mother wore to my confirmation in the 1960s," I told Sue. We took a picture of the dress and sent the image to Lori, texting: "Found my mother-of-the-bride dress for your wedding." We kept a few things and sent the rest to St. Luke's Mission.

Barbara Burns from WBEN Radio shared an email she had received back in February from Kathleen Dworak, a Clarence

Center resident, who kindly offered to paint a rendering of 6038 Long Street.

I responded:

`We certainly would appreciate the portrait.`

We were very proud of that 1920s house, and Doug had worked hard to retain the historical aspect of the home, while updating it for more modern living. We mourn for Doug, but also for the destruction of that little kit home.

Kathleen captured our home. The portrait hangs in my home office, but not where I need to look at it every day. Studying the rendition, I can reminisce about our life in that cozy home. Unfortunately, it also takes me back to the night of the crash and awakens visions of where Doug, Jill, and I were when the plane struck. I cannot look at the picture long.

The portrait also became the inspiration for an engraving of our home that was placed on an address plaque at the Long Street memorial.

At the end of April, I learned that the tragedy of Flight 3407 had touched me in another way.

Hearings were scheduled to begin in Washington, D. C. about the findings of the National Transportation Safety Board. My attorney would attend those sessions, but there would also be a live-feed set up for family members at a hotel near the airport. I thought it was time to watch those sessions, and realized that I would be meeting some of the family members.

Shortly after the crash, the Buffalo News had published short biographies of the passengers. I had glanced at the names and information, but admit I did not read them thoroughly. I had saved the newspapers, though, and wanted to read them before the hearings. I wanted to know more about the others who had died that night. When I came to the name of Lorin Maurer, I had to read her biography several times. I couldn't believe it. Lorin, a young woman in her twenties, had been on her way to Buffalo to attend the wedding of her boyfriend's brother. Her boyfriend's name was Kevin Kuwik. I was shocked because Keith Kuwik, Kevin's brother, was the principal of Ledgeview Elementary School in the Clarence District where I also worked. A few days before the crash, I had seen Keith and asked him about his wedding.

"It's actually this Saturday, February 14th," he told me.

I saw Keith shortly after I returned to work in March, and asked him how the wedding had been. He talked a bit about it, and never mentioned the crash. No one else at the district office where I worked had mentioned his connection. I felt terrible, and realized some of the fault was mine for not educating myself completely on the plane victims. However, I also was amazed that no one shared his involvement with me.

"We didn't want to upset you more," one of my office colleagues tried to explain.

I emailed Keith:

> I cannot express how shocked and upset I was to discover that you and your family had to share in the pain of that night. I especially feel terrible because when I saw you a few weeks ago I so casually asked about your wedding.

Keith assured me he had not been offended and completely understood.

His brother, Kevin Kuwik, is now one of the driving forces behind implementation of new air safety measures. I have spoken with Kevin many times and once had dinner with him while visiting friends in Columbus, Ohio. He is a wonderful young man, who was on the verge of beginning another chapter in his life with Lorin. His sorrow breaks my heart, and I only hope that he will allow himself to eventually find happiness with someone else.

In April, not only had I started the difficult task of encountering possessions lost and found from the crash, but more significant was the reality that I had started the painful walk among the shattered lives of the plane victims' families.

## SHARING A PASSION

Few people can say they have remained friends with their childhood acquaintances. Doug and Mace were an exception.

Doug and Jim met in 1955 in third grade at P. S. 43 on Lovejoy Street in Buffalo. Thus began a 54-year friendship that steadily grew as they discovered many shared common interests. In particular they shared a passion for sports in all forms. They played sports, watched sports, and collected sports memorabilia.

They played Little League, Police Athletic League (PAL) baseball at Houghton Park, and Municipal New York Baseball (MUNY). As they got older, they continued to play both fast pitch and slo-pitch softball.

They also played hockey together for years. In the mid-1970s, Doug, Jim, and his brother Jeff played on the same line and were dubbed the "Polish Connection" by other players in the Buffalo Senior-A Hockey League.

There was also basketball at the YMCA, Hennepin Park Community Center, or in friends' yards. Pick-up football games were also thrown into the mix.

Doug and Jim loved watching, supporting, and talking about their favorite professional teams. When it came to baseball teams there was a discrepancy. Doug was an avid Yankees fan who loved Whitey Ford and Mickey Mantle. Jim's favorites were Ted Williams and the Red Sox. They loved going to the old Buffalo Bisons Hockey games at the Buffalo "Aud" and playing ramp hockey with a crushed paper cup between periods. Needless to say, they were both fans of the Buffalo Sabres.

The guys supported the Buffalo Bills from their inception in 1960. They would go to Bills games on Saturday nights for a dollar at the old Rockpile (Buffalo's now demolished War Memorial Stadium) in the early 1960s. Jim tells the story of how one night, George Blanda of the Houston Oilers kicked a field goal and the ball came right into Doug's arms. Unfortunately, about twenty guys jumped on him and tore the ball away from him, despite his efforts to hang onto it.

After a game in December of 1964, Doug and Jim ran on the field at War Memorial Stadium after the Bills won their first AFL Championship against San Diego. According to Jim's recollections, Doug jubilantly pounded on Charger quarterback John Hadl's shoulder pads and shouted, "We won! We beat you! We're the Champions!" In this day and age, Doug would probably get himself arrested.

Mace had connections with the Bills, and he often included Doug in special events held with the Bills Alumni. At one of these events honoring Ralph Wilson and the members of the 1960s Bills teams, Doug brought along his Bills scrapbook and other memorabilia. After the dinner and ceremony, Doug was asked by several former players if they could look at his scrapbook. Jim and Doug sat for over an hour with Elbert Dubenion, Billy Shaw, Glenn Bass, Ernie Warlick, Booker Edgerson, and other childhood heroes and their wives as they flipped through Doug's scrapbook and reminisced. I always said it was one of the highlights in Doug's life. Some of the players even asked Doug to make copies of articles, which he was happy to send them.

Collecting sports memorabilia was a source of great pride for Doug and Mace. They had started when they were just kids, and things had escalated from there. In the mid-1970s they would

*Pictured left to right: Bill Macie, Bills Receiver Tom Ryleck and Doug.*

go on buying trips, often with money borrowed from their parents, for a big purchase. Jim recalls going to a Sabres game with Doug, jumping into his car after the game and driving all night to Wilmington, North Carolina to buy a large baseball collection. That acquisition required a U-Haul to bring it back to Buffalo.

In the late 1970s, they bought a Sportservice warehouse full of memorabilia and then went to Philadelphia for a convention. By then, I had entered the picture. That was my initiation into the wonderful world of sports collecting. Mace told me he thought I considered them "geeks" for collecting. I would disagree with that. You could feel and see the guys' excitement as they wheeled and dealed. They loved collecting. Jim's wife Betty would probably agree with me that their zeal was infectious. We came to appreciate the hobby.

I'm glad Doug never had to choose between me or his collection. I might have come in a close second.

Doug and Mace were loyal and devoted friends. An unwritten pact existed between them. If something happened to one of them, the other would be there to assist his wife and family, especially where the memorabilia collection was concerned.

It is true that much of Doug's collection was lost in the crash. It would have broken his heart. When Jim and I saw many of the destroyed items, our hearts ached too. Because space in the Long Street house was limited, though, some items were stored in the garage and had been spared. I swear Doug's spirit extinguished any flames that came near it.

What remained in that garage, much of it memorabilia (including the aforementioned Bills' scrapbook), is now in rented storage units. Boxes line the walls of these units, and every time I open those doors, I am overwhelmed. How will I sort through this? True to their agreement, Jim is there for me. We have started a process that will take years to complete. Every box we open holds a flood of memories. Mace remembers every adventure that led to the purchase of so many items. "I can't believe he still had this," Jim would say in amazement. The process is bittersweet.

Just as Doug cherished his childhood friend, I am thankful that he remains a presence in my life. Now, we share a passion— keeping Doug alive through special memories.

3/31/11

# MAY 2009

*"You gain strength, courage, and confidence by every experience in which you really stop to look fear in the face... You must do the thing you think you cannot do."*

~ *Eleanor Roosevelt*

How much emotional upheaval can one month contain?

I had the recording of Doug's voice, and now I would attempt to obtain his image. The Bills had unveiled a plaque honoring Tim Russert on November 30, 2008. Doug and I had season tickets for the games but that particular game we sat in a suite with employees from Doug's office. Part of that package included parking in the stadium lot. Usually it was just Doug and I who attended the games. This time Chris and Lori were in town and had tickets with friends. We had also given our regular seats to Doug's brother, Jackie, and his wife, Joan. This called for a bit more tailgating, so we arrived early and lingered longer in the lot.

Jenny Rizzo, a reporter from WKBW television, approached us and asked our feelings about the unveiling of the plaque. The evening news included part of Doug's remarks. Would the station possibly give me a copy of that video? I sent her an email. Jenny extended her condolences to our family, and indicated she remembered Doug. "I spent a few minutes trying to convince him to do the interview. He was very nice and good-natured about it and he gave us a good sound bite about Tim Russert," she replied.

She was kind enough to send us two copies. There he was, bundled up for the cold day, moving from side-to-side in an attempt to keep warm, Bills' hat perched on his head, curly grey hair peeking out from the sides.

"Why he (Tim Russert) was one of the Bills biggest backers since I've been living in Buffalo all my life, more than 40 years," Doug told the reporter.

Not a lot said, but it was so good to see him. At that point, I did not know what pictures would turn up in the items retrieved from the site so that video was important to me.

Discussions began with the Clarence town supervisor regarding the possible transfer of the Long Street site to the town. I, my attorney, and my brother-in-law, Billy agreed that it would be best to retain ownership of the property until a memorial was complete. That way I would have more control over what would be built. It was also the beginning of a possible plan to have a private memorial on Long Street, and a public memorial elsewhere in the town.

As Lori's bridal shower approached I was faced with "shit hitting the fan." One Long Street neighbor had called me a few times to say that a petition had been circulated to oppose a large memorial on the site. He sent me a copy of that petition. I was surprised to see that it opposed any memorial whatsoever, and indicated the neighbors preferred a new house being built on the land. I found those wishes very upsetting. I could understand their viewpoint, but I also knew my family and the 3407 families wanted a memorial. It was becoming clear to me that I would be unable to make everyone happy. Less than three months since the crash and I was expected to make decisions that would affect so many people.

A feeling of panic came over me, and I rushed out for a walk— anything to relieve the increasing pressure. It looked like I would need the wisdom of Solomon to solve this dilemma.

Lori's bridal shower was a success. About 60 people attended. The favors were magnets in tiny boxes resembling refrigerators—a fitting tribute to our family tradition of collecting magnets for our refrigerator.

All the gifts were brought to the duplex. It was a windy day and it was funny to observe the lawn care guys watching the girls attempt to bring in gifts and keep their dresses from flying up around their waists, invoking memories of Marilyn Monroe in *The Seven Year Itch.*

That evening the girls were off to Rochester for the bachelorette party and I attended a benefit being held by the Knights of St. John for our family. Both my brother-in-law, Eddie, and cousin, Peter, were Knights.

It was strange—actually very awkward—to be at the event knowing family, friends, and strangers were donating their money to help us rebuild our lives. Toward the end of the evening I was asked to go up front with the organizers. Luckily, they didn't ask me to make a speech—they talked for me and I motioned my thanks with my hands, tears welling up in my eyes. Amazingly, over $5,000 was collected.

I made my way to the back of the hall and headed right to the ladies' room. Inside I met one of my nieces who told me how she missed her Uncle Dougie. I mentioned how so many of her dad's (Eddie, Doug's brother) mannerisms reminded me of Doug.

The following day was Mother's Day. Although they were suffering from some of the effects of their celebration at the bachelorette party—and were feeling Doug's absence from the wedding preparations—my daughters were able to take me out for lunch.

For weeks, I debated whether or not to attend the National Transportation Safety Board's live-stream of the hearings detailing their investigative findings of the crash. I was apprehensive about meeting both the families and the press.

I did not attend the first day of the hearings. An animated

re-enactment of the crash was to be played. I couldn't bring my-self to be with the families when they saw the plane tumbling from the sky and imagined the terror their loved ones had experienced.

A report by the ERO News Network stated:

> The hearings conducted by the NTSB, Tuesday, are proving to be nearly as painful as the accident itself—to those left behind. The transcript of the cockpit voice recorder aboard Continental Connection Flight 3407, leaves little question that the pilots of the Bombardier Q400 violated anyone's definition of "sterile cockpit" while on approach to Buffalo Niagara International Airport the night of February 12th.
>
> In a conversation which continued until less than three minutes before the plane came down on a home in subur-ban Clarence Center, New York, First Officer Rebecca Shaw and Captain Marvin Renslow chatted about icing, including Shaw's near-complete inexperience with it when hired, and openly discussed shortcomings in both their own experience, and in training offered by the regional airline. About five min-utes before impact, Shaw commented to Renslow, quote "I've never seen icing conditions. I've never de-iced. I've never ex-perienced any of that."

I had gone to the WGRZ website on my work computer. I listened in disbelief to that statement. "You're probably experiencing it right now!" I said under my breath. Or maybe I just thought it. "Why aren't you paying attention?"

It was becoming obvious that pilot error would be a major issue in the crash.

The following day I did attend the viewing. My anxiety grew as I approached the hotel. Would I be greeted by a sea of report-ers? How would I react to meeting the other family members?

I arrived before the media and was met by Doug's brother Billy. He would be my protector throughout the morning—lit-erally walking in front of me and blocking any reporter who approached.

There were not many families in attendance that day but I did speak with a few. It would be my first encounter with their loss and pain. Meeting them was difficult.

The NTSB made no major revelations that day, and I prepared to leave. My attorney felt I should stop and talk to the reporters. I made a fast trip to the restroom and walked out to find the media assembled and ready to pounce. Microphones, lights, and cameras were everywhere. One of the first reporters to greet me was Donn Esmonde from *The Buffalo News*.

In the days after the crash Donn had written columns that seemed to mirror some of our feelings. I was thankful for his insight and I sent him an email to that effect. It was good to put a face to that brief email exchange. His description of me in his column the day after those hearings referred to my "friendly face…and golden ringlets." I got plenty of good-natured comments on that.

The press conference went well and I actually felt calm. Later in the day, it seemed surreal to watch myself on the local evening news and listen to the entire interview on WBEN and WBFO radio.

I couldn't put it off any longer, so I went to Wagner Monument to begin the process of obtaining a tombstone for Doug's grave. The design evolved around a tattoo Jill was considering. There would be two connecting puzzle pieces surrounded by the things we loved. Puzzles were prominent in our lives. A Buffalo Bison puzzle was on our dining room table the night of the crash and Doug had referred to puzzles when researching family heritage.

It isn't exactly calming to pick out a tombstone—especially when your name will be on it too.

Jill graduated from SUNY Brockport on May 16. All week the

*Jill and Karen*

forecast had called for rain and a cooler temperature, not encouraging for an outdoor ceremony. My preparation resembled packing for a football game—rain gear, blankets, and plastic covers to keep us dry. As often happens, the weather forecasters were completely off. There wasn't one drop of rain and the sun hovered overhead. I had lugged all that paraphernalia for nothing.

I was glad for the sun. I left my sunglasses on, hiding the tears that would flow. We felt Doug's presence throughout the day. A choir entertained before the ceremony. One selection was "Unforgettable," one of our special songs. The fact that Jill and I had survived to participate in this day was unbelievable.

May 19th had arrived. At the beginning of the New Year, I had drawn a heart around that date on my work calendar with the number "30." It would have been our thirtieth wedding anniversary. I marked the celebration of our union by visiting Doug's grave during my lunch hour—not exactly how I pictured reaching that milestone.

I suppose my memories tend to paint an idealistic picture of our marriage. Some probably would say, "Oh come on, it couldn't have been that perfect."

Sure, we had our moments when we'd roll our eyes and want to wring each other's necks. Divorce court was probably close at hand when Doug applied for two very different types of jobs and asked me to send his resumes out. I screwed up the resumes and both companies called Doug totally confused on what he was applying for. Of course, he didn't get invited to interview with either. There was also the time he was at the wheel and I was "map reader" (something I was never good at) as we left

Lori's apartment in Brooklyn and tried to find our way out of Manhattan—not a good experience.

We never had terrible arguments or went to bed mad. We probably both held our tongues when we wanted to scream. We had learned that patience and a sense of humor could always save the day.

"Flashing" my husband out the front window while he waited for the car pool hopefully made his day. I know when I would hear a knock on the upstairs bedroom window, and glance up to see my husband "mooning" me, it brightened my day. I can forget the little annoyances and hold on to the happy memories. We enjoyed each other and had a good life.

On what would have been that thirtieth anniversary my co-workers gave me flowers, Jill made Skyline Chili for dinner and bought some flowers too. The kitten, Belle, as usual scratched me up. I got through the day.

The biggest transition took place at the end of May. Jill and I headed to Pinehurst, North Carolina where she would begin her college internship. She had "walked" on graduation day, but would not receive her diploma until her internship was completed.

Originally, the internship was supposed to begin in April. After the crash, the Pinehurst Golf Resort had worked with Jill to postpone her arrival date. That gave her time to adjust.

As we approached the apartment building my stomach turned.

"This can't be it," Jill remarked.

"I think it is," I said.

It was a rundown building. Ripped curtains fluttered out of open windows. How could I leave my baby in a place like this? Did I have time to find her somewhere else to live?

We had arrived earlier than anticipated, so could not check out the inside of the apartment. Keeping most of my feelings to myself, we went to meet Dan, who was stationed at the nearby Fort Bragg Army base, for lunch. I was somewhat encouraged to find the town of Southern Pines to be quaint, clean, and apparently respectable.

When we finally could get inside the apartment, things didn't look too bad (the cockroaches would not make an appearance until later in her stay). Extra cleaning was needed, but the place had possibilities. Jill's roommate, Lana, who was from Russia and also worked at the resort, was very nice. Maybe I could leave Jill here.

My friend, Jeanette and her two daughters had volunteered to drive down to North Carolina so I would not have to fly home. The generosity of friends continued to amaze me.

New chapters were beginning, but what a range of emotions had been thrown into this month of May.

2/15/12

## ANNIVERSARY

*I hurried across the grass toward you.*

*Happy Anniversary, Doug. Can you believe it…thirty-three years? It seems like only yesterday—May 19, 1979.*

*Pictures reveal me as a thin twenty-seven year old, weighing in at about 110 pounds. I had crafted the wedding dress from Butterick Pattern #5746 and laboriously sewn individual tiny lace appliqués to the bodice. Back in those days, The Buffalo Evening News Sunday edition featured pages and pages of the weekend brides—all published for no fee. When I went to the photographer for that picture, those appliques appeared on the front, but still needed to be sewn on the back of the dress. To save money, I borrowed my girlfriend's veil and sewed a few appliques on to match the dress. White high-heeled sandals with double straps purchased at Hens & Kelly's in downtown Buffalo completed my ensemble.*

*The night before the wedding, I had inserted plastic/foam rollers in my hair and attempted to fall asleep. I lost that battle—how would the bride look in all the photos with circles under her eyes?*

*Meanwhile, you, your brothers, and friends gathered at the Wielinski Bailey Avenue homestead in the Lovejoy section of town for an evening of beer and cards. In the morning, Barb and I drove over and waited for a groomsman to drive us over to my parents in his "luxury" car. Tensions mounted when we encountered a traffic jam on Bailey Avenue.*

*We slipped into dresses, touched up make-up, and a photo session began. The bridesmaids wore different hues of the rainbow (a popular wedding fashion in the 70s).*

*I looked at my mother in bewilderment—never had I seen her so calm. Growing up I often saw her in a state of chaotic tension. There was a bottle of green medicine in the kitchen cupboard, taken to ease her nerves. Later in life, she suffered from obsessive-compulsive disorder, and many doctors asked me what that substance was. She herself had no idea.*

*On the day of my wedding, though, she was totally chilled out. Had she taken some sedative, or did relief and joy at finally seeing one of her daughters married produce this calm yet euphoric state?*

*How did you like that tan tux with brown trim you wore? Your hairdo proved that you, too, had curly hair (a definite clue that any future children would not have straight hair).*

*A family friend, Father Ed Schroeder, performed the ceremony at St. Lawrence Church on Delevan Avenue. Doug, remember how everyone thought your brother Jimmy, the best man, was so devoted with his head bowed in prayer when actually he was recovering from the all the beer he had consumed the night before.*

*Perhaps you subconsciously felt the urge to rebel against this life-changing step you were about to enter into—I had trouble slipping the ring on your finger. Persistence won out, and I claimed you.*

*As we greeted our guests after the ceremony, I witnessed a tender moment as my dad wiped away his tears. His baby was married, and he finally had a son.*

*Despite blue skies, rain drops fell as we dashed to the car. I have heard rain on a bride and groom is good luck. We had quite a run of that.*

*We were whisked away to Hilbert College in Hamburg for photos. Our "Just Married" sign, which was made by my co-worker in the advertising department at National Gypsum, kept flying off the car. We stopped twice to retrieve it, once on the Kensington Expressway.*

*Thinking we had plenty of time before the reception, we stopped at the apartment I had shared with Barb for a drink. We later learned that some of my mother's serenity had left as she anxiously waited for our late arrival.*

*At the Harvey D. Morin Post in West Seneca, the dinner included ham, roast beef, and, polish sausage with a variety of side dishes that certainly would have included a Wielinski favorite: baked beans.*

*Jimmy had sobered up enough to begin drinking again. Jimmy's toast had been short and simple. "A toast to the bride and groom," was all he said.*

*Perhaps there was a positive side to his brevity. I have to admit*

*I remember that toast, but not my sister's.*

*A memorable moment, especially for the men, occurred when one of my friends (to avoid embarrassment I will not divulge her name) caught the bouquet and, in the process, partially lost the top of her dress.*

*What great shots the photographer took. We asked him to capture each table of guests: the baseball team, work friends, the Wielinski, Schoenwetter and Schwab clans, and mom's pinochle gals. Years later, when those aunts, uncles, and my parents' friends no longer were with us, it was good to see their smiling faces in those pictures.*

*Perhaps that omen of good luck about rain on the bride and groom was with us as we drove to the Regency Hotel in Hamburg following the reception. We didn't have exact change at the exit, which delayed us getting through the toll booths. A car ran a signal*

Karen and Doug
1979.

*and smashed into another car directly in front of us. We avoided disaster by seconds.*

*I laugh at the vision of me following you down the hotel corridor—the docile new wife ready to take on the role of Mrs. Douglas Wielinski. We talked for hours about the wedding, reception, and tried to envision the future. There was lots of laughter.*

*Thirty-three years later and what a history we compiled. Now we have grandchildren on the way. I hope they inherit your zest for life. Maybe I can pass on the importance of humor to lighten life's burdens.*

*It was a good life, wasn't it Doug? We were just months away from that thirtieth anniversary when the unbelievable happened. I guess the time has come for me to stop adding on years to our anniversary total, but it is nice thinking that the number would have kept inching upward.*

I drive out of the cemetery. "Rest easy, Doug," I whisper. "Happy memories of you are keeping me going."

5/13/12

Author's note: Although much of the above remains in my memory, I unbelievably have access to these recollections compiled in a scrapbook entitled "Our Wedding Album." I had kept the book in a closet in our upstairs bedroom on Long Street. Granted, it is now waterlogged and charred, but how in the world did it survive such wreckage? Pages are curled, and the ink is streaked. Amazingly the engagement and wedding pictures that appeared in the Buffalo Evening News are not damaged, and a wedding invitation is preserved. As I've written before, such finds do really become relics. Our "official" wedding album did not survive, so the scrapbook record of events is a blessing. The remembrance of that memorable spring day can stay vivid and alive in a written form.

# JUNE 2009

*"Just as we hit water when we dig in the earth, so we discover the incomprehensible sooner or later."*

~ George C. Lichtenberg

June would bring the incomprehensible, but first the reality of everyday life continued.

I contacted Shea's Buffalo Theater, where we had Broadway Series tickets, explained our situation, and received replacement tickets in the mail. To compensate us for the performances we had missed, they gave us passes to the lounge area. Kim, Jeff, and I resumed that part of our lives and went to see *The Color Purple*. Doug and I had enjoyed nights at the theater, and that night some tears did escape in the darkness.

Doug held many titles for me: husband, lover, companion, and handyman. As a renter, I knew I could call my landlord for emergencies and major repairs. What about those general chores? My first test was a clogged bathtub. I had watched Doug unclog drains many times. It usually ended with some disgusting compound emerging from a sink or tub. I grabbed what few tools I had and got to work. Although I cringed throughout the process, I felt a sense of accomplishment when water easily flowed down the drain again.

The duplex, however, was in the airport flight path and it was time to start thinking about a new home. The constant flights over the house were unnerving, and I was ready to move on. Although I did not feel I would stay in the Clarence area, I did check out a few houses there. I noticed a "For Sale" sign pointing down one street and decided to investigate. I was shocked—it was *the* house.

When Doug and I had decided to downsize, we visited open houses in Clarence. Jill was a high school junior and we wanted to stay in the district. An older couple we met at one open house told us they had a historic home nearby and would probably downsize someday. Doug and I couldn't resist the urge to drive by. We loved that big, beautiful home. It had been built in the 1800s. We both agreed it would have been the perfect house for us when we moved back to Buffalo in 1998.

Now that house was for sale. I swore it was a "sign" and Doug had directed me to it. I immediately called the real estate agent and told her I had to see it. Kim and I both loved the quaint character of the house. I had to be realistic though. I didn't need a 3,200 square foot house. The yard would take a lot of maintenance, flooring needed to be updated, I would have to buy new furniture to fill the rooms, and most important, the price was too high for my budget.

I concluded that the "sign" was really practical advice from Doug: "Ok, you always wanted to look at the inside of that house, so go ahead, but just remember to think smaller."

Our names had been added to the 3407 families email loop. Any correspondence on that link automatically goes to all the family members. A few messages mentioned disturbing details.

Lori, who lived in the Kentucky/Cincinnati area, made the mistake of reading a particularly graphic email that was so upsetting she had to leave work. The distance between us made it difficult for me to console her, and that was painful for me. We had lived in Cincinnati for almost fifteen years, and many friendships remain. I found comfort in the fact that if Lori needed a motherly touch, my good friends Betsy and Gwen would be there for her.

As a group the email list members decided to limit sensitive material. We each had our own fears about what our loved ones had endured. We did not need descriptions to conjure up gory images.

Jill reported from North Carolina that not only had cockroaches appeared in her apartment, but a car was broken into at the complex's lot.

"Just remember it's only temporary and if anyone comes at you scream and kick them where it'll hurt—groin and throat!" was my motherly advice.

---

We had established a scholarship fund in Doug's name for a Clarence High School student with a love of history. The first award would be presented on June 9th.

Doug's brother Billy called late in the morning on the ninth, and asked if he could meet with me. I knew this couldn't be good news.

What he had to tell me was unexpected and incomprehensible. Doug's legs had been severed during the crash and had just been identified.

I could swear I had asked the coroner about the state of Doug's body when they first called to say he had been identified. Looking back, though, shouldn't I have realized that a house and plane could not fall on a person without causing severe damage to the body? I guess I had been naïve.

How could I comprehend that this runner of marathons, this hockey player dashing in for a goal, this ball player stealing a base, could have his legs torn from his body.

Why couldn't I have been told from the start that this had happened? Somebody with that information decided that if the legs were never found I would not have to be told. They were trying to spare me more pain, but I totally disagree. This incomprehensible news ripped open an emotional wound that was just beginning to heal. The heartache was fresh again.

Somehow I managed to return to work, but I was in tears when I told my boss about this news. Then my pain was multiplied when I realized I would have to tell my girls. I could not risk the chance that they would somehow find out from someone other than me. I told Kim before the presentation, and she urged me not to present the scholarship myself. I still felt it was something I had to do.

Kim's instincts were correct. I broke down as soon as I reached the podium, had to ask a teacher to announce the scholarship, and turned my back to the audience as I tried to compose myself. Luckily, I was able to hand the award to the recipient and congratulate him. His response that he had been honored to attend Doug's lectures was the highlight of a miserable day.

That weekend, a 5K run took place in Clarence Center for the memorial fund and first responders. Considering the events leading up to this run, I was apprehensive about facing the family members. I still had not met many of them.

Before the run, I had to face telling Lori and Jessica about the grim discovery.

Lori's reaction summoned something I never envisioned. We had been told that Doug's body was found outside the house near the neighbor's driveway.

"What if he was trying to crawl to safety!" Lori said in utter sadness.

I cannot allow myself to believe that scenario. I cannot picture him suffering in any way. I want to believe his death was instantaneous.

The turnout for the run was tremendous, and I had my own personal support group: three of my girls and their guys, family members, and so many friends. We all wore shirts printed with "I Love Doug" on the front and "6038 Long" on the back.

Large posters of each victim with a brief description of their life lined the route. This added to the emotion of the day. Speeches followed the run, and family members were called to the microphone. After my experience at the award presentation I asked

Jess' boyfriend to read my statement. It included how Doug had been a runner and would have appreciated this large assembly.

Some of the other widows gave heart-wrenching speeches. They expressed what I, too, felt about the loss of a dear husband, but was unable to say at the time.

I knew a procession was planned from the Fire Hall to 6038 Long Street. A bagpiper would lead us. What I didn't realize was that we would be walking on the property itself. I wasn't sure I was ready for that. It was hard to go, but the ceremony was very respectful and peaceful.

A few families lingered afterward. Lorin Maurer's father approached me. "Now what room would we have been standing in at this spot?" he inquired.

I struggled to get my bearings. "The porch I suppose."

Then he asked something that I suspected every family member must have wondered. "Did you hear anyone that night?"

"No, just Jill crying," I painfully said.

Although the day had been emotional, it was not as bad as I had anticipated. It had been good to join with the other families and my "entourage" of supporters to honor Doug, all the others who had been lost, and those who had responded that night.

I still hadn't made plans for my trip to North Carolina in July. I could not tell Jill about Doug's legs over the phone. I hoped to take her friends, Annmarie and Christina, with me for support, along with Kim. In the meantime, it would be difficult for Kim, Lori, Jessica, and me to keep this painful secret.

My nerves were on edge. On a Sunday night the plane activity seemed so constant over the duplex that at one point I found myself crouching on the floor in fear. That sound of an airliner passing overhead had always disturbed, but hitting the floor was a first.

Jill also had an experience of hearing a plane fly over her apartment. "I seriously thought it was going to crash because it sounded so close, she told me, "Let's say I didn't have a good night sleeping." Father's Day was also coming up, and that added to the emotional wrench.

That Father's Day, it somehow seemed fitting to visit the Clarence Flea Market, a place where I strongly felt Doug's presence. I bought a small pie from the "Pie Lady," just like he would. I was too late for Doug's favorite, cherry, but I settled for an apple pie. Several of his flea market buddies were there and it was good to hear about their remembrances of Doug and their sadness about his death.

Kim and Jeff had another reason for frayed nerves. After they had the foundation poured for their new house in Darien, they learned that it had been surveyed incorrectly. Part of the foundation was on their neighbor's property. Their original plan was to ask their neighbors to sell them a portion of their property—it was a five-acre lot and the neighbor's house was nowhere near the foundation. This was one of those times when I wished Doug could have given them advice. Kim and Jeff decided it was more advantageous to have the current foundation ripped up and the whole process started over.

Global BMS advised that we could now go online to see photos of the things salvaged from the Long Street site, along with the contents of the garage. Kim and I were about to embark on an unbelievable journey.

Every item, no matter the size or condition, had been sorted into categories: clothing, photographs, toys, collectibles, jewelry, household, and paper. There were thousands of items. Kim and I went through many categories the first night we had access to the site. Kim finally went to bed, but I felt compelled to keep going.

How can I explain my feelings? The song, "Traces" by the Four Classics came to mind with its poignant lyric, "faded photographs covered now with lines and creases." I also thought of lyrics from "The Way We Were." "Memories light the corner of my mind; misty water-colored memories of the way we were." The word "incomprehensible" also came again to my mind. I could barely grasp what I was looking at, all the bits and pieces of our life. It was inconceivable that so much could have survived such destruction, and that it had all been retrieved, cleaned, and sorted.

Some amazing items showed up. Doug's University of Buffalo undergrad ring was there. I always said he would be more upset about losing that ring than his wedding ring. The UB ring survived, the wedding ring did not.

My Grandmother Schwab's gold initial ring had been saved. It had been in our upstairs closet in a jewelry box. Jess' high school graduation ring had also been in an upstairs bedroom. There was a blue knit shirt of Doug's. At the beginning of our relationship, that shirt had been the first thing I had seen him wear other than his baseball uniform. I couldn't help but cry when I saw two Buffalo Bills' scrapbooks Doug had put together back in the 60s. They appeared unscathed. And there was my wedding dress!

There were over 200 web pages devoted to collectibles. I lost count of the number of tissues I went through. Doug had spent years collecting. My heart ached at how devastated he would have been at their ruin.

My attorney told me that Global would be sending photo catalogs and a CD that would make it easier for us to navigate through the huge inventory of items. Everything was being packed in Texas and would soon be transported back to Buffalo.

I thought I would burst with the knowledge of all that had been retrieved. I was now ready to share these discoveries publicly. Donn Esmonde of the Buffalo News came to mind. He had conveyed a sense of the turmoil we had gone through in the early days after the crash. Maybe he could help put my feelings into words again. Because of the pending lawsuits, communication with Donn would begin only after my lawyer had approved.

The trauma of these discoveries, the dread of still having to talk to Jill about the shocking information from the coroner, the fast approaching wedding of Lori and Chris. Incomprehensible!

2/25/12

## RINGS

I wish I could remember his exact words. My four daughters and I sat in the front pew of the church. Doug's casket rested slightly to our left. Monsignor Frederick Leising, Pastor at Nativity of the Blessed Virgin Mary, was delivering the homily at the funeral mass. He compared life to a circle—a ring—composed of many elements. The essence of Doug's being would continue to dwell in our circle, despite his death.

Look at any ring closely. Can you find where it begins or ends? A perfect blend creates a seamless surface. That is how life works. Our lives are comprised of multiple aspects that blend together to define who we become. It is no wonder that rings symbolize so many important events in our lives.

When I was a child, if an occasion called for a ring my parents never made a trip to a jewelry store. The jeweler, a friend of my mother and father, would come right to our house. He would bring a box filled with sparkling gems and settings.

Although I cannot recall the exact reason for my first ring (communion or confirmation perhaps), I know it was a small ruby stone set in a slim gold band. The band held some connection to a previous ancestor, and the ruby represented my July birth date.

A larger, square-cut ruby was presented at a later date, and I had worn it with pride until replaced by the long-awaited graduation rings. A silver ring, engraved with "SMS" for St. Mary of Sorrows, etched on a bed of blue was purchased during eighth grade, and worn during the beginning of my years at Bishop McMahon High School. Junior year brought with it the anticipation of senior year and a gold and green ring to announce the impending end of my school days.

I am sure it was a financial struggle for my parents to pay for these rites of passage, but my sister and I probably did not give much thought to the sacrifices they must have made to provide us with these rings.

Doug came from a large family—two sisters and six

brothers—so I can safely assume that he earned every dollar needed to buy his rings. That fact would have made the rings even more important to him. I find it quite amazing that all three of Doug's graduation rings were recovered from the Long Street crash site.

Two of the rings—from P. S. 43 and Hutch Technical High School—are kept in a safe deposit box now. The third, from the University of Buffalo, has found a permanent home on my right hand. I consider that fact somewhat of a two-fold miracle.

I had always kidded Doug that he thought more of that UB ring than his wedding ring, and that he would be quite upset if anything ever happened to it. He would usually set both rings on the antique dough cabinet in the dining room. So, did his wedding ring appear among the found items? No, but it seemed only right that the UB ring found its way to me. What other reason makes me consider this ring a miracle? It fits me perfectly. How can that be? Surely Doug and my fingers were not the same size.

Along with my "SMS" ring, my Grandma Schwab's gold signet ring was also safely returned. Both rings were kept in a jewelry box on a shelf in our bedroom closet. Someone had diligently sorted through the debris and managed to spot these precious things.

Grandma's small, gold ring displays the scrolled letters "CH" for Clara Hofmayer. That inscription solves a bit of the mystery surrounding the ring. It would have been given to her before her marriage to my Grandpa Schwab in 1910 when she was 23 years old.

My imagination kicks into gear as I picture her surprise opening a beautiful jeweler's box with the ring nestled in a soft, silky pillow on her eighteenth birthday. Clara would have slipped the ring from its secure bed and carefully used her fingertips to trace the letters and caress the tiny cherubs guarding those initials on either side. What joy her happiness would have given to whomever had presented this gift to her.

I like this scenario, and appreciate the gift of once again having the ring in my possession. Jill added another chapter to the story of Grandma Schwab's ring when Jill chose to wear it on her wedding day as "something old." I also wore it during our trial against the airlines. It strengthened my resolve to tell our story.

Fortunately, the crash did not claim my engagement ring and wedding band. I seldom removed them, and they were securely on my finger the night of the crash.

When I turned twenty-five, getting an engagement ring began to seem like an elusive dream. Then, when least expected, Doug burst onto the scene—an explosion of fireworks, splashing color, and excitement onto the blank canvas of my life.

It was July 1, 1977, weeks shy of my twenty-sixth birthday. My friend Cindy's husband coached a baseball team. They invited my sister and me to catch a game. I faced a weekend dilemma: should I go to Lake George with a guy from work, or stay in town and go to the baseball game? I am more on the conservative side so I chose the latter. That would prove to be a great decision.

A catcher with curly hair caught my eye. I watched that guy as the game progressed and was introduced afterward. Later, at a bar called the Crow's Nest we struck up a conversation. His name was Doug. He was a chemist, lived in Lovejoy, and came from a big family. When I was driving home, I let out a squeal of happiness. This situation seemed promising.

As the one-year anniversary of that first meeting approached, I wondered where our relationship was headed—as any good Catholic girl would. I tearfully confronted Doug and in so doing ruined the surprise he had planned. He told me he was going to propose on my birthday and that made me cry even harder.

We picked out the engagement ring together at a small jeweler. I liked two rings, but finally chose a small diamond attached to a filigree gold band. Doug decided to buy the matching wedding band later. Maybe he wanted to be sure this engagement thing worked out!

The engagement remained our secret. Doug had a baseball tournament on my birthday—July 15, 1978. He called to say things were running late. Excitedly he told me they were playing against some of the Buffalo Sabres. If Doug's team won, the dinner date we had scheduled would be postponed. I knew how thrilling it was for him to play those Sabres, so I said, "OK." Luckily, they lost the next game. The date was kept and Doug proposed by the whirlpool in the state park near Niagara Falls that windy evening. Why aren't his exact words etched in my memory? Did he bend on one knee? I think he did.

I can remember what I wore that evening—a short-sleeve silky red top with cap sleeves and a handmade tan skirt with red and yellow flowers. Doug wore a tan top and his brown and tan plaid pants. Oh the menswear of the 70s!

I witnessed the angry-side of Doug when we returned to the jewelers. The sales clerk told us that the matching wedding band was no longer available. Doug did not receive this revelation calmly. We took our business elsewhere and found brushed gold bands to match the engagement ring at a small jewelry store in Hamburg.

One of the happiest moments in my life came when that band was placed on my finger. May 19, 1979.

Our honeymoon included a few destinations usually not found on the list of dream honeymoons. Before we savored the fine cuisine of Boston (unable to find and settle on a better restaurant we ended up at a Burger King) we visited the Basketball Hall of Fame in Springfield, Massachusetts and stopped in Stockbridge, Massachusetts.

Anyone who knew Doug will understand why the Basketball Hall of Fame was on our list. The Stockbridge visit, though, was for me. I love Norman Rockwell, and Doug had learned that early on in our relationship. One of his first gifts to me was a beautiful autobiography by Rockwell that came in a protective box. Doug's rating as a boyfriend soared with that purchase.

How many honeymooners traverse rows of headstones in a cemetery looking for a deceased artist? For all Rockwell's great accomplishments and talent, his headstone was plain and understated. Of course, we took a picture of it.

In recent years a new, large Rockwell Museum was built in Stockbridge. When Doug and I visited back in 1979 the museum had been small and quaint, so fitting to Rockwell's style. We had stood in awe, gazing at the original *Four Freedoms* painted by Rockwell in 1943. These paintings were reproduced in *The Saturday Evening Post* over four consecutive weeks in 1943, alongside essays by prominent thinkers of the day. Inspiration for these works was derived from a 1941 State of the Union Address given by President Franklin Roosevelt, where he defined four essential human freedoms: freedom of speech, freedom to worship, freedom from want, and freedom from fear.

The museum curator stood before *Freedom of Worship*, and pointed out the old woman at the front of the work, hands folded in prayer. It was the ring on her finger that captured my attention. Not only did this famous painting portray her love of God, but the ring symbolized the love she must have felt for her husband of many years. It was a testimony to their lives together. As a new bride, I knew that was the type of relationship I wanted with Doug. That woman's image remains embedded in my memory.

I debate whether these symbols of love should remain on my left-hand? Right now, I do not feel any necessity to remove them. Last year, my chubby fingers meant that they needed to be enlarged. It took considerable effort to get them off. Because they had been on my finger so long, an indentation remained that magnified their absence. During that short period my other fingers automatically searched for the rings, and I felt another layer of loss. For now, at least, I do not want or need that additional reminder.

Rings always represent some sort of love, the romantic-type, of course, but a ring can also can signify a friendship, family connection, source of pride, accomplishment, or appreciation of the things that define who we are. When slipped on a finger they somehow find an immediate connection to our heart, which is a very good reason to wear them.

9/2/13

# THE FLEA MARKET

*"Searching is half the fun. Life is much more manageable when thought of as a hunt as opposed to a surprise party."*

*~ Jimmy Buffet*

I had not arrived that morning until almost nine—way too late by Doug's standards. "All the good stuff will be gone by then," he would say. He woke at five and would be at the market as the sellers unpacked their cars. By nine, he would already be back home. I walked through rows and rows of tables with items spread out in a way that would hopefully catch the eye of potential buyers. The occasion that prompted my perusal of these displays was a "garage sale" held at the Clarence Flea Market. It had been some time since I had made a Sunday morning jaunt to the market—a place I am certain Doug continues to haunt.

For Doug, the search was part of the fun when it came to his weekly visits. There was also that explosion of joy that came with the discovery of a long sought item or an unexpected encounter.

Often I would peer out our upstairs bedroom window and chuckle as I watched him—a glow of excitement on his face—carefully carrying his new treasures into the garage. Some rearranging might be necessary, but he would find a place for everything. Doug would bring special discoveries into the house, where we eagerly waited to see what his early morning run had uncovered.

It wasn't just sports or Buffalo historical items he sought for his collections. He often would produce old children's books for me, an old medical book for one neighbor, or a book on Indian artifacts for another neighbor interested in archeology.

When Kim returned from a trip to England he gave her an English "Bobby" teapot. After the crash, only broken china pieces were left. I was going to throw them out, but Kim salvaged a few jagged remains, now destined to become relics.

A friend had emailed an article by Sally Jenkins in the *Washington Post* about salvaged remnants from the World Trade Center. The article introduced Nancy Johnson who directs the

World Trade Center Artifacts project and had overseen the preservation of the Ground Zero wreckage since 2006. Amid "the twisted metal, a rack of bikes, a battered shovel, and dented file cabinet bursting with papers," there is a "climate-controlled room with giant statues of Bugs Bunny, Elmer Fudd, and the Roadrunner, the remnants of a Warner Brothers store once located in the Center."

"Isn't it something?" Johnson asks. "It brings a human element to all the inanimate objects...Wreckage becomes relic when it is associated with people and experiences that brought you joy."

I so understand that concept of wreckage becoming relic. We experience a feeling of joy wherever we come across a remnant that evokes a cherished memory.

Doug had brought home some things with no obvious future use. An Eastlake spoon-carved frame, devoid of its mirror, found a spot in the garage ready for deployment at a moment's notice. Also, carefully stored in cardboard were two large stained glass panels, which at one point might have graced a mansion window or luxurious cabinet. These items were "too good to pass up," in Doug's opinion.

Their location in the Long Street garage spared them from destruction. I found inspiration for their new life when adding a new mud room to my East Aurora home. I had a replacement mirror made for the Eastlake frame. It now reflects not only the image of those who stand before it, but the possibilities Doug recognized in it.

The addition called for a new window in the stairwell. I wondered whether the stained-glass panels could be incorporated into that window. The Craftsman style of the glass—almost Roycroft in design—perfectly fit my 1920s East Aurora home.

When I first saw the installed panels—sunlight producing golden ribbons through colored glass—I sat at the bottom of the stairs thinking how happy Doug would be with the transformation of his find. I wept.

As I walked this Sunday down one row of the bustling bazaar,

I recognized one of Doug's friends. He and his daughter mainly deal in books and other paper memorabilia. Often, when the weather was cold, Doug would bring hot chocolate for the daughter and coffee for her dad. This seller would have also received a gift card during the Christmas holidays—a small thank you from Doug to his regulars who kept an eye out for items he was interested in.

Before I could even say hello, the man approached me. "Hi, Karen. How are you and the girls doing?" I was surprised, but pleased, that he not only remembered me, but also my name. Some of his old sheet music caught my eye and would go home with me. I walked away from his table, happy that I had found a treasure, and with a feeling of warmth that Doug was remembered.

I saw groups of collectors throughout the market, deep in conversation about their recent sales or purchases. I could imagine Doug standing among them, and regret tugged at my heart. Doug was one of the regulars. The sellers knew what he liked, and would save items especially for him. He would have first dibs. They knew he was honest, and although he wanted a good deal, he would never take advantage of them.

There was a young guy who, according to Doug, probably relied on the proceeds from those Sunday sales to support himself for the rest of the week.

There was the school teacher, Alan, who loved history and sports memorabilia. Lots of bats and gloves changed hands between the two, but perhaps more important, they enjoyed sharing their knowledge with one another.

I love when I hear Doug's flea market acquaintances say, "Doug was a legend around here." Shortly after the crash, one of the market's signature garage sales was held in Doug's memory. The proceeds from that sale were donated to our family—such a show of respect for my "legend." I am honored by and proud of the memories he left with them.

My own personal hunt was not too productive that day. Besides the sheet music (a bargain at a dollar apiece), I did a bit of negotiating for a set of small leather books, which satisfied my weakness for old publications. The thrill of finding these tiny treasures justified the cost, especially when a bit of research shed some light on what they actually were.

Published by the Little Leather Library Corporation of New York between 1916 and 1923, they were inspired by cigarette companies that gave away free miniature copies of Shakespeare with each tobacco purchase. The corporation sold over 25 million little books through department, book, and drug stores, along with mail order sales. Whitman's chocolates used them in a promotion, a free book in each box, and Woolworth's later sold them for ten cents apiece. Synthetic binders replaced leather during World War I, and boxed sets often were given to the soldiers.

I now am the proud owner of 56 of these condensed books—an impressive group, including: *Friendship & Other Essays* by Henry Thoreau; *Sherlock Holmes* by Conan Doyle, *A Child's Garden of Verses* by Robert Lewis Stevenson, *Speeches & Addresses of Abraham Lincoln, Memories of President Lincoln* by Walt Whitman, and even *A Message to Garcia* by East Aurora's own Elbert Hubbard. I think Doug would be proud of the collector I have become.

Keeping with Doug's spirit of giving, I plan to give two small volumes by Edgar Allan Poe to one son-in-law, and a book of poems to a friend.

Doug once came home with several narrow ledgers from the Clarence Center Creamery. The ledgers were filled with distinctive examples of Palmer Method penmanship. That writing style, easily considered an art form, is now abandoned. The neatly-recorded ledgers give a glimpse into the workings of that early business. Coincidentally, that business was located on the corner of Clarence Center Road and Long Street. The site now is a Verizon sub-station. Doug wanted to give the ledgers to the Clarence Historical Museum. He never had the time to do so.

We discovered pieces of those ledgers in the retrieved items. It was sad to see the remains of such historically important records. Yet, the museum expressed interest in what had survived—relics that preserve a part of Clarence Center's past. I felt Doug's wishes had been honored as I passed the ledgers on to the museum.

The hunt at times can produce memories of the past. Of course, when I see an item from my childhood at antique sales, it does make me feel pretty old. Most memories are pleasant, though. I once found a small, striped juice glass—its cup perched on a tiny pedestal—just like the one I used for Welch's Grape Juice when I visited my Grandma Schwab. The glass was another casualty of the crash, but Welch's still evokes memories of Grandma when I take a sip.

Continuing with my new-found treasures, I was hit with a blast from the past as I saw a small, three-legged stool topped with a piece of leather. I had purchased one exactly like it many years ago in Mexico. Three friends and I had hit the then popular vacation destinations of Acapulco and Mexico City. We faced monsoon-like rain storms, just missed an earthquake in Mexico City, consumed a large quantity of alcoholic beverages, and tried not to succumb to the very convincing selling tactics of cute little boys offering us souvenirs on the beach. Amid all that activity, I had bought the little stool that was part of my household furniture for years.

Since the crash, when I come across an item that was lost in the destruction, an impulse automatically tells me I should buy it as a replacement. I have done that often, but this time I resisted the urge. Of course, now I regret that decision. It would have been fun having the stool again. Perhaps I will go back sometime and see if it is still available.

"If you pass an item by, and when you return it is still there, then it was meant to be yours," Doug always said.

Early morning clouds dispersed. The hot sun contradicted the fact that it was still spring and not a summer day in mid-July. The sun—once a welcome friend—had become a foe. I was running out of energy. My hunt would end for the day.

A sonnet by Edna St. Vincent Millay portrays the seemingly never-ending pain of losing a loved one. In my search for Doug's presence, it often enters my mind:

TIME does not bring relief; you all have lied
Who told me time would ease me of my pain!
I miss him in the weeping of the rain;
I want him at the shrinking of the tide;
The old snows melt from every mountain-side,
And last year's leaves are smoke in every lane;
But last year's bitter loving must remain
Heaped on my heart, and my old thoughts abide!

There are a hundred places where I fear
To go, — so with his memory they brim!
And entering with relief some quiet place
Where never fell his foot or shone his face
I say, "There is no memory of him here!"
And so stand stricken, so remembering him!

I definitely understand that fear of facing Doug's memory and my regret that he never entered those quiet, new places. Like my visit to the flea market, though, I find that I can overcome that fear and welcome his memory.

As for new places, where "never fell his foot or shone his face," I hope that I can rise above the pain and experience what the hunt uncovers—for both of us.

5/15/13

# JULY 2009

*"Bad things do happen; how I respond to them defines*
*my character and the quality of my life. I can choose to sit in*
*perpetual sadness, immobilized by the gravity of my loss,*
*or I can choose to rise from the pain and treasure the*
*most precious gift I have—life itself."*

~ *Walter Anderson*

There never seemed to be idle time, and my mind constantly needed to stay alert to what details needed attention.

Doug had always taken the responsibility of sorting through the maze of college loans for the girls. I wasn't sure where to start making sure all that was in order. Jessica contacted her financial aid advisor at SUNY Oneonta for some direction. We discovered that Doug had taken out a PLUS loan in his name, one that would be cancelled upon his death. No one else would have a financial obligation to repay the loan. The cancelled balance was more than $13,000. Jessica and I were both thankful to Doug for arranging that particular loan.

I made the effort to resume some sort of social life. A friend from work invited me to her cousin's restaurant one Friday night. Kim, Jeff, and I spent the Fourth of July at the "Clarence Day in the Park", and watched impressive fireworks in a neighboring town. For the first time I attended Shakespeare in Delaware Park where I saw *The Tempest* with my cousins Michael and Marty. These outings were pleasant but did little to relieve the ache I felt for Doug.

I had been seeing a social worker but I now would be meeting with a psychologist. My lawyers said that if the case went to court the report of a psychologist would be beneficial. I found the social worker to be helpful and I liked her as a person too, so I did not welcome having to begin all over with the psychologist.

My first trip to see the psychologist did not ease my frustration. Her office was located at Erie County Medical Center (ECMC), an imposing and scary edifice. As I started to walk toward the building, a Mercy Flight helicopter appeared overhead. It hovered directly over me and seemed to follow my path. I tried to put my apprehension aside and told myself that the helicopter would soon leave. It did, but my already shaky nerves were even more on edge.

I immediately liked the psychologist, Lisa, but felt almost claustrophobic in her tiny, windowless office. That first experience probably wasn't the greatest but it turned into a good professional and personal relationship. A quote I found about a year ago brought Lisa to mind:

> Oh the comfort—the inexpressible comfort of feeling safe with a person—having neither to weigh thoughts nor measure words, but pouring them all right out, just as they are, chaff and grain together; certain that a faithful hand will take and sift them, keep what is worth keeping, and then with the breath of kindness blow the rest away.
>
> ~ Dinah Maria Mulock Craik, *A Life for a Life*

In July, a new doctor entered my life. After years of treatment for glaucoma, I was referred to a specialist. Daily application of numerous eye drops did not seem to be controlling the progression of the disease. Implants needed to be inserted in both my eyes to provide lubrication. This would involve two surgeries, and a recuperation time of probably two weeks following each surgery. Just what I needed, I thought, more time away from work. The surgeries would have to wait until life settled down.

The Remember Flight 3407 foundation was organized. Funds donated by various people and organizations would now be under the control of the foundation. Specific amounts were earmarked for a memorial and the needs of the families. The board consisted of me, several community leaders, 3407 family members, and a Long Street neighbor. Meetings would be scheduled each month.

Not long after the crash, the 3407 families began their efforts to fight for safer airways. Kevin Kuwik was a leader of this campaign. Although I did not accompany the group to Washington, D.C., whenever Kevin requested a barrage of emails to political officials, I complied.

One email was sent to Florida Senator Bill Nelson. He had travelled aboard the space shuttle Columbia January 12 through January 18, 1986, the last successful shuttle before the Challenger disaster. In my note to the Senator, I had shared the fact that Doug had enjoyed collecting space memorabilia.

"I love how you mention the astronaut link in Senator Nelson's email," Kevin told me. We talked about how emotional an experience reviewing the retrieved catalog items had been. "Lorin's suitcase was essentially intact—just some water damage," he said. "None of her jewelry yet, but thankfully they found the watch I got her for Christmas—it was stopped at 10:35. We wonder if that is when the fire trucks got going with the heavy water." He also said that the NTSB people had told him there were over 40,000 items, the high number due to our household items.

I had been thrilled to see Doug's UB ring appear in the catalog. My brother-in-law Billy brought me down to reality by mentioning that several people on the flight had also attended UB. The only part of the date that was visible on the picture was "1969." Doug had graduated in 1969, so I felt fairly confident it was his ring, but some doubt crept into my mind. My lawyer had said that Global BMS wanted the families to know that if we had any questions about a particular item we could contact them directly. I called and they quickly reassured me that the date was 1969 and the initials "DCW" were indeed inside the ring.

Doug's friend Jim had been given access to the online catalog. He agreed that looking at it was very emotional. "I almost cried several times reminiscing about how we acquired some of the items that were left, many were from our Sportservice warehouse deal in 1979," he said. "There were even items there that I had traded to Doug over the years."

Even though many of the things were badly damaged, he said that there was still a lot of good stuff. "I'll do my best to help you realize the best return on the items without making the liquidation of the materials a lifetime chore," he assured me. "I'll certainly do my best for you. I know Doug would have done the same for me."

His support meant so much to me, but I still felt sorting through what remained could indeed be a lifetime chore.

The time had come to visit Jill in Pinehurst, North Carolina, and tell her that Doug's legs had been severed in the crash. Kim and Jill's friend Christina would go with me. Another friend of Jill's told Dan the reason for the visit. Although he did not tell Jill, he gave her the impression that I had a specific reason for visiting. That did not make things any easier. When I first arrived Jill did not want to discuss the crash. I needed to relieve myself of the burden I held but I did not push it. The second day, she allowed me to break the news. We needed to assure ourselves that he did not suffer. Will we ever really know the answer though? I was so grateful that she finally had the courage to hear my news.

We basked in luxury that weekend, staying in the Pinehurst Resort's Holly Inn and The Carolina. It was luxury we never could have afforded were it not for Jill's employee discount. For a few days, we tried to push the events of February 12 behind us. Reality made that unrealistic. I kept thinking how much Doug would have loved being there, playing golf and brushing up on the rich history of Pinehurst.

On the way home, we stopped in Lexington, North Carolina. I had learned from a rest stop brochure that the streets there were decorated with pigs. Just as Buffalo had its fiberglass buffaloes, Lexington had its pigs. I have a fondness for pigs. Perhaps it's their laid-back attitude toward life, flat button noses, or curly tails that attract me. A detour to check out these pigs wouldn't take us too far off course, so we decided to visit.

It was pig heaven. Pigs were decorated as a pirate, a picnic basket (which included "pigs in a blanket"), a peppermint, an old-fashioned pop cooler, a hunter, and "Bambino," the baseball player to mention a few. We passed a bridal shop with a large sale sign. Although Kim's wedding was still a year away, Christina and I encouraged her to investigate. She found a dress but was hesitant about buying a wedding dress in North Carolina. Kim is not impulsive, but it was getting late and we had to get back on the road. She needed to make a quick decision. She mulled it over while we grabbed lunch, and considering the very reasonable price, made an uncharacteristic decision to buy it. It seemed remarkable that we had ended up in this little town, especially on July 13th, Doug's birthday. He was with us.

My bags were barely unpacked before I was on the road again. This time I headed to Cincinnati/Kentucky to help Lori with some last-minute wedding details. We worked on table assignments and name cards. They had chosen a beer theme—each table centerpiece would hold a different brewery glass filled with flowers, and name cards would be matching coasters. Doug would have approved. It was my responsibility to safely deliver the glasses to the florist and carry the wedding dress back home. Being in charge of that dress certainly made me nervous, but I carried out my duties successfully.

Despite all my comings and goings during July, I managed to find a house I liked in nearby Lancaster. My bid was accepted. It concerned me that Jill thought the house looked similar to the one on Long Street. The entrance, living room, and dining room layout was somewhat the same, but the entire house was larger than the Long Street house and the upstairs and kitchen areas were completely different. After an inspection that revealed considerable problems, though, I withdrew my offer. The hunt would continue.

3407 was back in the news on July 21. WBEN had obtained more information on the flight data. I stared at an online photo of the plane and site that had probably been taken the day after the crash. I could see the exact area I had emerged from. It was such an eerie feeling to realize just how close that plane had come to me. It seemed unbelievable that I had survived. That image stayed with me the entire day. Luckily, I had scheduled an appointment with my psychologist that same day. I needed to talk about my reaction to that picture.

My attorney continued to discuss a possible meeting with Donn Esmonde, who indicated he was honored that I was reaching out to him and he would jump at the chance to interview me. There would be ground rules—no details about the night of the crash. I was warned that as a columnist his piece would include his point-of-view and impressions as to how I was doing and my appearance.

We met on July 23 at the duplex. It went well. I certainly gave him enough material. My lawyer kidded me that he hoped Donn wouldn't make it into a series. Allowing him to see the nine volumes of categorized items we had received, I was surprised that he only glanced briefly at them. If I were a reporter, I would have appreciated the opportunity before me and spent considerable time flipping through those pages. I was also concerned when he indicated his report would include more quotes than his opinions. One reason I particularly wanted him to do the article was to see how he would interpret the craziness we were facing.

His column appeared in the July 26 Sunday issue of the News. I was not disappointed, and he did mention the catalogs—his quick glance at them apparently had made an impression.

Donn likes to describe the people he interviews in some detail: "She is 58, pleasant and conversational, wearing a denim skirt and turquoise top. Her heart-shaped face is fringed by golden curls." Except for throwing my age in there, I was pleased with his perception of our story. We exchanged emails.

Donn:

Once again you have managed to put into words feelings that I would like to express. I was happy to see you did include your insights into the article and did not just "quote" my words...that is why I wanted you to do this article. Thank you for referring to me as 'conversational'. Reflecting on our talk, I was afraid I rambled on too much and did not give you enough time to ask questions. In summary, when you are reading the work of a good writer, you wish there was more! They should have given you another column. Hopefully, another time.

Karen:

Thanks much for the kind words, I'm glad you think it worked out well...It was a little difficult deciding what anecdotes to include, what to paraphrase and what I simply did not have room for, but I also was pleased with how it worked out... Continued good luck as you continue to 'repair'.

(A reference to the John Mayer song, "In Repair," that seems to sum up my life at this time.)

Jess flew to Ireland in 2011. I will never forget. Jess called from the Newark Airport just minutes before she would board the plane. She was hunting for the flight information in her purse and I said, "Just tell me what airline you'll be on."

"Continental."

Chills went up my spine as a vision of the Continental logo on the tail of the plane the night of the crash flashed through my mind. In case she hadn't made the connection, I said nothing about the airline. The minute I hung up the phone, I burst into tears.

The second Jess arrived home and landed at Newark Airport, she called me crying hysterically.

"The realization that I was flying on Continental caused me anxiety and stress on the flight and while in Ireland," she told me between sobs. "I hated that I was in a foreign country with no cell phone connection. I was so worried something would happen to you guys and I would have no way of knowing."

July was winding down. Chris and Lori's wedding was just days away. Jill, too, was flying for the first time since the crash. As I anxiously waited for her arrival, I experienced a moment of déjà vu.

A luncheon at work had brought the school principals to the District Office. Keith Kuwik, Kevin's brother, was included in that group. We spoke and again those chills went up my spine when he asked, "When is your daughter's wedding?"

I replied, "Actually this weekend."

I remembered saying similar words to him the week prior to the crash. Kevin's girlfriend, Lorin, was on Flight 3407 to attend Keith's wedding. Jill would be flying in for Lori's wedding. The timing and similarities were frightening.

Thankfully, all my girls arrived safely and wedding festivities began.

I joined the bridal party for Thursday in the Square, a summer outdoor concert series in downtown Buffalo. A rented minibus took the bridal party to the square. That was quite a wild ride with Lori, Chris, and their friends who fit the description of party animals. Several of the Wielinski cousins met us there, and I thoroughly enjoyed my first experience in the Square.

Friday rehearsal went well, followed by dinner at a local restaurant. Doug would have appreciated the Cooperstown baseball bat presented by Chris' parents to the newlyweds, inscribed with their names and wedding date. Apparently that was a popular idea, as bats were also Chris' gift to his groomsmen.

Reflecting on the events leading up to this celebration, I had to wonder how we managed to rise above such pain. Doug was constantly in our thoughts. We fought sadness and were trying to treasure the most precious gift we had, life itself.

3/3/12

# In Repair

Mainly, I will listen to my CD's when I am driving by myself on longer trips. My first long road trip after the crash was a visit to see my daughter, Jill, in North Carolina. As I listened to John Mayer's *Continuum* Album I was struck at how "In Repair" could be my theme song.

The beginning of the song recalls "too many hours in this midnight." How many nights have I tossed and turned either thinking about where I have been, who and what I have lost, or where I am going?

Just when I feel like things are coming together and I am moving on, reality pops up and I'm forced to deal with some issue related to the crash. As the song suggests, my heart is "still unsteady" and "I am in repair."

I am waiting to see what the future brings, although I certainly do not want my "old ways" to desert me. When I was looking for a new home, I also saw through Doug's eyes. What would he think? I'd look at some larger places and see a huge upstairs room and think, Doug would love this for his collection.

I suppose I do hope some "brand new luck" will find me, but I cannot complain. Luck, fate, or divine providence were with Jill and me the night of the crash.

John Mayer's lyrics bring hope: "Maybe when things turn green again, it will be good to say you know me." Several springs have already passed, and it is uplifting to see nature come to life again. The first spring, two of my daughters and I went to lunch at a little restaurant in Clarence Center. I found my spirit renewed by the blossoming of the trees, but I was angry that this beautiful, friendly setting that once was my home had been taken away from me.

It's just human. We all want people to like us. I still feel like I am doing a balancing act, and especially felt that way concerning the Long Street property. I wanted to make everyone happy, but I concluded that in this scenario everyone would not be satisfied with the memorial result. The debate over who will say it is good to know me continues.

I love the last line of the song: "I'm not together but I'm getting there." When people ask me, how I'm doing, that is how I want to reply. It is unbelievable what my family has accomplished and the journeys my girls have started. "You're so strong," people tell me, but I feel my girls have been amazingly strong too. What else can you do? I think Doug would be proud of us. We're in repair.

2/7/11

## The Story Behind the Story

Little did I realize how my life would be impacted by these words: "Erik sent you a message."

This request came from Erik Brady, a reporter for *USA Today*. Somehow you just know that someone whose Facebook picture is a cartoon caricature with fuzzy hair sticking out of a Buffalo Bills cap is a person with a sense of humor, whom you would like to learn more about. In this case, my first impression was spot on.

Of course, it helped that he was requesting permission to do a story about Doug. Now that I know him, I can picture him poised over the keyboard, carefully choosing the words to introduce himself and make an important request. I imagine that it took a few reflective moments before he summoned up the courage to press that "send" button.

He wrote:

```
I have been thinking for a long time that I would
like to tell the story of Doug's life and of his
collection of Buffalo sports memorabilia. Though
we never met, we were roughly the same age with
many of the same interests (I have a minor col-
lection myself) and I think a national audience
would be deeply touched to learn about the life of
the man behind the headlines of a few years ago.

The little I know about Doug tells me he loved his
wife and daughters most of all but that he also
had interests in American history and Clarence
schools and Buffalo sports. I would appreciate the
chance to talk to you about the sort of story I'd
like to do, but only with your permission.
```

His timing was perfect. The message arrived on January 24, 2011, a few weeks shy of the second anniversary of the crash. It would once again become a media topic. Although I knew it was not intentional, many stories referred to the "victims on the plane," omitting Doug on the ground. If he was remembered, it always seemed like an after-thought—"and one man on the ground." I realized that part of the reason stemmed from the fact that I had not exposed myself and family to the media. The interest had originally been there, but I had not granted many interviews. Donn Esmonde had written some moving articles at the time of the crash about our family in The Buffalo News. I had also met twice with him to discuss some of our struggles following the crash, and those interviews also resulted in wonderful stories.

As much as I immediately wanted to respond to his inquiry, I knew the proper thing for someone in my position to do: contact my attorney. Thus began the long process of confirming that Erik was who he said he was, that he was interested in Doug's story and not just the events of the crash, and that this story would not interfere with the pending law suits. I have had to learn to be more patient since the crash, but I was so anxious to do the interview for this story that I pushed hard for a definite agreement.

In May, that patience was rewarded when I finally met Erik —via a three-way phone conversation with my attorney. It wasn't the best introduction. He was calling from a train station, and our connection was not the greatest, but we agreed that he would come to Buffalo for a weekend in the near-future.

As the first weekend in June loomed I prepared for the meeting. Days before I had pressured my attorney to make sure all arrangements were in place. "He's only going to be here a few days and I want to make sure we have people and places lined up to make it a worthwhile trip for him," I insisted.

I didn't sleep well the night before our meeting. I kept thinking of everything I needed to take down to the law office: a huge scrapbook filled with 1960s Buffalo Bills news clippings; several heavy binders showing items retrieved from the crash site and the garage; a family photo album my daughter Jessica had given me after the crash depicting not only a loving family but Long Street itself. I wondered how I would lug all that from a downtown parking ramp to the law office. It's no wonder that I was up by four o'clock in the morning searching for pieces of letters from the high school students thanking Doug for his lectures. I didn't find them.

So there I was, early morning, pulling a large suitcase behind me, while still juggling a hot paper cup of tea. I worked my way down from the roof of probably one of the oldest ramps in downtown Buffalo—no elevator—and continued to maneuver the several blocks to the law office.

My tension mounted as I waited for Erik's arrival. What would he look like? All I had in my mind was that Facebook caricature with the football cap. Finally, there he was, the smiling face and firm handshake that brought that caricature to life. Sometimes you feel you're going to get along with someone from the start. I liked the real-life version.

We talked from nine-thirty in the morning until four o'clock in the afternoon, breaking for a brief lunch before continuing with Doug's friend, Jim. We covered a lot of ground: how Doug and I met and our early years together, how Jim and Doug had been lifelong friends since third grade, the last time they had spoken on the telephone, Doug's relationship with our daughters and the students at Clarence High School. We flipped through the 1960s scrapbook. Erik was fascinated with the articles and enjoyed seeing the by-lines of his old acquaintances at the now defunct Courier Express, where he, too, had started his journalism career. He commented on the good condition of those yellowed clippings as well as the time and effort Doug had poured into this boyhood recollection of his beloved Bills.

When we finally ended the day's session, Erik offered to lug my suitcase back to the parking ramp. "Even though I never met Doug, I feel I now know him," he told me. I now knew that the right person was working on this story.

The next day, under threat of rain, we met at the storage sheds which held the boxed remains of items from the Long Street garage. Every time I pull up the doors to those units, I am overwhelmed with what I face. Where to start? I began to open boxes and pulled out the plastic bags filled with random items: tins, programs, coins, advertising items—just a sample of the contents of two sheds filled to capacity.

Our next stop would be the Long Street site. Before heading over, I pulled a framed, colored picture a neighbor had given me shortly after the crash from my car. 6038 Long Street came back to life in that picture—a small 1920s home proudly standing among trees and flowers. I wanted Erik to have that vision before he encountered the barren place that now was 6038 Long Street.

At the site, I pointed out where the house and garage had been. We stood at the curb—not stepping onto the grassy emptiness, perhaps as a sign of reverence for the events that had occurred there. I can count on one hand the number of times I have walked on my property. As often happens when I visit the site or my former neighbors, a plane passed overhead. My eyes were drawn up to the sky. If I can see the planes, I feel safe.

Erik and I stopped at the cemetery. By now, the threatened rain had arrived. I held an umbrella to stay dry. His ever-present cap shielded Erik. I explained the carvings on the headstone. Shortly after we had taken refuge in my Aunt's home, I discovered a small drawing on the dining room table. It depicted a baseball bat, hammer, and history book on a lone puzzle piece. I recognized it as one of Jill's drawings and asked her if it was an idea for the headstone. She surprised me with her reply. "No, it's a design for a tattoo I'm thinking of getting."

To me, it also seemed a fitting symbol for Doug's headstone. I had told people, in the months following the crash, how we had been working on Buffalo Bisons puzzles in the weeks prior to the crash. Lori had also uncovered an email Doug had sent her while she was living in Brooklyn. Since his dad had been born in Brooklyn, he thought she might be able to check records there for further details on the ancestry of the Wielinski family. He referred to it as "putting together another piece of the puzzle." The addition of a second puzzle piece on the tombstone would stress the connecting of Doug's and my lives to form our family.

Early the following morning, Kim and Jeff joined Erik and me at the Clarence Flea Market, one of the places where I feel Doug's presence the strongest. He loved his early morning hunts.

Alan Tober, a good friend of Doug's and regular at the

market, shared stories of Doug arriving with canvas bag and tiny flashlight in hand ready to explore the day's offerings. I've heard it before, but I am always touched when Alan says "Doug is a legend around here."

Kim shared her remembrances of a loving father with Erik.

He would later contact all the girls, and I appreciated his kindness in making them all feel part of his story.

One further stop remained. Erik followed me as we drove to the location where the destroyed collection items were stored.

*USA Today reporter, Erik Brady, interviews Doug's daughter Kim at the Clarence Flea Market.*

When Kim and I originally went through the items retrieved from the site, any sports collectibles were boxed and sent to one location. This was the first time I had visited that location, and once again I was amazed by the stack of boxes before us. How heartbreaking it is to see what remains of the things Doug had taken such pains to collect throughout his life. His joy of collecting, not for financial gain, but for the pleasure and memories it brought him, was evident.

Doug's brothers, Billy and Eddie, greeted us. This was also the first time Eddie had seen the ruins of the collection. He recalled helping Doug sort cards. He told us about making the trip down to the wholesaler's at Seneca and Bailey to pick-up boxes of the new sets of sports and non-sports cards when they arrived. His payment for that job—he could keep the bubble gum. During the year Doug was in Vietnam Eddie had been delegated to obtain copies of all Buffalo Bills' home game programs. When Eddie got his hands on those programs, he knew the routine: put them in plastic and slide them into the zippered pocket of the stadium cushion seat.

Both brothers lent me support after the crash. Eddie and his wife Maureen were there for Jill and me at the hospital that first night and drove us to the hotel. Except for the clothes we wore and the toothbrush and toothpaste provided by the hospital, we had nothing. Eddie and Maureen were the ones who filled carts at Target with basic needs to help us start over.

Billy has been my rock, my financial advisor, and especially my defender against anyone who does not have my best interests at heart. As I told Erik about the role Billy had played in my life since the crash, I had to walk away. Tears told the story of the emotional impact this weekend had on me. How wonderful it had been to focus on Doug all weekend, but what a painful reminder of what I had lost.

Our weekend reflection was finished. It was now up to Erik to sort through his notes and write the story of the forgotten victim of Flight 3407. It was a story I sincerely wanted to be told. The estimated publication date was July 15, coincidentally my sixtieth birthday. What a perfect gift that would be.

Erik called on July 11 to say that the publication date would have to be pushed back. When he originally said the article would run on the first page, I assumed he meant the front page of the Sports section. Now he told me that the article would be the cover story on *the* front page! I couldn't believe we were that newsworthy.

The publication date all hinged on world events and available front page space. I had just emailed my attorney on July 19 to see if he had heard anything about the date when Erik called. The new date was now July 29, a Friday. That would be good because the paper would remain in circulation the entire weekend.

I sent emails to friends and family who were aware of the interview:

```
Rec'd word today, that barring any worldwide crisis,
our article will run this Friday, July 29th on the
front page. Here's hoping for "peace on earth,
good will toward men!"
```

I was on pins and needles that Thursday. The day couldn't go fast enough. Luckily, it was a busy day for me—filled with a 3407

Foundation meeting where motions were made to settle disputes on the Long Street memorial. Progress was being made and after more than two years of planning ground would be broken with a possible completion date in September.

To help relieve the tension of anticipation, I scheduled a massage. As I drove home my cell phone rang. It was Erik. I flipped open my phone and yelled "Hang on. I'll pull over!" I could finally relax, the presses were running, and the article would be available on-line shortly.

Jess called shortly after that to say we were online. During the evening news, Channel 2 aired a clip of Erik saying that he considered the story a "Buffalo love story—a story of Doug's love of Karen and their girls and theirs for him; his love for sports and his love for Buffalo."

Reading the article online that night did ease my anxiety level, but seeing it in print the next morning was the best feeling in the world. Erik had included so many aspects of Doug's life and had woven the stories of Jim, Alan, our girls, teachers, and me into a beautiful tapestry. It was everything I wished for and more. I was thrilled that millions of people could be reading Doug's story.

Feedback on my end was so positive: "fantastic read," "just wonderful," "beautiful story," "he's a fantastic writer." Many people told me that reading the article brought tears to their eyes, and of course, that was my reaction too. I hoped Erik's feedback was as positive.

I was euphoric about Doug's story having been finally told, but there were also moments of disappointment because all that excitement and thrill of anticipation was gone. Does that make sense?

I decided I had to write this "story behind the story," a small gift to Erik Brady to thank him for sending me that caricature, and for bringing his writing talents our way to capture the Doug we all loved.

8/1/11

http://usatoday30.usatoday.com/sports/2011-07-29-Doug-Wielinski-sports-memorabilia-plane-crash_n.htm

"Recalling a Collector's Life, In Bits and Pieces"
by Erik Brady, USA Today

# AUGUST 2009

*Tangible: capable of being felt, seen or noticed, substantial; real.*

This was the real deal. Less than six months after the crash, we accomplished what Doug had started when he gave Chris his permission to marry Lori. On a beautiful summer day, August 1, 2009, the first of four weddings took place. One-by-one my daughters and I would take that walk down the aisle in a time frame of only 26 months. That August wedding would set the tone—bittersweet. Doug's presence was felt and missed amid the happiness.

The girls and I had no idea how we would handle this first wedding emotionally. The evening before the big event sisters, bridesmaids, and the mother-of-the-bride gathered together in the hope of relieving the ever-present tensions. Lori's sisters and bridesmaids surprised her with a photo album that rekindled many happy memories.

Lori also gave me a book, *Dear Mom...Thank You for Everything* by Bradley Trevor Greive. When she was in college, I had given her his book, *The Blue Day Book*, during a rough time in her life.

We had borrowed a Hallmark *Hoops and YoYo* panic button and found ourselves hitting it in the days before the wedding. It produced laughter and lightened the mood.

The day unfolded. I took the emotional first steps down the aisle with Lori. I noticed crumbled tissues scattered on the floor of the pew where the bridesmaids sat. At the reception, when it was time for the traditional father-daughter dance, Lori surprised her sisters by calling them up to dance in a joyous circle to Reba McIntire's "My Sister, My Friend." Lori asked me to dance with her during Billy Joel's "Don't Go Changing," one of Doug's

and my special songs. I rejoiced in the beauty of my daughters—
inside and out.

Despite the veil of sadness caused by such a recent tragedy,
I was thankful for our ability to proceed with this wedding, and
the blessing that Jill and I had miraculously survived the crash to
share in the celebration.

*Pictured above from
left to right: Lori, Kim,
Jess and Jill. Wedding
photos courtesy of
Sarah J. Carr.*

The search for a new home continued. Even though my attorney and brother-in-law both questioned the wisdom of it at this time, I was determined to move from our flight path town house. I found that houses in my price range went fast. There was not much room for debate, and if you were interested you had to get your bid in quickly.

I had originally considered East Aurora, but at the time I thought it was too far from my job in Clarence. Homes in Lancaster, Snyder, and Williamsville were possibilities. But then Kim found something in East Aurora online. Previously, I had come upon this particular house but dismissed it as it was only 1,100 square feet. I was drawn to the area, though, so Kim and I went to check it out. It won me over with its charm. The staging also helped. Casually placed on the couch was a copy of Northanger Abbey, one of my favorite Jane Austen novels. It had to be a sign; I wanted to place a bid. My attorney advised me to proceed cautiously.

The salvaged remains from the Long Street house, along with the items from the garage, arrived back in Buffalo. Global representatives personally delivered boxes to the families of the plane victims, and some even had media at their homes as they sorted through the contents. Our items from the site were being stored in a warehouse at the Buffalo-Niagara International Airport. The Wednesday after the wedding, Kim and I braced ourselves as we prepared to meet the Global representatives along with our attorney and my brother-in-law. We did not know what to expect.

As I prepared to leave work to face a dismal task, a co-worker pointed out that a Long Street resident had written a letter to the editor of the Clarence Bee opposing any proposed memorial on the site. That neighbor certainly had the right to her feelings, but it was not something I needed to see before viewing the remains that had been retrieved from the ruins of my home and from the garage that had been spared.

*Partial view of Wielinski items at airport warehouse.*

The warehouse room measured approximately twenty-five by twenty-five feet and the walls were lined with cardboard boxes stacked in rows, six boxes high. Everything was numbered, inside and out. A few tables were placed in the middle of the room where we could look at the articles. We were shown a separate room equipped with a couch. We could go there when the emotional burden became too great.

Some ground rules were laid out by Global. If we decided to claim any items, documents would be signed in duplicate before removing them from the warehouse; if there was any doubt that the items were ours, they would be boxed separately and documented for the plane victims' families to review.

My attorney and brother-in-law also had instructions for us. All sports items would be boxed separately. This would include destroyed items. Kim and I would also have to record where each item we looked at had been in the house. You have got to be kidding me, I thought. The stress just kept being added to the situation.

What had survived the crash and inferno were no longer just pictures on the internet and in catalogs. They were tangible articles to hold in our hands.

The first items we examined were jewelry. We left that day with Doug's UB ring and my grandmother's gold initial ring. And there was another amazing find among the jewelry.

I was wearing small, silver hoop earrings on the night of the crash. My cousin, Stacey, had given them to me years ago. When we finally arrived at the hotel after the crash, I realized that I was wearing one earring and the other had fallen off. Unbelievably, that earring had been salvaged from the ruins.

The next day we began the tedious process of taking everything out of the boxes and sorting each item into a specific category: those that were damaged and we did not want to keep, those that did not belong to us, sports collectibles, those things that we would keep for further inspection.

As we went along, we had to identify where each article had been in the house. This was especially difficult to determine with the sports collectibles. Doug had these in his den, in the dining room, and in the basement cistern room. Since the den and dining room were directly above the cistern, how could we assign an area?

It was unbelievable how many pieces of paper there were—pages from books, personal notes, pieces of magazines and yearbooks, school assignments, newspapers, and legal documents. They had been trimmed to remove traces of burnt or mildewed material. Some were the size of postage stamps. Bundled together with rubber bands, there was no way to review every single scrap. These were put in the "keep" pile for more extensive review.

Quite frankly, there was a lot of shit going on in my life. My attorney should not have been surprised when I dashed off an email at 5:55 a.m. on Friday, August 7:

```
Well, here I am again up at the crack of dawn.
The referral of "good" in the subject is ques-
tionable. I have decided that this has been the
hardest week emotionally that I have had since
```

the accident. First, I think I'm suffering from
post-wedding depression. After all the preparation, and a wonderful weekend and beautiful day,
I think it's an emotional letdown to have it all
over. Then, how do I describe dealing with the
burnt remains of what was my house...going thru
literally the shreds of paperwork is especially
tedious and emotionally draining. It's a relief
to come to a solid item. And wouldn't you know
that I had to find out about my old neighbors suddenly writing all their letters this week (about
a memorial)—great timing! You and Billy—when I
tell him—will say this was not the time for me
to continue my house hunt. You're probably right,
but I feel this drive to find some "roots." I feel
100% that this house in East Aurora will be a
good thing for me. I want to take walks in the
nice neighborhood...go to the park right down the
street, walk down to the Roycroft area and even be
able to walk to a church. The house is comforting
and cozy. I don't think the inspection of this
one will turn up much, if anything, wrong with
it. I don't want to be rational and take my time
with this. Basically, I do not want to lose this
house...I hope we can get moving on this.

I write you because this week I don't feel like
I can say all this to you without bursting into
tears. (I'll take a copy of this when I see Lisa
(psychologist) on Thursday...it'll be quite a
session).

So now, I'll get ready for work and get thru a
day of "normal" activities. Thanks for listening.

I did place a bid on the house and it was accepted. The inspection
took place and the main problem seemed to be a slightly high
radon reading. I could deal with that.

---

A "mental" journey also began as I met with the insurance adjuster at her office to talk about Long Street. No daughter, attorney, or brother-in-law accompanied me. This would be a walk I took by myself. I drew a floor plan and the inspector, Dana, and I "walked" room-to-room. The only hesitation came when I was asked for specific numbers for clothing, canned goods, bathroom items, books, CD's, etc. That was all a guessing game. I needed to ask Kim and Jill what brands of clothing they bought, and if they could recall all the little things that were in their bedrooms.

I spent two mornings with Dana in this pursuit of possessions. You would think having to recall everything that was in your home would be an emotional minefield, but somehow it seemed to give me comfort. Although it sounds crazy, my narrative to her let me once more "see" the items that my family possessed and thus unleashed a flood of memories. Later, I wrote about this experience in an essay entitled "Requiem." Until that was written I do not think I officially mourned the loss of my home. It was not a lament for lost possessions, but rather a story recounting the memories associated with those possessions, basically a history of our life as a family.

The journey through the salvaged items at the warehouse continued. Kim and I finished the tumultuous task of sifting through the Long Street remains on August 18. It had taken seven days, three to four hours at each visit. It was emotionally impossible for us to stay beyond that. The Global representatives seemed amazed that we had finished in such a short time. In the end, there were thirty boxes of sports collectibles transported to another place for my brother-in-law to sort. Thirty additional boxes would eventually end up in my garage, boxes filled with items that we either definitely wanted or needed to review further.

I never did retreat to the "couch room," but I did need to step away several times during the sorting process when something triggered intensified emotions.

We came across a piece of a tie. When Doug and I went to our first Luvata company Christmas party all the men were wearing Christmas ties. That year the girls gave Doug a snowman tie so he would fit in the next year.

A fragment of a pink newspaper article caused tears to well up in my eyes. My Grandma Schwab had kept a scrapbook filled with articles about her brother-in-law, Francis X. Schwab, the Mayor of Buffalo in the 1920s. I had been honored to be the custodian of that family keepsake. Now it was reduced to jagged scraps.

Clothes from our master closet were difficult to look at. It was eerie handling hunks of things I had worn. "I always liked that dress," I said to Kim. It seemed crazy to even have that thought cross my mind. Sorting through Doug's clothes was especially hard. He had always looked good in that grey turtleneck with his curls slipping over the collar. Yes, I had to walk away every once in a while for a respite of a few minutes.

There were many scraps of Doug's baseball uniforms. What memories they invoked of our early days when we were young and discovering the joy of new love. T-Shirts commemorated the many races he'd participated in. Sometimes I thought his three marathons were more mentally stressful to me than him. I'd wait at certain points when he assumed he would be reaching that mile and panic when he didn't show up. Was he crumbled in a heap on the street somewhere, totally exhausted? No, there he would come, looking strong. A friend offered to take all these scraps and make a quilt for us.

The girls had all worn my father's baptismal dress. Their tiny little bodies almost engulfed in the flowing fabric, but what a lovely family tradition to carry on. I held that heirloom in my hands and mourned the fact that a brownish-yellow scorch mark now marred the front of the dress.

We did come across items that were not ours. As we held these things, our reaction always seemed to be one of shock. "Oh my gosh, this isn't ours. We shouldn't have it in our hands!"

Months later, I came across pages from a yearbook that I

assumed were from my Bishop McMahon High School days. Then I realized that the students weren't wearing McMahon uniforms. These were pages from a Sacred Heart yearbook. I knew immediately whose they were—Beverly Eckert's. Beverly had been on Flight 3407 to attend an event celebrating her husband's birthday, but she also was scheduled to speak at a gathering of Sacred Heart alumnae. Evidently she had brought her old yearbook along. Once again I felt that odd sensation of trespassing on someone else's emotions. I knew that Beverly's sister, Susan, lived in East Aurora. I found her phone number and called to tell her I had the yearbook pages. Susan came over that day to get them and was thrilled to have this small part of her sister's life.

August brought new beginnings. Lori and Chris began the adventure of marriage filled with hope, promise and unlimited possibilities. We were beginning to face the path of destruction left in the wake of the crash, and we saw that this avalanche of piecemeal possessions would result in bittersweet memories.

Added to the tangible items we had been inspecting grief and loss were now part of our possessions.

*"Sorrow cannot all be explained away in a life truly lived, grief and loss accumulate like possessions."*
~ Stefan Kanfer

3/18/12

# PHOTOGRAPHS

Our toys were limited when I was growing up in the 50s and 60s. I had a Tiny Tears doll. It had a head hard enough to knock someone cold and the ability to drink from a bottle which would result in the emission of water not only from a small hole in her bottom, but also through her leg joint, a feature I was eventually not allowed to use. There was a wonderful metal doll house. There were building blocks, 101 Dalmatian cutouts, a Mickey Mouse Club coloring book. My sister and I shared games: Go to the Head of the Class, Monopoly, and Uncle Wiggly. I remember being crushed when I opened the Uncle Wiggly game on Christmas morning to make the shocking discovery that instead of the advertised plastic "bunny" markers, ours included only round, wooden pieces.

Mine was a far cry from the playroom of my daughters. Their playroom often resembled the wind-tossed aftermath of a tornado with toys covering every square foot. Luckily, the door could be closed to conceal the wreckage from visitors. Every so often we sent the girls on a cleanup mission.

Perhaps my limited toy supply enabled me to find other means of entertainment, like flipping through family photo albums. I could spend hours tracing the lives and times of our family through this array of photographs. Little did I realize that in the future I would be seeing these images in a very different light.

Part of the clean-up process following the crash required many people to comb the site and retrieve our remaining possessions. A neighbor described lines of workers in hazmat suits working their way through the site. I cannot comprehend how they could do this job, and I remain amazed at what they collected, including hundreds of photographs—or shall I say pieces of hundreds of photographs.

The majority were trimmed to remove burnt or moldy edges. Some were intact, including the pictures from my parents' wedding album.

One picture is an eerily ghost-like image of our home at 6038

Long Street. It gives the illusion of wax melting on a candle, dissolving from sight.

Numbered bags were inside the boxes of photos. Their contents seemed random. An example: bag number C.406.0025 held pictures of our family celebrating the dawn of a new century. We are happy revelers with crowns announcing "2000" perched on our heads. There are pictures of my girls and their guys—the same guys who have become, or soon will become, my sons-in-law. A few of the girls' school class pictures are in this group. An 8x10 photo of my dad is there, taken when he lived with us in Ohio.

Two books were also included in this bag. One is the *"Deluxe Edition: Write Your Own Book."* It was a gift from a friend on the birth of my first daughter. I was not a faithful writer at that time, but what I did record makes me smile. The first entry involves Doug and me first considering parenthood. "Our first serious try was in October," I had written," during a baseball playoff game between the Yankees and Kansas City." It figures that sports were part of the equation! If I calculate correctly that attempt was successful.

The other book is a 1947 *Saga*, the Clarence High School Yearbook. Doug had found that in one of his flea market hunts. He chose it because a Long Street neighbor is pictured in it as a senior. The cover of the yearbook is gone but the contents remain intact. All in all, bag C.406.0025 held considerable treasures.

We removed the items from those bags and they're now stored in plastic bins in my basement. A smoky odor persists along with the overpowering smell of the dryer sheets inserted to keep things fresh. I have a real problem with dryer sheets now. They not only trigger memories of what was taken that night, but also make me relive the process of going through what remained.

Many of the photos are from the albums I flipped through as a child. Most of these had been in the basement on Long Street. The photo albums of my life with Doug and the girls were mainly upstairs, in rooms directly hit by the plane. They had little chance of surviving yet they do turn up. Relatives and friends have since shared their photos with us, some even compiling books for us. I treasure the images of my ancestors and my childhood as these could not be replaced.

Treasures. How could a newspaper clipping from the 1950s be replaced? It heralded the fiftieth anniversary of Mr. and Mrs. Otto Schoenwetter, my paternal grandparents, that was celebrated with a mass at St. Ann's church on Saturday, June 11. It includes a short biography of my grandfather:

> The 76-year old husband was born in Germany. He came to this city with his parents in 1887 and entered the upholstery trade while he was still in his teens. Mr. Schoenwetter was employed at the old Pierce-Arrow Motor Car Company for many years before joining the Pullman Company in 1918.

Priceless.

Yes, I am thankful that these bits and pieces survived, but sometimes I can't help feel that it would have been easier if they hadn't. It is a mixture of joy and torture. I could have mourned their loss once, and not had to deal with the heartache and tears that can occur while looking at them over and over again. They are curled and discolored but what remains of so many of them is the center, the heart of the photo—the smiling faces of my family. Those faces make it worthwhile.

3/3/11

## REQUIEM FOR A HOME

Close your eyes. Now, mentally go room to room in your home. Can you visualize every piece of furniture and every item in that home?

That was my task when I met with the insurance adjuster after the crash. I would begin to visualize the contents of 6038 Long Street.

I started up the stairs to the front porch. I saw well-worn wicker furniture that we first bought for the sunroom added to the house in Loveland, Ohio. Doug's Aunt Diane and Uncle Eddie visited us one weekend. We came across a great wicker rocker, but since I had already purchased other things for the room it was not bought. Shortly after that visit, we received a note from Aunt Diane along with a check to buy the rocker. It became a lovely haven to rock Jessica and Jill when they were babies.

As we swung open the front door, I remembered accidentally cracking the bottom panel of that door. Lacking the courage to mention this to Doug, I hoped if he noticed it I could claim ignorance. I had my story all ready. I would say, "It's an old door and must have been cracked before we moved in." I am a terrible liar, probably because of my days as a Catholic school girl. Luckily, the subject never came up.

An old Eastlake spoon-carved dresser was in the hallway. Doug found it at the Caesar Creek Flea Market near Cincinnati after picking up Kim and her friend from Girl Scout camp. The owner was packing up and didn't want to take it back home so he gave Doug a great deal. Doug squeezed it in with the girls and their gear. It needed lots of loving care. Doug stripped off years of paint, restoring the dresser to its original beauty.

"What was in it?" the adjuster asked me. It was a catch-all, a little bit of everything. So I struggled to remember and came up with an assortment of children's handmade Christmas ornaments; window cling-ons, including the "Happy Birthday" one that the girls always looked for on their special day; personal phone books; candles; and eerie Halloween music tapes brought out each year to set the right mood.

In my mind's eye, we turned into the living room. There was a lovely Eastlake desk, discovered in an Ohio antique shop's outside barn. It was one of those pieces that called out, "Take me home!" Another small desk came from the church festival. It had been donated by the nuns who taught at the school. I'm not sure how receptive the girls were to having a piece of furniture that came from the convent.

The chaise lounge had recently been acquired. It was something I had always wanted and Doug bought it for me in the fall. Spots had enjoyed nestling there. No doubt she was on it that fateful night. Had Doug bent down to say goodnight to her? Her remains were found by his legs.

Bookshelves flanked the front window. What was on them? There were books on Lincoln, Lindberg, the Pan-American Exhibition, sports figures, and children's holiday books. My mother's Roseville pottery rested there, along with a small Sebastian figure of Lincoln given to me by Doug after Jessica was born, and my dad's old "Schultz & Dooley" beer mugs. There were pictures from a trip to Ireland with my sister-in-law, Maureen, and our wedding album. After the crash, I came across our wedding photographer's name. I found his phone number. He was amazed when I explained who I was, but lamented that he had retired and no longer had any negatives.

The dining room was next. There was much to see. The 1900 dough cabinet was the first antique we had bought in Waynesville, Ohio, a Mecca for antique shoppers. Originally purchased for our kitchen in Loveland it was too big for any of our other kitchens. It had made a graceful transition to a family room and then to dining rooms in subsequent homes.

Waynesville also was the source of another Eastlake cabinet. This one we saw through the window of a closed shop. We called the owners and requested a deal. It was the day after Christmas.

Once again I had to give numbers to the adjuster. "Details, please, on dishes and crystal," she asked. How many Desert Rose dishes had been passed on to me from my mother? Were there platters, vegetable bowls, and a gravy boat? Were my mother's and grandmother's silver settings for eight, ten or twelve? Napkins, table cloths and lace doilies? How about those china cups and saucers given to me by my godmother Carol as a wedding gift? Grandma Schwab's sister, Aunt Frances, had hand painted some china. How many of those did I have? Don't forget the tiny advertising tins Doug had collected.

A beveled chest filled to the rim with photo albums was there. "How many albums did you have?" One special album had been put together by Doug for the first year anniversary of meeting each other. He had saved ticket stubs, napkins, newspaper clippings, and playbills. He had even gone back and taken pictures of where we first met, the Crows Nest and Duff's. There was a picture of rocks on the shore of Lake Erie in Wannakah where we had shared one of our first kisses. Yes, he was a romantic and definitely a "keeper."

A huge antique trunk sat by the window. I found it at a garage sale one Saturday on the way to the radio station where I worked part time. If it was still there on the way home, I would call Doug about it. Sure enough, there it was. Doug drove out to see it, and although he questioned where such a large item would go in our little Long Street house, we bought it. It became known as the "Buffalo" trunk where historical artifacts from the area were kept, including binders filled with old postcards.

The dining room table told another tale. After the dining room had been built in Loveland, the search was on for a table. No store-bought table for us. We wanted something old. I saw an ad in the Cincinnati paper for a table and chairs in a part of town I was not familiar with. Doug was out of town, so I packed all four kids in the van and headed out. In the age prior to GPS or directions from Google I managed to find it. I bought the table—a small refraction table and six slat chairs—all for a hundred dollars. The seller loaded the purchase on top of the van and we slowly made our way home. Doug had just pulled in the driveway when he spotted us driving down the street. What a sight that must have been. He appreciated the bargain, and we shared a multitude of happy meals at that table.

The night of the crash, that table held Buffalo Bison Baseball puzzles from the 1930s. Only one more had to be finished. I picture Doug stepping into the room to add a few more pieces. Is that where he was at 10:17?

Now we stood in the den. Well, it was never easy to stand in that room. It was filled to capacity. Furniture included an old desk, two legal cabinets and an antique cabinet. I can't say I ever saw Doug sitting at that desk. The room was basically a resting place for collectibles. It seems everyone wants to know what was in that room. I know there were Hartland statues and bobble head dolls. Complete Topps and Fleer sets were stored in an upper cupboard. Stacks of newspaper and magazine articles were piled on the floor. Doug would tear interesting articles out and keep them for future reference. Articles on the girls' sporting achievements were also saved. Binders of sports cards were there too.

The kitchen was big enough to include a vintage table from the 1920s. A colorful design had been stenciled on the top, and orange vinyl covered the chair cushions. My parents' corner cabinet, a wedding gift from the 1940s, fit nicely into a corner. "Let's review what was in the cupboards," the adjuster began. "How many canned and baking goods did you have?" Does anyone really know how many of these items they have? When was the last time you counted your canned goods?

Our refrigerator sported many magnets. That had started years ago. Whenever we took vacations or Doug was travelling, we would find a magnet from that area. Soon even the girls' friends were bringing us magnets from their excursions. When we moved to Long Street the real estate agent told us to remove the magnets to create a cleaner image. I thought our magnets showed potential buyers that we had a love of adventure and fun. Wouldn't you want to buy a home from people like that?

An old milk can stood in the hallway leading to the family room. It had been dragged from a storage shed at our cousins' farm in Langford, probably just before my sister and I spread our wings and got an apartment. There, as well as in the Eden and Loveland homes, it made a great telephone seat. All the weight it had borne had jammed the lid permanently closed. It had been retired from telephone duty on Long Street and had become the resting place for a basket full of pigs.

A brief stop in the downstairs bathroom brought up the question of how many towels and wash clothes had been in the house—along with shampoo, conditioner, body wash and other hygiene items.

The vision of one scared cat also came to mind. Several years ago, Spots had wandered across the street and under a van with an oil leak. Despite Doug's efforts to catch her, her fur was soon coated with oil. I was not home to witness this drama but according to the girls Doug's language was quite colorful. We hoped that the neighbors, who happened to be having a prayer meeting, were not interrupted by this display. Getting back to oil-slicked Spots, the next day we were still trying to deal with the mess. We corralled her into the shower stall, where Lori held her as I attempted to wash the oil off. It's a miracle Spots did not have a heart attack. Kim and Jess peered over the stall to watch the proceedings. A soaked cat is quite a sight, but I am sure Spots did not enjoy the laughter.

We added a new mud room by the back door in 2007. Instead of having a closet constructed we had found a vintage armoire. Doug's brother, Jackie, and his friend, Turk, laid the tile floor.

Adding a new family room to the back of the house had increased our living space. It was a bright, cheerful room and became the gathering place for family and friends. Unlike many of our homes, the majority of the construction was done by others. We had tackled the hardwood floor though. In all honesty, Doug did the bulk of the work. The girls and I assisted. I did not have the patience Doug had when it came to staggering the planks. The result was beautiful.

Building the new room allowed us to buy more antique furniture. Doug found pieces at garage sales and through his connections at the Clarence Flea Market. The workmanship of a

Kittinger desk, manufactured in Buffalo, was especially impressive, as was a beautiful oak storage cabinet.

Nothing could beat the story of how a bar in Connecticut found its way to Clarence Center. Doug discovered it on the internet and paid about a hundred dollars. The only catch — he had to pick it up in Connecticut. He and Lori's boyfriend at the time jumped in the van and headed east. "We're crossing the Tappan Zee Bridge!" Doug exclaimed, in one of his many phone calls, as they inched closer to their destination. The bar was heavy, but they got it into the van and made it back home. Since the room was not yet finished that bar stayed in the van for a while. It came out the day of our niece's wedding. There was time between the church service and the reception, so dressed in our wedding best the entire family maneuvered the piece into the family room. The wooden bar was flanked on either side by two lion carvings, which we affectionately referred to as "Sid" and "Leo," uncles who had both enjoyed a drink or two in their day. One lion survived the wreckage.

The mental journey through downstairs was complete.

Ascending the stairs, we lingered at the landing to consider the bookcase that held Jane Austen books, along with "Willow" statues. The hallway and three bedrooms were up a few more steps.

Kim's was the first room. It faced the front of the house. Her room reflected her life and times: teaching supplies, wedding magazines, trinkets from a trip to London, Monet prints, dragonfly items. Clothes were neatly hung in the large closet.

Jill's room was more haphazard. She had brought all her college stuff home. Piles of things she was planning to take with her to North Carolina for her internship were being organized. There were also possessions of her boyfriend, Dan, stored there since his enlistment in the Army. Another large closet, which was so unexpected to find in this 1920s house, was filled with her clothes and those of her sisters. A good assortment of homecoming and prom dresses hung together, an aura of special teenage times surrounding them.

The bedroom Doug and I had shared waited at the end of the hall. We had far too much furniture in there already, but we couldn't resist buying an Eastlake bedroom set. Ironically, we found the dressers at one antique shop in Canandaigua, New York and the bed in a different shop the same day. There was always a stack of books on Doug's side of the bed waiting to be read: sports, religion, history. He was always seeking additional knowledge, while I'd be reading "fluff."

The adjuster continued to press for details. How many pieces of clothing? What name brands did we buy? Let's break that down by tops, pants, dresses, suits, shoes and even underwear. Let's list jewelry and trinkets in all these rooms. This was crazy.

We stopped in the bathroom. The previous owners had intended to redo the bathroom before it sold, but we wanted to put our own touch on it. It came to us completely gutted. We saved the claw-foot tub, and Doug found an old dresser that he transformed into the vanity. Again, Doug's brothers Billy and Jackie and their friend, Turk, helped with the restoration. Before new floor boards went down, we decided to slip an envelope with our Christmas family newsletter and picture into the space. Perhaps someone would find our impromptu time capsule in the future.

The opening to the crawl space was in the hall. Holiday decorations waited there in anticipation of next year's celebration. Doug would swear, as he handed down box after box, that each year the number of Christmas decorations increased. The ornaments and Santas were treasures to us, as each told a story and recalled special holidays. All was lost, though, except for Jill's small "Baby's First Christmas" ornament.

Pictures of my ancestors hung on the walls. Because the hallway and pictures were both dark, the girls called those stoic images "creepy."

The dress I had found for me to wear to Lori's upcoming wedding hung in the small hallway closet. At thirty-nine dollars it had been an unbelievable bargain. After the crash a friend of mine was able to locate that same dress on the internet. She snagged it for the same bargain price.

The mental journey through upstairs was complete.

The last stop was the basement. Where to begin? There were old photo albums, family videos, computer and file cabinets packed with information, tools, and the cistern. Doug had decided the wall to the old water cistern should come down and the area cleaned for additional storage. Many of the things from the garage found a new home there: books, sports memorabilia, decorations, things from my parents' home, a wood box of mementos from my dad's World War II service. Ironically, we thought these things would be safer inside the house. The first time we visited the site after the crash a portion of the blue wall of the cistern was still visible.

My task was finished. The adjuster had been compassionate, kind, and yet professional. She had made a difficult undertaking more bearable. Now she had the job of putting a monetary value on our possessions.

Open your eyes. Did your mental vision match what you now see? I do not have that advantage. I must rely on my memories. I see nothing but an empty lot.

4/11/11

# THE QUILT

*"Life is a crazy-quilt of suffering and joy."*

~ *Jonathan Lockwood Hule*

The package fit perfectly between the screen and front doors. I had forgotten that my friend Cindy planned to drop something off. I figured it was a Christmas gift, but the minute I picked the parcel up, I knew it was the quilt. Tears welled before I even opened it and continued to flow a good half hour after the wrapping came off.

Cindy had thought that a co-worker of hers, Connie Grimsley, would be interested in making a quilt out of the fragments of Doug's old baseball uniforms and race shirts that had been salvaged.

It had been almost two years since I had met with Connie about a quilt. Time passes and the quilt had slipped silently to the back of my mind.

Now I slowly unfolded this treasure in my hands. Memories of Doug swirled around me.

Doug's uniforms from his days playing baseball for Wylie Distribution Warehouse appear twice on the quilt — home game orange and away games black. He'd been wearing that orange uniform the first time I laid eyes on him—the catcher with the curls. I could not resist watching on that warm July night back in 1977. As our relationship grew, the two of us would lie on my apartment floor after a game and my hands would slip under the folds of that uniform to explore this man who shared my feelings of love.

There was a T-shirt from Super Bowl XXVIII in Atlanta when the Buffalo Bills clashed with the Dallas Cowboys on January 31, 1994. My sister-in-law Maureen picked me up in Cincinnati, and then we drove down to Atlanta where we met Doug and his brother Bill. The guys, who were on out-of-town business trips, would be flying into Atlanta. Doug managed to get a flight out of Newark just before a snow storm cancelled takeoffs. Any frustration he might have felt with the tension of that situation dissolved when he learned the Buffalo Jills were staying at our motel. During the course of our stay we managed to take a photo of a beaming Doug with those cheerleaders.

*The quilt*

The contingent of Bills fans at the motel included a priest who conveniently said mass in his room. Unfortunately, all those prayers could not help the Bills beat the Cowboys. The half-time lead of 13-6 kept us in our seats, afraid that by moving we might upset some cosmic force that would change the momentum. Despite our euphoria the Bills' Thurman Thomas was stripped of the ball less than a minute into the second half, and a downward spiral began. The result was a fourth straight Super Bowl loss for the Bills with a somber score of 30-13. My brother-in-law, Billy, driving at what seemed like about a hundred miles an hour (thankfully I slept through most of that), took us straight home, almost five hundred miles, to Cincinnati after the game.

Doug's hockey days are featured on the quilt, both with a piece of Doug's Knotted Bar uniform and with a patch announcing them as Senior "A" Champions 1973-74. Doug and his friend Jim Macie played both baseball and hockey for the Knotted Bar, a restaurant/pizzeria on Lovejoy Street. The guy who ran the place was known as Pizza John. He had sponsored the hockey team during that winning 1973-74 season.

Doug and Jim played on many teams together. One team was sponsored by a teammate's father who owned a restaurant in downtown Buffalo. Many times the guys would stop by the restaurant after a game to show their thanks for sponsorship.

One Friday night the group went out drinking (the usual routine after games of any sort). After the bars closed at 4 a.m. (yes, when you are young staying up that late is possible), they went to another teammate's house for breakfast.

Doug and Jim would often go out drinking Friday nights and then go to the Depew Rink where Doug's brother Joe had ice rented from four to six a.m. "You would sober up fast once you got on the ice," Jim said.

A cartoon character, puffing on a cigar, was the mascot of the Huttons baseball team that Doug played for when we lived in Eden after our wedding in 1979. It was probably one of the first times Doug played on a team that did not include some of his Lovejoy buddies. He was readily accepted by the group, and I can recall picnics that included sports trivia contests that Doug would usually win. Such events included young couples with cars full of baby paraphernalia to accommodate their growing families. We were just fitting into the social scene in Eden when the offer of a job in Cincinnati intervened.

That job change to Quantum Chemical is represented on the quilt by a piece of material from a jacket. The Pierce and Stevens logo, from the job that moved us back to Buffalo in 1998, also appears. Both moves took a leap of faith, and made a big change for our family.

Running was a big part of Doug's life, which is well illustrated by the quilt. The Run for Your Life competition held in 1982 and the Cincinnati Mini Marathon from 1992 appear. How many races did the girls and I attend, cheering from the sidelines as

Doug streaked past? The Mini Marathon was a yearly event, but I recall others at the Cincinnati Zoo (very hilly), and Lunken Airport, which had a convenient play area for kids. I looked up the race results for the Run for Your Life 20k. Doug's time was 1:33:28. I was probably not there for that race. It was September, 1982. Kim would have been about a year and a half and I was seven months pregnant with Lori.

The Daemen College Charles McDougald Memorial 5k Walk and Run from 2002 found its way on to the quilt. Kim attended Daemen and every year we participated — Doug running and Kim and I walking. After Doug completed his run he would always make his way back to accompany Kim and me to the finish line.

There are remnants of Doug's time as a referee. A small patch indicates this was during the 1972-73 season when he refereed for a youth hockey league. He had given that up, he told me, because dealing with the parents was so unpleasant. Through the years the girls wore the referee uniform for Halloween.

A T-shirt from Paris symbolizes a trip Doug and I took to Germany and France for our fifteenth wedding anniversary in 1994. I regret that among the many fragments of photos that have emerged from the remains there is not one from that journey. It was my first European experience and deserves a story of its own. We arrived in Paris after a stay in Germany, where people were friendly, cities were pristine, and communication was easier, as Doug could speak the language. I was not as comfortable in Paris. Neither Doug nor I were fluent in French, and the public restroom facilities, consisting of holes in the floor and cement areas to place your feet while squatting, made me think that cleanliness was not such a high priority for Parisians.

We arrived on a Wednesday, parked our rental car in a small square near the hotel. When checking in were informed that The Louvre we planned to visit the next day would be closed for Ascension Thursday. Luckily, it was open that night so we rushed over. It was amazing. We spent hours walking through the various halls. My biggest surprise was how small the Mona

Lisa actually was. We continued toward the Arch de Triumph and then to the Eiffel Tower. These landmarks are a considerable distance from one another, which was another surprise to me. Doug had been to Paris with his friend Bernie in 1977, and he told me that the grating on the tower was not solid at the top. As a person afraid of heights I declined when asked if I wanted to go to the top. I probably am one of a very few to pass up that opportunity. Still, it was thrilling to be in Paris standing at the foot of the Eiffel Tower.

Unfortunately, when we returned to the hotel we learned that the square we had parked in was being transformed into a market. In the morning, when approaching the car to retrieve an umbrella, we were met by an angry woman. Although we could not understand what she was saying, we knew she was not happy about having less space to display her strawberries. There was a ticket on the car, and when we asked the desk clerk at the hotel if we should pay the fine, he laughed. "The car surrounded by strawberries? A German car rented to Americans? Who will track that down?" We never did pay.

When people say Paris is romantic they are telling the truth. Walking along the Seine River banks, exploring offerings of vendors' paintings and books (we bought a small Parisian scene), cruising down the river at night in view of the illuminated Eiffel Tower, and attending mass at Notre Dame Cathedral were all breath-taking experiences, definitely romantic while arm in-arm with your love.

We wanted to drive past Euro Disney in Paris. Although the park had opened in 1992 it was desolate when we went by. There were no crowds and we were able to explore venues near the park. We picked up souvenirs for the girls, including a shirt now on the quilt.

All these memories surround the center of Doug's life— his family. Connie incorporated one of my favorite pictures of our family into the quilt. It was taken in the fall of 2002, after we had returned to the Buffalo area. Many of my Schwab and Schoenwetter cousins were invited to our Everwood Court home that day. It provided a perfect opportunity to have someone take the photo that would be sent with our yearly Christmas card and letter. I love this picture of Doug. He's wearing a Bills shirt, smiling contentedly, and I like that his wedding and UB rings are visible. That photo encompasses what he loved in life.

*Counterclockwise from left: Kim, Doug, Jill, Jess, Karen and Lori (Autumn 2002).*

Under the picture, puzzle pieces of different colors represent each member of the family—woven together to form a complete picture of togetherness. We had arrived at a good place in life. I like to think we made the most of those moments before we learned how quickly things can change.

What a perfect gift this quilt is to our family. I can see it being passed from person-to-person, especially in times of stress or confusion. "Wrap it around you and feel the warmth it can bring," I will tell my girls and their children. The warmth comes not only from the material of the quilt, but from the tenderness and love Doug shared with us during his life.

I will let that warmth permeate through loneliness and feel Doug's arms wrapped around me. I will release a sigh of contentment.

12/26/14

# September 2009

*"At some stages of your life, you will deal with things, and at others you are overwhelmed with misery and anxiety."*

~ *Nigella Lawson*

I believe my girls wanted to keep me busy so I wouldn't have too much time to think about Doug being gone. They were being kind and helpful, even in their own grief.

I headed to Goshen, New York on Labor Day weekend to visit Jessica. Finding affordable housing in the New York City area was difficult and Jess had moved frequently. She had a new apartment, and this one was tiny but cozy. She had arranged a schedule of activities including a visit to Cold Spring-on-the-Hudson, a little town filled with a variety of shops and restaurants, and a stop at Boscobel, a Federal Period home surrounded by beautiful gardens. The mansion overlooks the Hudson River valley with West Point in the distance.

As I sat on a garden bench enjoying the scenery, my thoughts drifted to another visit in the Spring of 2008. Doug and I were visiting Jess at yet another apartment. We drove to West Point and the three of us posed for a picture with the Hudson behind us. That trip also included dinner at a well-known German restaurant.

On this Labor Day trip in 2009, I sat in the beer garden at that same restaurant during their Octoberfest, and drank from a giant Bavaria Wheat beer glass, missing Doug.

Later that weekend, Jess and I took a walk in a small park and talked about the night of the crash for the first time. Jess told me how relieved she had been to learn that Jill, Kim, and I were safe. But she added that the relief had made her feel guilty. How could she feel relief when Doug was dead? She mourned for him, but couldn't even imagine how she and Lori would have dealt with the loss of Jill, Kim, and me, in addition to Doug. I assured her there was no need for any guilt. "It's only natural to feel relief for our survival," I told her.

The autopsy report had arrived, my attorney emailed me on September 10. We could discuss it at my convenience. Evidently neither of us was ready yet because that discussion did not take place until March of 2012.

Kim and I attended our first Bills game since the crash. It seemed so strange to be going without Doug. Luckily it was a sunny day so I could hide my tears behind sunglasses. I had debated whether or not to renew our tickets that season, but the team was celebrating their fiftieth year and I knew how much that would have meant to Doug. At that particular game the "50 Year All Star Team" was introduced during halftime.

Macie and I met several times at the storage facility that September to begin sorting through the thousands of collectible and personal items from the Long Street garage. I panic whenever I try to comprehend what I will do with it all. Jim Macie will certainly guide me, but it is overwhelming. One box at a time—that is how you begin.

We made some progress as we went through about two-thirds of the contents of one shed. We consolidated and removed empty plastic bins out of big boxes. Jim used a marker to identify the contents. Another shed contained about twelve 24 x 24 flat boxes filled with sports cards. These he ranked from one to five. Five were those with the highest selling value. The lower value cards were probably worth only a half cent each.

The majority of the collectibles were familiar because Doug had shown them to me at one time or the other. Jim was amazed that Doug still had so many of the items they purchased from a warehouse in the 70s.

He suggested that I hold on to several items that could be sold on eBay. What an assortment there was. Examples included: an inauguration banner for President Dwight D. Eisenhower dated January 20, 1953, a Chicago Cubs Bobble Head—ceramic not plastic, a complete set of 1989 Score National Football League cards in the original box, Coke hockey cards, 1971 National Basketball Association-American Basketball Association cards, and, Kahn's hotdog package strips.

There were World Series Programs from 1960 to 1982, along with others dating from the 1940s and 50s. The illustrations on the older programs were drawings, not photos. Two from the World War II era captured current events of that time: one showed a little baseball player buying war bonds and stamps, while another depicted men from all branches of the service listening to the games on their radios. Those programs originally sold for 25 to 50 cents.

The oldest program came from the World Championship series of 1928 when the Yankees faced the Cardinals. According to the Baseball Almanac, "After coming off a magical season, the defending champion Yankees managed to hold off the Athletics to win their third consecutive pennant by two and a half games." That team included Babe Ruth and Lou Gehrig.

There were photo album stamps of 1972 National Hockey League players—a set of six players in each pack for only 10 cents; and war gum cards from 1942 depicting battles, generals, and heroes. The backs reminded collectors to "Buy War Bonds & Stamps for VICTORY."

We also set aside a set of Icee Bear NBA Basketball cards from 1972; Post-season football cards from 1962 in a box Doug had marked "Auction" and, Mecca cigarette "Series of Champions" cards. These cards depicted champion athletes and prize fighters and were issued from 1910-1912.

Doug liked collecting first day covers and there were albums commemorating such events as Hall of Fame inductions, Super Bowls, and basketball point records. One album held a collection of Salada plastic coins from the 60s.

Perhaps someday I'll consider selling these items, but for now they surround me with Doug's spirit and the joy found in finding and collecting them. His excitement somehow lives on in me. I am not sure I want to part with them, but considering the quantity of things stored in the sheds I guess I'd better change my mind. Such decisions in the future, I suppose, are going to bring sadness and anxiety.

I still felt the need to keep busy so I took a dulcimer class at the Roycroft Campus. Strumming my cardboard dulcimer seemed pretty easy in the group but attempting to master it at home was more difficult. Although Doug did not play an instrument, around the Christmas holidays he would bring out a harmonica, my old guitar, or finger a melody on the piano. "I really admire people who can play an instrument," he would say. "Maybe I'll take some lessons."

Two days before the Bills game against New Orleans, we learned that the Bills organization planned to present us with a game ball at the opening ceremonies. Kim and I wore our "I Love Doug" shirts from the June race as we joined first responders along with the families and co-workers of two firemen killed that summer. It was quite a thrill to walk on the field and have Thurman Thomas present a ball inscribed with Doug's name. The announcer paid homage to Doug as a life-long supporter of the Buffalo Bills and mentioned his contributions to the sports memorabilia hobby. It was an honor Doug would have appreciated. As we walked out of the stadium shouts of "We love Doug too!" made us smile. We never did learn who arranged for this very special moment.

Jill had finished her internship at Pinehurst Golf Resort and was offered a full time job. She drove back to Clarence Center at the end of the month. We would begin packing her car and mine with her remaining stuff.

Keep moving, keep busy, and try not to dwell on the overwhelming anxiety that loomed in an uncertain future. Take it one day at a time.

4/11/12

## STORAGE SHEDS

"I must be a masochist." I find myself saying that more and more. I seem to keep finding ways to inflict pain on myself, especially where Flight 3407 is concerned.

When writing about the crash or its aftermath I often find myself Googling "3407" and sitting, eyes glued on the screen. For what? I could call it research, which is partially true. But one thing is certain, I will find pain.

I can try ignoring reality but there are some things that will not go away—things that are my responsibility to resolve. I can delay decisions but putting it off will not make a problem disappear.

Perhaps that is why on a warm spring afternoon during my lunch hour I found myself driving to the facility where the contents of the Long Street garage were stored. It is definitely remarkable, and miraculous, that amid flying debris and raging flames that garage stood in defiance of destruction.

A few days after the crash we received word that the garage, along with its contents, would be leveled. I recall contacting my attorney. I pleaded, on the brink of tears, that these items should be saved, "That is all we have!" He assured me that although smoke had crept through cracks and crevices, tainting the boxes housed inside, everything would be carefully removed and sent to Texas for cleaning.

When they pulled up the doors, I am sure the workers who came to clear out the garage were astonished at what they found. There was no space for cars. Anyone entering would have to navigate through the boxes solidly stacked inside.

Those boxes are now stuffed into two storage sheds. I do not go to those sheds often. It is an overwhelming experience. How will I sort through all this? What will I do with it all?

Sports memorabilia prevails. "What were you thinking, Doug?" I can't help but ask. I know the answer. He loved the history behind it all, and he knew it could have value in the future. That afternoon I wasn't looking for sports related stuff. I was seeking something else. I longed to find personal things, things that related to our past. Perhaps the arrival of grandchildren has sparked this need. I want them to have at least a few bits and pieces of their ancestry.

I began searching through the sealed boxes. I found weights, a circular saw, sports cards and coins, golf clubs, a box of spindles from the deck at the back of the Long Street house, swords, and sports books. There were old photos of people that Doug must have bought as references to the historical period when they had been taken and miniature stadiums. Except for the girls' old green blackboard, with the alphabet etched on its side and a long tray to hold chalk, I could not find any personal items.

I left, sweaty and dusty, after the lunch hour had ticked away. My search would continue on another day, but perhaps not during a lunch hour while I was wearing dressy pastel cottons. My mind drifted back to Doug's old work jeans and torn sweatshirt. Now that was the right attire for digging through dusty old sheds.

Every item that had been sanitized in Texas was photographed and we had been sent catalogues with thumbnail pictures. It had been almost four years since I had flipped through those catalogs. After my trip to the sheds, I was drawn to the basement to retrieve a canvas bag filled with four of those thick catalogs. I rediscovered forgotten items in them—many so simple. They brought me joy and sorrow.

One photo showed baby treasures: shoes, Baptismal candles, knit caps, tiny "Life Begins at Sisters" t-shirts, a small baby bottle containing the two teeth Lori was born with, and Doug's baby shoes. For years these items stayed in my bedroom dresser drawer. When had they been moved to the garage?

A construction paper snowman smiling on a red card reminded me of the first Christmas card I received from Doug. Other items included a ceramic squirrel my dad had won on a boat cruise with the seniors in Cincinnati—he was so proud of that, the "Just Married" sign from our wedding and our cake topper, a box marked "German Bible and family documents," and an ash scoop. This tool did remove some ashes from fireplaces in past homes, but also was used to remove dead mice that Spots would proudly sneak into the house after a successful hunt.

When I was a child I often took naps in my parents' bedroom. I was fascinated by a plaque that hung on one wall, the head of a man and a woman, cheek-to-cheek—a wedding present they had received from an artistic friend. Perhaps I liked it for the affection and love it conveyed, or maybe I found it interesting that the woman, with her pale skin, seemed to be protected by the darker man. It appeared unscathed in the catalog and rekindled warm thoughts of lazy afternoon naps.

I found other items from my childhood. A group of small dolls included Betsy Ross in a red, white and blue flag-inspired dress and Martha Washington in a purple satin dress with a matching triangular hat over white hair. These patriotic ladies had been kept in my mother's china cabinet. We could look at them, but rarely got the chance to actually touch them.

I spotted hard cover books that my sister and I had received as Christmas presents: *Lassie*, *The Bobbsey Twins*, and *The Five Little Peppers*. Copies of *16* and *Teen* magazine brought back memories of crushes, and reminders that as a teenager I had longed for the confidence those stars and models seemed to radiate.

A *Bing Crosby Christmas Album* containing old 78 records took me back to our living room on Herman Street. My sister and I would play our parents' records, and we often put on "shows" for their entertainment.

I was thrilled to confirm my assumption that the linoleum block forms I had carved for my early Christmas cards had been in the garage. There was my first endeavor—a cross and soldier's helmet, never actually used, but a sign of the turbulent 70s. One cutting showed a sail boat—my one and only "commissioned" piece. My sister's friends had asked me to design something for their first daughter's birth announcement. As avid sailors, they were pleased with my creation.

I was glad to see some items my girls will be able to share with their children, an assortment of Fisher-Price toys and a lineup of dolls in all shapes and sizes. OK, so maybe my grandsons won't be impressed with the dolls. How nice, though, to pass these childhood toys on to another generation.

It was late. I had spent almost two hours looking at the catalogs. The masochistic process had certainly brought some pain, but feelings of relief and joy far outweighed the pain.

If I could buoy my spirits just by flipping through catalogs, imagine the happiness I will feel when the search ends and those items are in my hands once again. Tangible items plus memories equal great reward.

5/30/13

# The Kiss

*By Karen Wielinski*

Why do eyelids drop like fruit sweet and lush,
Clinging to a tree, yearning to be free?
Afraid to gaze into a vivid sea,
Waves of passion clearly come into sight.
Is it too much to bare this burning light?
The faintest breath from lips that barely touch,
Anticipated and wanted so much.
Cheeks—one rough, one soft—nuzzle in a rush.

Electric sparks ignited by desire,
Like dry twigs come to life when touched by fire.
Blush of color unfurls on one so fair,
Hue to match the flower placed in her hair.
Eyes open with a start—what will this bring?
A simple kiss now changes everything.

*6/29/13*

*1940 Alexander Baker Company "Chalkware" plaque*

# FRAGMENTS

I reached for the two bags. My brother-in-law had discovered them, out of place, in boxes of sports memorabilia. He thought I would want to have them. A quick glance revealed that bag C1183.000 contained a wooden index card box with envelopes of pictures belonging to my dad. No number appeared on the second bag, but it clearly contained items retrieved from the Long Street site.

There were pictures of my dad that chronicled the years he lived with us in Cincinnati. These items, in perfect condition, must have been in the Long Street garage. The images of Grandpa and his little girls, smiles beaming, reach out to me as they celebrate birthdays and other family events. They hover around him as he reads birthday cards and books to a captive audience. I am glad Dad lived with us for five years so that the girls could get to know their grandpa.

"Did you ever give us baths?" my daughters often asked of the pictures that showed them with crumpled clothes and tossed hair. The reason they so often looked so tousled was that their days were filled with lots of activities. As a mother of four I did not have the energy to bathe them every night, but I did keep them fairly clean. I assure them that they will understand when they become mothers themselves.

There were lots of the tiny school photos that traced the school days of my girls. I found a gem hidden among them, my own seventh grade school photo. A white Peter Pan collar peeks over a blue uniform. I am tight-lipped, consciously avoiding a smile that would reveal my chipped front tooth, the result of an encounter with a wooden paddle (remember those paddles with the red balls attached on an elastic string?) during a backyard baseball game.

Some pictures show Dad at Lake Cumberland, Kentucky spending time with my sister Barbara and her husband Bill. He loved going for rides on their boat, and occasionally Dad was allowed to try his hand at steering the vessel. In these shots he appears in his T-shirt and shorts—showing off his very white legs.

Dad never owned a pair of shorts until he was 80. We were driving to Arkansas to spend a Fourth of July weekend with Doug's brother, Joe, and his family, and the heat was getting to Dad. We stopped in St. Louis to get him a much-needed pair of shorts. He proudly displayed those white legs from that point on.

I moved my attention to the unmarked bag. I never know what to expect when I pull a stack of ragged papers from these larger bags. What an assortment this one contained.

Doug was an avid newspaper reader. I doubt that he would have ever considered stopping his paper delivery to read the news on line. After reading articles, he would tear out those that especially caught his attention with the intent that he might just want to refer to them in the future. That accounted for the piles of clippings that filled boxes and covered the floor of his den.

The first article reported the closing of the Peter Cooper Corporate offices in Gowanda, New York. Shortly before we were married Doug had taken a job as an adhesive chemist with that company. That was the reason our first home was in Eden, located halfway between Gowanda and downtown Buffalo where I worked. Doug had left that position for the job in Cincinnati. Apparently he had saved that clipping because he had once worked there.

He also liked to keep obituaries. There were interesting ones in this group:

> Cornelius McGillicuddy died October 3, 2004, at the age of 81. He was a walking "history book" and distant cousin of Hall of Fame Manager Connie Mack. He participated in the official statistical team for the Bills and served on the statistics crew of the old Bisons and Bills in the All-American Football Conference.

I could see that Doug had probably saved the obituary of Cornelius because of his interest in the Bills, but as a movie buff he would also have been interested in an obituary of "Janet Leigh Actress of Psycho Fame" on the same page.

A clipping from October 4, 2004, was headlined "Leroy Gordon Cooper, Jr. Mercury Astronaut." The early space program was another of Doug's interests, one that he shared with a young neighbor to whom Doug often passed on space "finds" from flea markets.

The obituary of Orval Cott, Senior, dated December 26, 2003, was one that I know Doug would have considered a "keeper." Orval was a former professional basketball player and lifelong resident of the Lovejoy area where Doug had grown up. If I'm not mistaken, Doug used to play sports with Orval's sons.

What else did I pull from this bag? There was the sad report that "Jeopardy" whiz, Ken Jennings, had lost after a seventy-four game run. Doug tried to catch "Jeopardy" most evenings. The engagement announcement and bridal picture of his niece and goddaughter, Amy, were tucked in this group. An article about Arthur C. Clarke, the author of 2001: A Space Odyssey, was information he might need one day.

I tried to pry apart the stuck together pages of an Easter card, and was rewarded with the squiggly signatures of the very young Kim, Lori, Jessica, and Jill. I discovered a partial cover of the Niagara University Commencement program from May 23, 1976. That was when Doug proudly received his Master of Science degree in chemistry.

Pieces of a calendar emerged. No date was visible, but Doug had written in the Yankee scores for each day, along with the names of the pitchers.

"You pamper me…Happy Anniversary to the man who spoils me," read an anniversary card I had apparently given him. There was a shard of a Graig Nettles Topps baseball card. That was eerie. Doug and I had considered naming any son we might have Graig.

There were remembrances of Doug's service years: a Certificate of Achievement from the U.S. Army Quartermaster School in Ft. Lee, Virginia for a "Distinguished Graduate" dated June 30, 1970; and a diploma naming Pfc. Douglas C. Wielinski on the completion of the "Automotive Repair Parts Specialist

Course" and "Stock Control & Accounting Specialist Course" dated April 30, 1970. Bits and pieces of Doug's report cards from P.S. 37 and P.S. 43 showed he mostly earned Bs. There was a fragment of "Certificate of Birth" for his mother, Arleen Flading.

Doug had started to collect old photos of various subjects. He bought them for the cars, airplanes, sports teams, store fronts, and retail spaces they depicted, and he was always eager to delve into the history behind his finds. What an assembly I sorted through: a young man in front of an old plane with writing on the back identifying the subject as one John Muffit, "Ruth's high school boy friend?"; an old gas station pump; what appeared to be a blimp of some sort with writing on the back "Friedrichshafen 1936;" World War I soldiers; a shot taken from a car window showing a law office and café, taken perhaps for the African Americans in front of these establishments; an unidentified baseball catcher; a German family, circa 1914; a sports card written in German from the Summer Olympics of 1936; women factory workers circa World War II; Frederick C. Pries, merchant tailor and his salesmen in front of a store in Buffalo; Cowan's Confectionery & Bakery; and someone in a casket. Amazing stuff!

The smoky/dryer sheet odor had started to give me a headache, or was that caused by the ordeal of sorting through these bits and pieces of the past? At that point I came across an emotional find. Although the date is clipped off, I think that Jill had made that faded Christmas card when she was eighteen. The faint image of a large cat stretched out before a fireplace festooned with holiday decorations was drawn on the front. I had to strain to read what remains of the personal note she wrote to Doug:

> "Thanks for always being there for me, like coming to all my games. I appreciate it a lot and I wouldn't do as good without you there. I'm happy that you got another job. You deserved it…I love you!"

It was time to stop sorting. Emotional weariness had settled into every bone in my body.

I have come to the conclusion that this process is both a

blessing and a curse. In a sense I have been given a gift—the opportunity to review my own life and the lives of those I love. Many people simply don't take the time to scrutinize lives this way, but I have been forced to. The fact that I have these fragments of my life to shake up my memory is a blessing, as is the fact that I had Doug to love. But I curse the sadness it carries with it.

8/26/11

# OCTOBER 2009

*"All you need is the plan, the road map, and the courage
to press on to your destination."*
~ Earl Nightingale

October would be a month of journeys.

After Jill's internship at the Pinehurst Golf Resort in North Carolina, she had been offered a job there. This was convenient because her boyfriend Dan was still stationed at Ft. Bragg only 45 minutes away. She had returned home and we would spend the next few weeks packing her up for her permanent move back to North Carolina.

As we organized and packed for Jill's start on her career, I took my own trip into the past

My career as a working girl began in July, 1969 when I got a job at National Gypsum Company, then headquartered on Delaware Avenue in Buffalo. Bishop McMahon High School turned out secretaries (that's what they were called then and that's what McMahon was known for). There was a steady stream, year-after-year, of local companies who always seemed to have positions for McMahon graduates. I landed the job at National Gypsum, but I had really wanted to work at either the Courier Express or the Buffalo Evening News. Even then, I was drawn to the printed word and wanted to be a part of the hustle and bustle of the newspaper world. It wasn't meant to be. I sent resumes and I even connected with the daughter of one of my mother's friends at the Courier. Nothing was available. I finally had to put that dream on the back burner and accept a practical offer. Fate had dictated my course.

It was boring. I found myself in the "Steno Pool," sitting

around waiting to type up letters from a Dictaphone, and hoping someone would go on vacation so I could fill in. Eventually, I worked in the Credit Department and then Advertising (which I loved), and the girls I met became life-long friends. One of those girls actually was responsible for me meeting Doug, so it turned out that fate knew what it was doing.

Six to ten of us would eat lunch together. The numbers varied. Our ages ranged from eighteen to twenty-five. The Monday lunch hour was always crammed with stories about weekend dates (I had few). There was a group of older guys who ate and played cards at the table next to us, but we always suspected them of listening in on our chatter. Oh what hopes for romance and setbacks of heartbreak we girls experienced over those lunch table years. Conversations were never dull.

National Gypsum left Buffalo in 1978 shortly before I was married. The lunchroom girls went off in many directions but we still managed to keep in touch over the years of weddings, children, and occasional divorces. One of our group who had moved to Minnesota visited during October and we gathered once more. It was the first time I had seen many of them since the crash, so the reunion was bittersweet. Lori's wedding turned conversation in a happier direction. We meandered down memory lane, laughed a lot, and wondered how so many of us could possibly be approaching the big six-oh. Our non-stop chatter made it seem like we were sitting around that lunch room table once again.

The closing on the South Grove house finally took place on October 14. Early that morning, I met my attorney and we entered the courthouse to process the paperwork. We were in and out in no time—a completely different scenario than Doug and I had faced when closing on the Long Street property.

That experience had been exhausting. Doug was unemployed at that time, and the deed listed me as the owner and major bread winner. That was not a role I was used to. The day of the closing, we waited for a call that would tell us what the final costs would be. We were still waiting by mid-afternoon. Our decision to downsize had been difficult and my nerves were shot. I retreated to the basement of the house we would be leaving on Everwood Court and cried. Finally, we learned the amount, rushed to the bank for a check, and then downtown to sign papers. We made it within minutes of the time when the county clerk's office closed.

Now I clutched the paperwork making me a home owner once more, this time in East Aurora, and I again found myself in tears. I was determined to find another home for my family, and had done so even after many people had said I was rushing.

"It's too soon," I was told. "Give yourself time." To me, though, this move was a quest—a goal I felt driven to reach in order to lessen the pain of losing our Long Street home. Now that I had reached that goal, I could concentrate on helping Jill move down to North Carolina. We loaded up both of our cars and headed out.

I do not like following people on the highway. It's always a battle trying to keep another car in sight and keeping up. All through West Virginia and Virginia we were pelted with rain. I am not a fan of the hills of West Virginia, and navigating them and keeping an eye out for Jill was not easy, especially as night approached. There were times when I actually wondered if that was really Jill in front of me. Had my gaze strayed? Had she branched out in another direction. It was a relief to finally stop and rest in Virginia for the night.

Jill and Dan were not officially in their new apartment and they still had no furniture. That meant that we would have to stay in the village apartment that Jill had occupied during her internship. We would have to share those digs with the occasional cockroach. But first, we were meeting Dan and a few of his Army friends the next day in Fayetteville so we put off the roaches for another day and stayed in a Fayetteville motel.

The next day brought an adventure — a trip to IKEA in Charlotte. Although I had visited the IKEA in Cincinnati with Lori and Chris, I had never experienced an IKEA furniture-buying expedition. We were joined by two Army couples and one little girl. A miniscule U-Haul trailer was attached to the one guy's van. We listened to a John Mayer CD over and over again during the two and a half-hour journey.

It surprised me that the little girl was so excited about going to IKEA, but I saw why when we got there. They had a huge play area to keep kids occupied while their parents shopped.

I bought a filing cabinet. Dan and Jill found something for almost every room in their apartment: bed, mattress, dresser, table and chairs, lamps, coffee table, and couch. That's when I found out that buyers were responsible for loading stuff (that they would later have to assemble) onto carts and through the check out. The friends also purchased big things and I marveled that everything fit into the U-Haul and the vans.

It was inevitable. I would have to sleep in the unappealing apartment. We were greeted by two big bugs as soon as we walked in. Having never seen a cockroach before, I suggested they might be crickets, which made me feel better. They scurried away before we could end their residency and we didn't see them during the evening. I decided to sleep on the couch. I placed a sheet on it so I wouldn't stick to the leather (or was it plastic?) all night. Jill retired while I watched one of the two TV channels. Reception was limited. I had finally settled down when a large cockroach dropped out of nowhere onto my lap. He escaped but I slept with the lights on.

I spent several days helping Dan and Jill organize their new apartment. Then it was time to say good-bye to Jill. Previous good-byes in North Carolina had been easier to handle because it was only an internship for a few months. This time was different—exciting for her, but difficult for me. This time she was leaving the nest.

Kim was still living with me, but she and Jeff were almost finished with the construction of a new house in Darien. When I moved to East Aurora I would be living on my own.

From North Carolina I covered almost 500 miles to visit a friend, Janet, in Westerville, Ohio, a suburb of Columbus. Although I had occasionally travelled without Doug, I realized that travelling alone was now a fact of life. Now my travel companions became music and a book-on-tape. Rush hour traffic was in full swing when I neared Columbus and the last hour of the drive seemed to take forever. I was relieved to finally reach my destination.

My visit would be short, but Janet and I worked in a visit to the German Village section of Columbus which has been listed on the National Register of Historic Places since 1974. Doug and I had always enjoyed this little piece of the "Motherland" with cobblestone streets lined with quaint homes and shops. The Book Loft always occupied a big chunk of our time—a maze of 32 rooms filled with every imaginable form of the printed word. The bookstore occupied several pre-Civil War buildings that had housed a general store, a saloon, and a nickelodeon cinema in earlier times. As I wove my way through its many passages, I recalled the happy hours Doug and I had spent browsing there and selecting yet another book or two to add to our shelves.

My last stop was in Sandusky, Ohio. I attended an OCCL Convention. So, you ask, what in the world is OCCL? It stands for Ohio Child Conservation League, and that organization had been a lifesaver for me when we first moved to Cincinnati in 1983.

It seemed strange to me that the word "conservation" was in the organization name. Perhaps it does make sense, though. Webster's Dictionary describes that as "controlled use and systematic protection of natural resources, as forests and water-ways." Well, the group did try to find ways for mothers to "con-trol" their children, and of course we always want to protect them. It is also true that sometimes we felt like we were wading through "forests" of toys, technical devices, and strewn clothing. Potty training, bathing, washing, and tears provided waterways.

The League was really a support system for moms. There were monthly meetings to discuss the joys as well as the trials and trib-ulations of motherhood. It also provided an endless variety of activities for our children, especially the youngest.

After we had moved to the Cincinnati suburb of Loveland, Ohio I found myself completely on my own during the day. Since the girls were not yet in school I needed to find other ways to connect with people. Our home was not in a development, but I would put Kim and Lori in the stroller and head over to more populated areas. If I saw anyone with little children I would in-troduce myself. One woman connected me with OCCL, where I met women who remain my friends to this day.

Each year the state convention is held in various districts of Ohio. I attended many over the years. The most memorable was in Marietta, Ohio in October, 2006. I was scheduled to leave for Marietta on the morning of October 13 when a surprise October lake effect snow storm hit Western New York. That morning we awoke to find our cars buried in massive mounds of snow. I decided not to go. That was disappointing because my friend, Gwen, was being installed as the state president.

Doug, however, encouraged me to head out. "You'll regret not going," he said. Long Street looked passable, and a glance down Goodrich Road didn't look that bad. Forget that President George Bush would declare the area a major disaster. Doug sent me off with a kiss and a wish for a safe trip.

Once on Goodrich Road, I knew I was a fool. The road had not been plowed and my car lurched though ruts created by other fools. When another car approached in the opposite direction I knew I could not stray from those ruts and risk getting stuck. Instead, I swear when we passed my eyes were shut and braced for a collision. Miraculously, there was no crash and I made it to Main Street, where I barely missed downed wires and proceeded to a very rutty Transit Road. By the time I reached the southern suburbs, the snow had disappeared. I could not get on the Thruway until I reached Fredonia, but I made it to Marietta in time for dinner. I experienced slight flashes of guilt throughout the weekend as I thought of my family coping with a power failure and all that snow. But hey, Doug had told me to go. As it turned out, he coped just fine. He found a bar with electricity and watched a Sabres game.

The 2009 convention in Sandusky was held at the Sawmill Creek Resort. The setting was rustic but there were none of the hardships of camping. The furniture was constructed of rough logs, but padded with comfortable pillows and placed near roaring fireplaces.

I wasn't sure what my friend, Gwen, had told the delegates about the crash. I wondered how I would handle questions that might arise and I admit that I was apprehensive. It also did not help my emotions that a Christmas theme had been chosen that year.

At the dinner itself no one asked questions. A local high school choir sang carols, but I did leave the room before the singing of "Silent Night." There were limits to what I could handle.

That night, I joined a group of Gwen's friends from other districts and the subject of the crash came up. I had been anxious, but was surprised to find that I did not feel uncomfortable talking about the crash. In a way it felt therapeutic.

After another 250 miles I was back in Western New York. I had travelled over 1500 miles in nine days (transporting an IKEA file cabinet most of the distance).

*"In life you need one thing to survive: the ability to realize shit happens. You step in it, accept it, get over it and keep moving."*

*~ Author Unknown*

Yes, shit happens, but I had kept moving. It was a way to keep sane.

6/18/12

# HOME

*"I long, as does every human being, to be at home wherever I find myself."*

~ *Maya Angelou*

I find myself in a wanderlust state—aimlessly trying to figure out where I belong. Where exactly am I at home?

A house becomes a home as a result of the love felt there, whether it is the love between husband and wife, parents and children, individuals and their pets or possessions. The feeling of home provides security and warmth.

I was introduced to those feelings of home as a child at 221 Herman Street on Buffalo's East Side. There I was surrounded by family—my mother, father, sister, grandmother, and an assortment of aunts, uncles, and cousins. Comfort was readily available.

Snippets of memory burst into my mind—tiny recollections of day-to-day events that would seem insignificant to an outsider: Dad thinking he could get a bit more whipped cream out of that aerosol container by opening the end with the can opener, resulting in a spray of whipped cream decorating our kitchen; being tiny enough to fit in a large cardboard box in our kitchen and lulled to sleep by the sound of my mother cooking dinner while I clutched the small rubber mother from my dollhouse. In fact, the smell of rubber can often trigger that particular childhood memory.

The recollection of warmth on my back from the living room heater brings contentment. That was a favorite spot for flipping through the Sunday comics or playing with my Barbie doll, using plastic mint candy dividers as her furniture. I remember listening to my parents' old 78 records. They included such favorites as "Peg of My Heart," "Lavender Blue (Dilly, Dilly)," Bing Crosby's "White Christmas," and Spike Jones' "All I Want for Christmas is My Two Front Teeth."

I shared a bedroom with my sister, Barbara. Some nights we would join hands as we fell asleep, hoping to see if that bond would hold throughout the night. Of course it didn't. Our bedroom was a getaway for listening to music. We tucked tiny transistor radios under our pillows so we could listen after our bedtime until the airwaves were silent—or until we fell asleep. One of our aunts gave us an old 45 record player. The Beatles' "Hey Mr. Postman" was my first purchase. We graduated to a 33 and a third record player, and I remember the excitement of rushing down to Sattler's at 998 Broadway whenever a new Beatles' album came out.

I easily felt at home.

We moved when I was fifteen. Before we left, I picked up pad and pencil and carefully drew the floor plan of 221 Herman. I loved that house, and I thought perhaps when I grew older I could ask an architect to design a replica.

Our next home was on Hagen Street off East Delevan near the city line. During our ten years there I evolved from an awkward teen to a young adult. There were boys to dream about, proms that required a girl to find a date, and life-changing decisions to be made. On Hagen Street I experienced many firsts: first kiss, first car, and first job.

My sister and I had a huge bedroom in the attic, and we were allowed to paint it any color we desired. We chose a golden yellow, somewhat for the bold color, but mainly because the price of the paint had been reduced. Again, it was a haven for music. While most kids my age were listening to the Rolling Stones, Grateful Dead, or Chicago, I was listening to Rod McKuen—does anyone remember Rod? Ah, "The Earth," "The Sea," "The Sky."

I easily felt at home.

Our independence was emerging and my sister and I wanted the freedom to do things our way. Hagen Street was feeling more like a house and less like a home. After several days stranded in the house with my parents during The Blizzard of '77, we decided that the time had come to make our move.

We rented an apartment in a Hamburg complex. Now we were no longer city dwellers but suburbanites. It was great, especially when this guy named Doug entered my life. The concept of home intensified as he spent more and more time in that apartment.

Again memories streak across my mind: peeking through the peep hole in the door and seeing Doug after a three week trip to Europe with his friend Bernie running up the stairs sporting a new mustache, suede jacket, and jaunty cap; looking out the window and watching Doug's Monte Carlo roll down the parking lot toward a milk machine; trying—not too successfully—to impress Doug with my very limited cooking abilities (such as trying to fry potato pancakes without oil); snuggling on the couch watching Joe Ferguson and the Bills; venturing into the explorations of human relationships and falling in love.

I easily felt at home.

Doug and I wanted to share our lives and so we got married on May 19, 1979.

Doug worked in Gowanda and I worked in downtown Buffalo. We found a house in the middle—Eden. "I've found our dream house!" he said, and took me out to see it. The house was surrounded by corn fields, and we reached it by driving down a dirt road. I'm not talking about a dirt driveway—part of the town road was dirt. It was a good-sized ranch but there was no garage door and we walked a plank over a hole of a porch to enter. Inside, the house was partially finished but the majority was definitely a fix-it-upper. I was stunned at his enthusiasm.

"We're going to finish all this?" I asked.

"Sure," he said confidently. That was my clue that this would be the first in a series of future home improvement projects.

In Eden we proved the theory that possessions do not make a home. We had little in the way of furniture. The house was a work in progress. The living room, dining room, kitchen and bedrooms needed to be finished, so we slowly became carpenters and painters. We had my bedroom furniture from the apartment, but it was at least a year before we added a living room couch.

Besides his carpentry duties, Doug also built a Heath Kit television. Until he got the TV built our viewing was done on a tiny portable television Doug's brother had given us for a wedding present.

We were surrounded by corn fields as we tried to fit into the agricultural community by growing cucumbers, zucchini, beans, watermelon, and yes, corn. Our success was limited.

My cooking skills were honed, and we invited parents, aunts, and uncles over for pinochle and dinner. Joy and pride surfaced as we welcomed two baby girls into our home. We were enveloped in love.

I easily felt at home.

Just as we were adjusting to parenthood, we faced a new dilemma. Should we move to Cincinnati, Ohio where Doug had been offered a new job or remain in Western New York? Married life and parenthood were still relatively new. How would we adjust to such a major change away from family and friends? It was an exciting challenge, though, so off we went to Ohio in 1983.

We went from living in the Garden of Eden to Loveland, a suburb of Cincinnati and home of the Reds, Bengals, Skyline Chili, Graeters Ice Cream, and Flying Pigs. It proved to be a good decision. Our family increased with the arrival of two more little girls, and we developed a definite feeling of home in our house on Paxton-Guinea Road. There was also a feeling of community with the town of Loveland and parish of St. Columban.

Doug, still very much the jock, didn't seem to mind the absence of a boy. The girls became involved in sporting activities and could still follow in his footsteps.

As our girls grew, so did the Paxton-Guinea home. After attending a home show Doug decided it was time to build a dining room. Later we built a wing for my dad. The home was filled with a whirlwind of activities: special birthday parties with character cakes, games, crafts and sleepovers; moms gathering to discuss the perils and pluses of motherhood; the arrival of Spots, the cat. She brought the joy of pet ownership to our family along with the experience of watching her kittens grow. We saw the extension of our family when both my sister and dad joined the household at different times, and we witnessed the amazing transformation of our baby girls into pre-teens and teens.

*Pictured from left to right: Lori, Doug, Jill, Jess, Karen and Kim in 1991.*

When the girls started school at St. Columban, I attended my first PTA meeting. "We need someone to do publicity," one of the officers announced. Should I volunteer or stay in the background? I wanted to jump up right there and then and say "I'll do it." I seized the opportunity. I wrote and took pictures for the local newspaper, *The Loveland Herald*. My next project was creating a monthly newsletter for the school. Soon after, I added taking pictures for the school yearbook to my duties. I loved every minute of this volunteer job. I wrote about all kinds of subjects: a Russian visitor, an astronaut, a holocaust survivor. One newsletter was devoted to the history of the school, and every year I made up a humorous prophecy about the eighth grade graduating class. My need to write was being fulfilled. I had become a super-mom volunteer.

I easily felt at home.

My sister in California got divorced and decided to move to Cincinnati. Doug cleared a space in his basement card room to set up a makeshift bedroom for her. She remained with us, surrounded by Doug's sports collection, for about seven months.

A curve-ball came our way when my parents' health declined.

We decided to move them from Buffalo to Cincinnati. We faced the difficult decision to admit my mom to a nursing home, and we added a room to our house where Dad would stay for five years. Doug willingly accepted my family into our home.

The room addition for my dad was quite an undertaking. We had previously added a dining room and sitting room, so we had some experience. Much of the work we did ourselves. As handy as we were, however I couldn't help but call Doug at work the day the local building supply truck dropped off huge rafters in our front yard. Flash back to that first encounter in Eden.

"Are we really going to put these up ourselves?"

Again, without hesitation, Doug said "Sure."

Much to my surprise, we did. Even my 80ish dad helped!

When my youngest, Jill, turned five, I returned to the work force. I held a series of secretarial jobs working for a concrete company, a chiropractor, a medical doctor. It felt good to be contributing financially to our family. Having my dad living with us made this transition back to work easier.

Doug found fulfillment in his job, I found fulfillment in my girls and volunteer activities, and Kim, Lori, Jessica, and Jill had a childhood filled with the love of family and friends.

We would have been content to stay in this nurturing environment but fate had other ideas. Doug's company was moving. Should Doug stay with his company and move to Houston, or should he accept a position he'd been offered in Buffalo? Our extended families were always a big part of our lives, so in 1997 we decided to return to Western New York.

Our decision seemed contradictory to our girls. We had taken a family trip to Buffalo a few months before all this upheaval. We had stayed near the airport, directly across the street from a dilapidated Westinghouse building. "We got out of this city just in time!" Doug and I had said with conviction.

Opinions can change, and once we were settled it was wonderful rediscovering Buffalo and the surrounding areas. The city had always remained in our hearts, and returning after fourteen years made us appreciate what this area had to offer.

We moved into a house on Everwood Court South in suburban East Amherst during December, 1997. This was an affluent neighborhood. Catered parties and lawn services were the norm for our neighbors, but Doug often puttered around inside and outside our home with his beat-up old blue shorts and torn sweatshirt. When new neighbors first moved next door they assumed Doug was the groundskeeper. We liked our new neighborhood but we retained our blue collar heritage.

We made use of the 3200 square footage of that home. The older girls had their own bedrooms, and Jess and Jill shared a spacious room. A huge master bedroom featured a French door entrance, cove ceiling, two closets, and a massive bathroom. Guests would gravitate to an island in the kitchen. The adjoining family room had floor-to-ceiling windows. The partially finished basement became a hangout for the girls and their friends. Doug found the unfinished area perfect for collectibles that had overflowed from his den.

There were many good times in that home: homecomings, proms, and high school graduations; ringing in the new millennium with homemade crowns and a rousing game of "spoons" that generated the loudest laugh from Doug that any of us could remember; Doug adding Victorian trim and "Painted Lady" color to the house; and family reunions where over-flow guests lounged on the wrap-around porch.

It was easy to feel at home.

Doug's employer downsized and his job was cut, so we had to reconsider how much space and expense was truly necessary. We decided to downsize too and moved to a smaller home at 6038 Long Street in Clarence Center in September, 2003.

Don't get me wrong, Everwood Court was nice and very enjoyable but somehow we felt more at home on Long Street. Less space was cozier and brought our family closer together. Doug and I both loved the history of Long Street, and especially the fact that our house was originally a kit home. Perhaps the kit had arrived on the old Peanut Line Railroad—now the Clarence Bike Path. Doug treated anyone who visited to a history lesson, embellished with the various bits and pieces of historical information he had unearthed during his antique explorations.

It was easy to feel at home, but life can change in an instant.

The bond that held our family together was severed on February 12, 2009, when Continental Flight 3407 plummeted from the sky and crashed into our home. With Doug's death and our material history shattered would our family ever be able to salvage that feeling of home?

The aftermath of that night left little time to sit and ponder such a question. Finding a place for the girls and me to live was just a necessity. An aunt provided temporary lodging until a town house on Kraus Road in Clarence Center would become our new home.

It would become a home, despite all the sadness surrounding our arrival. Our stay there lasted less than a year and yet there are times I miss the closeness I felt with Kim and Jill, and the comfort we gave to one another. Lori's scheduled August first wedding, less than six months after the tragedy, was orchestrated from Kraus Road. That wedding was something that gave us a happy goal.

It is true that this home held many moments of sadness and fear—revelations and discoveries were around every corner during that time. Tears were almost a constant, and fear and panic were companions because of the location of the apartment directly on the flight path.

I felt compelled to find another house. It became an obsession and I ignored the advice of my attorney and brother-in-law to not rush into becoming a home owner again. The discovery of 365 South Grove ended the obsession.

So, where do I feel at home?

East Aurora and I are a good fit. I love the small town feel. Whenever I drive into the village I feel like I am on a vacation visiting a quaint, historic area. It also gives me the feeling of community that I felt as a child growing up in Buffalo. It is wonderful to be able to walk places; I don't have to always hop in a car and drive someplace to eat, drink, or shop. New friends and activities have become a part of my life.

I have adjusted to a new life and feel at home.

Adjustment: "the art of making fit or comfortable; conforming or adapting, as to new conditions." Boy, that sums up life, doesn't it?

Despite the warmth of home I feel in East Aurora, I still retain a sense of being at home in Clarence because I still work there, being with friends from the community and enjoying activities there.

I feel at home in both Buffalo and Cincinnati, and I love what each offers.

I am coming to a conclusion—Doug made wherever I was home. I continue to carry him in my heart so I can feel at home no matter where I am.

7/6/12

---

*"How will you know I am hurting, if you cannot see my pain? To wear it on my body, tells what words cannot explain."*

~ C. Blout

I did not want to see the pain on their faces. That is what I feared. For weeks, I debated whether I would attend a memorial service at Forest Lawn Cemetery in Buffalo. It was scheduled for November 8. Families would meet at the Millennium Hotel where buses would transport them to Forest Lawn. My encounters with the 3407 families had been limited so far. Seeing their pain added to my own. I wasn't sure I wanted to put myself through it.

There was much debate among the families about wording on the memorial plaque. The plane families did not want the original phrase "which crashed into 6038 Long Street." They did not like the word "crash." To me, that described what happened that night. It was changed to "all who perished aboard Continental Flight 3407 and on the ground at 6038 Long Street." As long as Doug's name and our address appeared on the plaque I was satisfied.

The families debated about the role of the media. Kevin Kuwik, whose girlfriend Lorin was lost that night, was a leader of the families' Washington campaign for improved airline safety. Kevin emailed:

```
I almost feel like this was more of a challenge
than any meeting we've ever had in Washington,
due to the sensitivity of the subject. We have
touched base with all the local media regarding
our group's wishes for privacy. They are aware
that the service will be private, and that there
```

will be family members available after the main
body has departed the site.

My brother-in-law, Billy, planned on going to the service and
a luncheon afterward. He felt people wanted to meet me and he
encouraged me to attend. I would go, but I did not want to ride
on the bus that would be available to transport families between
the Millennium Hotel and Forest Lawn Cemetery. I preferred
that he and I drive to the cemetery. I wanted a means of escape, if
necessary. I also told him I would not attend the luncheon.

Continental Airlines had arranged with Forest Lawn to bury
additional remains of those killed on February 12. It was chilling
to think what the two caskets that greeted us contained: one held
the unidentified remains, the other identifiable remains too small
and numerous to return to the families. These caskets would be
placed in a crypt bearing the name plaque. There was a real possibility that some part of Doug's remains were cradled in that
casket.

It was an unseasonably warm November day—blue skies
with temperatures in the 60s—as over 600 people gathered inside
a huge tent. The service was moving and emotional. An amazing
thought entered my mind. *All of these people are here because of
something that happened at our home.* It was surreal, bizarre, and
so hard to comprehend. After the service we filed past the caskets, placing a red rose reverently on top in remembrance of our
loved ones.

I changed my mind and decided to join the other families for
lunch. There was time between events for Billy and me to talk. I
told him how much I appreciated everything he had done for us
since the crash. At times I am remiss and forget the pain he feels
because of his brother's death.

During lunch we sat with the family of Mary Abraham. Mary,
44, was the youngest of four siblings, a retired Army Reserve first
sergeant who lived in West Seneca. Her sisters turned their energy toward the improved air safety measures to ease their pain.

I sought out Kevin Kuwik, and asked him to introduce me to
the Mossop and Ferris Reid family. Donald and Dawn Mossop

along with their son, Shawn, had been travelling with Dawn's sister, Ferris, to Toronto via Buffalo. How does a family deal with the tragic loss of four loved ones? I needed to extend my condolences. We were introduced and hugged. I cried. It really was too much pain. It was time to leave.

Despite my apprehension and tears, being a part of the day had been good.

I had planned to be in the South Grove house by Christmas. That goal was not going to be reached. Although I was disappointed, it just made more sense to make a few improvements before moving in: a new furnace and air-conditioning seemed a priority, as did some electrical details that needed updating. I also decided to replace carpeting and laminate floors with hardwood in the living room and kitchen.

Another visit with the glaucoma specialist indicated that some surgery was necessary to help relieve the pressure in both eyes. A tiny stent would be inserted near the iris. I would have to basically be housebound for two weeks following the surgery, and that was not welcome news. To make matters worse, only one eye could be done at a time. Reading and watching TV were allowed but no lifting, bending or straining. There was one thing I definitely needed to know. "Can I cry?" Tears were a big part of my life now, so luckily crying was allowed. The first surgery was scheduled for January 11.

When we had first moved to the Clarence area in 1997, joining the Clarence Women's Club had helped me become involved in the community. I learned that East Aurora also had a Women's Club. Even though I wasn't officially in my new house I decided to attend a meeting. The ladies were enjoying a pot luck dinner and made me feel welcome. It was inevitable that they would learn about my recent tragedy. They didn't dwell on it or ask for details, which eased my anxiety about meeting this new group.

I was surprised a few days later, to receive a long email from one of the members, Zoe, who reminded me of the actress Blyth Danner.

> I sat across from you at the pot luck—the one you said looked like someone (I have forgotten who already). We are so happy that you have decided to join Aurora Women's Club...it is welcoming and caring (and we probably eat too much and some of us enjoy our wine a lot!).

She proceeded to tell me that she and her husband, Rod, had moved to the area three years ago, and also mentioned several December events that she felt might be of interest to me.

> I hope you join us," she said. "I admire the path you are taking in your adjustment. No one can ever fully understand what you are dealing with. Please know you will have as much support here as you need to continue to move forward. I look forward to a meaningful friendship.

This was a woman I definitely wanted to get to know better.

I was involved in both the Long Street Memorial Committee and the Flight 3407 Foundation, attending meetings two or three times a month. It was the general consensus that there would be two memorials: a more private one on Long Street, along with a public memorial. Ideas would be solicited from the 3407 families, neighbors, and community. The committees visited various locations in the Clarence area where a Civic Memorial could be erected. The Dean of the Architectural Department of the University at Buffalo, Brian Carter, and graduate student, Joe D'Angelo, were part of the Memorial Committee. The decision was reached to bring all these groups together in December for an update on ideas submitted and the work being done by the committee. Some progress was being made.

During one of the Flight 3407 Foundation meetings, a Long Street neighbor mentioned that she was surprised that someone had placed an American flag on the site. I admit my initial reaction was one of shock that someone would do this without my permission. After a few moments of reflection, I asked her, "Is this a large flag?"

"No, it is a small flag," she answered.

"Where is it located?" I asked, as I began to realize who must have placed the flag on the site.

"Near the McGreevy's house," she responded.

A chill went through me.

My brother-in-law Billy mentioned a few weeks before that he had asked the coroner to mark the spot on the land where they found Doug. Although he did not tell me this had been done, I was convinced that the small flag marked that spot. Later that day I drove to Long Street and parked in front of what was once our home. The small flag barely fluttered. What a sense of sadness overcame me as I realized that Doug's body rested on

*Karen and Kathleen Dworak with the Long Street Painting.*

that very spot amid the destruction. At that point I could not find the strength to open the car door and stand by the flag. I would not summon the courage to do so until the day after the first anniversary of the crash.

Kathleen Dworak, a local Clarence Center artist, had offered to paint a portrait of our Long Street home. Her work had been completed and Kathleen brought the painting to me at work. She had captured the heart of our 1920s home, including small details: the impatiens that grew profusely on the shady side of the house; the flag perched on a porch pillar, hints of that "painted lady" look Doug liked to add to our homes, exemplified in a touch of maroon interjected here and there, the old wood dolly with a bag of flowers draped over the front; and inviting wicker furniture on the porch. I was grateful to Kathleen for once again making 6038 Long Street visible to me. I knew this portrait would be a part of any new home I might have. It would not hang in a prominent spot where it would be readily visible though—that would be too difficult to endure.

Thanksgiving was approaching fast, and the girls and I, along with my sister, Barb, and her husband, Bill, would gather at Lori and Chris' home in Bellevue, Kentucky. How much thankfulness would we feel on this first major holiday without Doug? My answer to that question crossed my mind one morning and I composed an email:

> This is what happens when I go to bed early for a change...I wake up in the wee hours of the morning, wide awake! It does, though, give me time to send this email.
>
> As Thanksgiving approaches and the holiday season looms in front of us, the sadness and deep void felt on a daily basis since losing Doug certainly intensifies. Yet, there are some things I am thankful for:
>
> - I am thankful for the 30+ years I had Doug in my life. Some people never have that happiness and love in their lives.
> - I am thankful for my four beautiful daughters...

beautiful inside and out. They have grown into good people, and I am proud of their many accomplishments and strengths.

- I am thankful for my daughters' guys…they love my girls and I feel confident they will protect and care for them. They have supported me since February 12th and been willing to ease my sorrow in any way they can.
- I am thankful for a wonderful network of family, friends, co-workers and even complete strangers, who have been so supportive and understanding. It is amazing, and they certainly help me to carry on.
- I am thankful for Jill and me being alive... miracles do happen.

To my girls and family I'll be sharing Thanksgiving with, these are all things I would like to say that day as part of the blessing, but that would be too emotional.

So, Thanksgiving blessings to all. Embrace those who share it with you and remember the love and memories of those not there.

After we arrived at Lori and Chris', Jess announced that she wanted to run in the Cincinnati Thanksgiving Day 10k Race in remembrance of Doug. It would be the first time she would run in a 6. 2-mile race. I was apprehensive about accompanying her —not because I was concerned about whether she could handle that distance, but because it would be the first time since the accident that I would be in that running environment. Again, it was one of those instances when I didn't trust my emotions.

Arriving early Thanksgiving morning I felt the excitement that always emerged when I saw the runners' enthusiasm before a race. Of course, Doug was on my mind. How many races had I wished him luck and rooted from the sidelines? This race began and ended at the Paul Brown Stadium. We found the starting line, I gave Jess some encouraging words, and walked about a half mile to secure a spot to watch the race. Looking back toward the stadium, I was amazed at the sea of people assembled—hundreds or perhaps even a thousand people as far as the eye could see. Despite the number of people, I was able to catch a glimpse of Jess streaking past me. I walked back to the stadium, entered a rest room stall, and cried as I thought of Doug and how proud he would have been of Jess following in his footsteps.

I went to about the five-mile point where I hoped to see Jess. Her anticipated finish time had passed and I still had not seen her. Finally, she called and asked where I was—she had finished and was concerned that she couldn't find me, so much so that she called her sisters to see if I had returned to Lori's. I fought my way back to the stadium through the crowds and finally we reconnected. In tears she told me "I kept thinking about Dad and how great it would have been to run with him."

Our family managed to get through the holiday—thankful to be together and for the memories of Doug we carried with us.
The legal process took a giant step forward as our wrongful death suit was filed. I have such mixed feelings about the law suit. Somehow it just does not feel right to profit from an event that claimed so many lives and affected so many people. Despite that emotion, I know Doug always wanted to provide for and help his girls. He would want us to pursue financial security.

There had been far too many opportunities to see the pain of others during November. My heart felt battered. I hoped opportunity would not knock that often again.

7/16/12

## GOING THE EXTRA MILE

My nephew Brian had asked me several times, "If you need any-thing, Aunt Karen, I am always willing to assist."

Looking at the array of clutter in my garage, I decided to take Brian up on his offer. We had a productive day as he removed items left by the previous owner, and he helped me organize what needed to stay.

It became obvious that the garage was a popular hangout for the critters of the neighborhood during the winter months—the floor was littered with the remains of their feasting on nuts. Brian also located the secret entryways that gave them access to this vermin speakeasy I was running.

I was thrilled with the transformation, but one downside to the cleanup was that it once again forced me to deal with a group of boxes in the center of the garage. These held assorted items retrieved from the Long Street site—things that Kim and I had briefly examined back in August, 2009—fragments of paper we felt deserved closer inspection at another time. Brian rearranged the boxes on a now cleaned off workbench.

At the end of the day, I told myself it was time to delve once more into the memories. I would start with one box. What would the contents reveal?

A gloomy day greeted me in the morning. Nothing was planned and Jill, who was staying with me until Dan was dis-charged from the Army, was currently out of town so I had no ex-cuse not to open the cardboard box that beckoned on the kitchen floor. The odor of cleaning fluids and dryer sheets, which were inserted during the Texas sanitation process to cover that smell, served as an omen to my senses. Brace yourself, be prepared.

Photographs had been thrown together in a random order—a lifetime of moments captured from Christmas, Halloween, school days, visits with family and friends, a convention to Las Vegas in 2000 where the keynote speaker was Colin Powell.

There was Doug working on the additions to the Loveland, Ohio house—a dining room and a "wing" for my dad. One showed him working on the roof, and I remembered the time he told me "I just sat up there and listened to all the activity of you and the girls below. I stayed a moment to enjoy the calm before the storm that would be unleashed when I went down."

I was thrilled to find photos of Jill referred to in my stories that I never thought I would see again—one in the Santa suit worn during the "Kokomo" song Jill had played (in remembrance of Doug) during her wedding, and one where she is sitting on the kitchen table picking grapes off the stems during my jelly making attempt. A few minutes into this inspection and already I had to reach for the tissue box. Might as well put the whole box on the table.

At the bottom of the box, I almost missed a small plastic bag that contained a silver medal from the Tri-State German-American Schools in Cincinnati. For several years Doug and the girls all took German classes—his special time with his girls.

Several times I mentioned to people that Doug ran in marathons. Flipping through pieces of paper, I now found the details involved with those races.

His first marathon was the Skylon International Marathon, from downtown Buffalo to Niagara Falls, Ontario in 1982. Doug was 35 and completed the race in 3:48:22. I was pregnant with Lori and more than a little concerned about his running a marathon. He had certainly trained on the roads surrounding Eden and was no stranger to running a variety of shorter events. I stood by City Hall and cheered him on, and nervously waited to head to Niagara Falls for the finish. At his estimated arrival time, the blur of runner after runner streaked by me, but I didn't see Doug. I finally stopped a race official and inquired where I might be able to learn the names of those who had finished. "Check out the medical tent first," I was told.

Thankfully, Doug appeared before that became necessary. He had completed his first marathon.

Doug again participated in the Skylon International Marathon, on October 7, 1984. A certificate indicates he was 207th of 686 entrants with a time of 3:38:25. Once more the again pregnant wife hurried to the finish line and this time actually saw him cross. After that marathon we stopped at the Skylon Tower for after-race festivities, and Doug helped change a flat tire for another runner in the parking lot.

He would run two more marathons in Columbus, Ohio. On October 24, 1993, he was 188th out of 471 entrants with a finishing time of 3:40:14. His last marathon was on November 13, 1994, but I found no record of his finishing time.

I did find a handwritten note where he recorded his experience during one of the Columbus marathons. The ink is faded and the edges of the paper have been cut, so I am left with bits and pieces:

> At the beginning of the race, people were dropping gloves, hats, bags, etc. because of the nice weather. . . the 5-8 mile hills weren't too bad...running at about a 7:40 pace at 13... decided even at that pace, it would be hard to make the time required overall for Boston...at 18 I began to feel slower pace about 7:50...after 20 really began to slow.

A brochure was in this box for the Boston Marathon. Even though he never participated, I know he at least wanted to have the satisfaction of knowing he could qualify for that prestigious race. Men in the 35—49 age bracket needed a time of between 3:15—3:25. Doug came close, but never reached his goal.

His running numbers provided testimony of a variety of events while we lived in Cincinnati: the Brewery Run, Cincinnati Zoo run, and several Cincinnati Mini-Heart 5Ks. There was one adventure I could have done without—the Little Miami Mini-Triathlon in Ohio.

A mini-triathlon encompasses three events: a swim (100 yards to a quarter mile), biking (six to twelve miles) and run (one to three miles). Doug decided to challenge himself to compete in a triathlon in September of 1996. He later wrote to a friend, "It was a sprint-type, half mile swim, 20 mile bike and a five mile run. I surprised myself by making it through the swim without drowning."

As a spectator, along with four little girls, I can definitely report that the swim in Caesar Creek Lake seemed to take forever. A herd of people (to me that's what they looked like) in identical swim caps entered the lake. It was impossible to distinguish one from another. Who would even know if someone got pulled under the water? One by one swimmers emerged until only a few dots remained in the horizon. I was trying to keep calm for the girls' sake, but my nerves were quickly fraying. (Jess reminded me that she and her sisters were all sobbing by this time.) I also kept thinking, *He better not drown and leave me dealing with these little girls today.* I was ready to call in the rescue team when he finally popped out of the water in his little Speedo and swim cap, and ran to his bike. (Jill recalls Doug glancing at the girls and saying, "What are you crying about?"). I hope to find that picture some day. Doug in his Speedo. It was a real classic. Unfortunately, I did not come across the results of that day.

What did turn up was a portion of a note from Jill. "Dad you did it. You did the Triathlon." The words were surrounded by blue swirls—perhaps symbolizing the memorable swim—and hearts. It had been another sports adventure, and I'll admit he looked good in the Speedo!

I was happy to come across Doug's achievements—a solid, although partial record. He certainly gave himself goals to go that extra mile—in his running but also in life, whether it was spending time with his girls, helping a fellow runner in need, or building additions to provide comfort for his family and for my dad. I was reminded of all that from a box partially filled with remnants.

I will continue to sort through my wreckage, painful as it can be sometimes, because I know there is always a good chance I will discover more "relics." I just have to remember to keep the tissue box close at hand.

4/15/12

# DECEMBER 2009

*"Like snowflakes, my Christmas memories gather and dance —
each beautiful, unique and too soon gone."*

~ *Deborah Whipp*

The month of December would release a flood of memories.

It was my Christmas tradition, started almost 40 years before, to make cards for family and friends. My first boss at National Gypsum and his wife created their cards. Their practice intrigued me. They showed me the process of cutting linoleum block and rolling the design with ink to create the image on paper.

It was the Vietnam era and my first attempt pictured a grim scene: a helmet draped over a graveyard cross, indicating my plea to end the war. I reconsidered and opted instead for two hands linked together offering a hope for peace.

As the years went on, I graduated to a silk-screen process. When our Wielinski brood multiplied I took my creations to a printer. Later I welcomed the advent of the color home printer. I also was one of those people who sent, to some, the dreaded family update letter. Personally, I enjoy receiving annual news from others, and I thought it was a great way to let out of town folks on my list know how we were doing.

I faced yet another decision that first Christmas after the crash—was this a tradition I could continue? After much soul-searching, I decided it was something I needed to preserve.

My card was simple: a blue outline of Mary and Joseph proceeding to the distant city of Bethlehem, where a bright, golden star beckoned. A quote from Willa Cather proclaimed "Where there is great love, there are always miracles." Despite our tragic loss, a belief in miracles seemed apropos. Inside was a wish that "the light of hope, the warmth of friendship, and the comfort of love" would surround our friends and family throughout the New Year.

It was difficult for me to write my traditional letter, but then it gradually began to take form:

> I debated whether or not to send the annual Wielinski update this year. The sadness and emptiness felt each day definitely has intensified this holiday season, but there is some comfort in keeping traditions alive.
>
> First, I must begin with a huge "thank you" to everyone who has supported us since February 12th. I've said it many times, but such thoughtfulness at times was overwhelming. During the early days we looked for and received comfort from the amazing numbers of cards that were forwarded to us. So many included warm thoughts and remembrances of Doug, which confirmed what we knew...he was a man of many interests, impacted many and as some phrased it "a gentle man."
>
> The last ten months have brought many emotional situations...meeting with the families of Flight 3407's victims, meetings with psychologists, unraveling financial matters, sorting through the scorched remains of what was a home—30 years of my life with Doug. Through it all, though, were good memories and the creation of new memories...

I gave updates on the girls: Kim and Jeff building a new home and preparing for their wedding next July, Lori and Chris' wedding in August, some of the special moments and the belief that Doug was with us in spirit, Jess overcoming her fears and flying to a conference, and the pride Doug would have felt as Jess completed her first 10k run; Jill's graduation from Brockport and her internship at Pinehurst.

> So, life goes on...difficult at times, but we know Doug

would want us to carry on. He is with us at all times, helping us cope with this new life dealt to us on that cold, February night.

My Christmas gift to you is the advice to remember to hug your loved ones and don't sweat the little things! Have a happy & safe New Year.

I have always hoped that those who receive my cards will consider them a gift, a small part of me. An email from a complete stranger made me realize that their reactions are also a gift to me:

> You don't know me, but my Dad worked with your husband at Outokumpa and forwarded me your holiday letter, as he knows I followed this story and felt great sorrow for the loved ones of the victims of the February tragedy. I grew up in Buffalo and now currently reside in Florida, but still have strong ties to Buffalo and will always call it home.
>
> The real reason I am writing though is to thank you! You have such a positive outlook that was expressed so sincerely in your letter. It's truly amazing to have gone through what you did and still be so very strong and encouraging. You inspire me and I hope everyone lives by your words of advice…" Remember to hug your loved ones and don't sweat the little things!" Please know that you have people all over the country thinking of you and your family during this holiday season.

A note from an acquaintance—the mother of one of Jess' friends from kindergarten in Loveland, Ohio—indicated that not everyone had heard about our experience:

Dear Old Friend:

I read your Christmas letter with horror…trying to figure out what you were referring to. I ran to the computer to

Google the flight you spoke of. I had no idea that you had been through so much pain and tragedy this past year. I am so sorry I had not written to you before now…please know I did not know of the accident! How in the world have you coped with all of this? I have thought of you so much these past two days. I have thought of your walking Lori down the aisle. I have thought of you trying to find a new home. I have thought of your trying to put your life back together and missing so many of the pieces. I am sure this email is not helping make you feel a bit better, but please know I am sending you all my prayers and thoughts for the strength to make it through this pain. Your girls will surround you with love and hold you tight as will your friends and family. I will stay in touch and we will hold you tight…I am broken-hearted for your loss.

She was wrong, the note did make me feel better—a kind thought usually does. This brings up the reality I must face though. After tragedy hits, support is a great comfort, and almost overwhelming. I have written that notes we received following the crash carried "quite an impact—one that provided my girls and me our daily bread, which we greatly needed to face another day. I would gladly receive more." What people sometimes forget is that as time marches on the pain remains, and just the brief words "Hello, how are you doing?" can bring still needed consolation.

I made an unexpected discovery at work, an archive of emails on my computer. Some dated back to 2006, and it was fun to read once again the girls' adventures as they started college and new jobs. There was one special message from Doug, dated February 14, 2007:

```
Hope you had a good lunch. I'm thinking of you.
Love, Doug.
```

The discovery of that short and tender Valentine's gift from my romantic husband called for a retreat to the ladies room for a cry.

One of my National Gypsum friends, Marilyn, brought me a Christmas tree she no longer needed. It was crafted to resemble a real tree, complete with pinecones and dew. The tree also was pre-lit so no struggling with lights.

What should I decorate it with? A special part of Christmas tradition involved unwrapping ornaments, and recalling the memories each invoked: the girls' baby ornaments, angels fashioned from handkerchiefs, and clothes pin reindeers made by the girls during art classes, a tiny train inscribed with "Rothenberg," a souvenir from Doug's and my trip to Germany, a golden shoe which had hung on my grandmother's tree so many years ago, and an embroidered angel to top the tree.

Jill's and Jess' "Baby's 1st Christmas" ornaments were salvaged from the wreckage. Two work friends had given me an ornament box and presented one ornament each month since March. I went online and successfully searched for a duplicate of Kim's baby ornament and a few others that held special memories. Still more friends gave us ornaments to replace those lost.

The painful task of cleaning out Doug's office had resulted in many sentimental discoveries. I decided that some of the souvenirs tucked in his desk drawer could be repurposed into ornaments: a small Liberty Bell represented my first trip with him to Philadelphia for a baseball card convention, a replica Eiffel Tower served as a reminder of our trip to France, and a small Alamo building, brought back the memory of when I joined him in San Antonio, where he had travelled for a conference.

The tree was up and the next chore on my list was gift wrapping. Our mischievous kitten, Belle, made completion of that task difficult as she jumped on the paper.

Howling wind continued to be a persistent problem in the town house. I found it nerve-wracking enough that I welcomed all invitations that got me away from the abrasive sound.

I accepted Zoe and Rod May's invitation to join them at an open house held in one of East Aurora's old mansions. We were able to tour the house which was now a bed and breakfast. Afterward, Zoe and I joined a few members of the women's club at the Roycroft Inn for drinks. I planned to stay at my new house, even though I had not yet moved in, and brought an air mattress to sleep on. Zoe wouldn't hear of it and insisted that I use their spare bedroom. Zoe and Rod barely knew me and yet they welcomed me with open arms.

A cookie exchange at work meant that I would have to face another tradition—making sugar cookies. This endeavor was touched by sadness because I no longer had my Grandma Schwab's cookie cutters: Santa, the Christmas tree, the star, and the bell. Lori found similar shapes for me, but somehow the cookies just looked different. Belle caused another flashback as she approached to sniff at the cooling cookies. I thought of our old cat, Spots. We would always give her a bit of sugar cookie, which she loved. I instinctively went to grab my tins and Tupperware to store the finished cookies but then realized they, too, were gone. Little daggers of pain seemed to emerge from the simplest activities.

A meeting was scheduled that December by the Memorial Committee at the Clarence Middle School to give everyone an opportunity to present their ideas for a 3407 memorial. One of the 3407 family members emailed to complain that the public should not be consulted on this project. I reminded her that this accident affected many people—the families of the plane victims, the Long Street residents, and the community. All should feel welcomed to submit ideas.

I was already tired of debates and complaints and did not want to find myself in the middle of controversy. My attorney and brother-in-law Billy would represent me at that meeting.

The crash again appeared in the news. Colgan Airlines claimed the accident was caused by the pilots' error, and the Pilot's union claimed it was a combination of things, including lack of pilot training.

My mind raced with all these claims and revelations. My mood felt like PMS used to, I told my sister.

The girls—and their pets—began to arrive. Jill and Dan drove from North Carolina with their new puppy, Isabelle. Lori and Chris brought their dog, Ginger, and Belle's sister, Mises, whom I was adopting because their former roommate had moved. She was named for an economist whom I knew nothing about so I decided to call her Mia.

Doug would not have approved of this menagerie. He was not in favor of Ginger visiting us on Long Street, although I admit he was mainly concerned about how a dog would affect our old cat, Spots. Personally, all the critters provided a diversion for me. They helped block the realization that Doug would not be with us this holiday season.

On Christmas Eve we attended mass at our old parish, Nativity. That proved to be difficult but also comforting. I continued the custom of putting presents under the tree, and sipped a drink, feeling the solace of Doug's spirit.

Our childlike excitement comforted us Christmas morning as we opened presents, and we ate breakfast on familiar holiday dishes. One bowl had survived the wreckage, and the girls had found a partial set at a garage sale, salvaging another holiday tradition.

Jess presented me with one special gift. In the years before I met Doug, I crafted ornaments from clothes pins, including Santa and Mrs. Claus. Jess surprised me with new versions, which I placed on the front of the tree. I loved the thoughtfulness of her handcrafted ornaments.

The end of 2009 approached. We were all happy to see it go. Lying in my bed on Long Street with Doug sleeping contently beside me January 1, 2009, I could never have envisioned the nightmare lurking around the corner. 2010 just had to be better.

The other girls had returned to their homes, and Kim kept me company as 2010 inched closer. I knew she would like to ring in this New Year with Jeff and his family. I told her to go celebrate with her fiancé—2010 would be their wedding year, and they should be together. Being alone did not bother me. Happy memories surrounded me.

We'd been snuggling together on the couch a few months after we'd met in 1977, when Doug asked "Would you like to be my date on New Year's Eve?"

Of course I said, "Yes!"

He would be my date for every New Year's Eve that followed. As 2010 arrived, I raised my glass to my husband and friend for all the holiday memories that we had created—"each beautiful, unique and too soon gone."

8/10/12

## A Special Gift

Our family lived in the Cincinnati area for several years. Jill had met Will Hillenbrand, a children's book illustrator, almost twenty years before when she attended the Loveland Branch-Hill Guinea Kindergarten.

I was reminded of this when Jill included the book, *I'm the Best*, on her Christmas wish list in 2010. It is the story of an orphaned dog searching for a new home. She had received a signed copy of that book when Mr. Hillenbrand visited the school.

Unfortunately, there was little salvaged from 6038 Long Street. Material things lost that night are of little consequence compared to the loss of life, but every now and then some item will cross our minds and bring a special feeling of regret for its loss.

I thought how surprised and pleased Jill would be to receive another signed copy. I located Mr. Hillenbrand's website but found no email address. There was, however, the name of a bookstore called The Bookshelf in Cincinnati that handled his speaking engagements, and I hoped they could put me in touch with him.

I contacted the shop and told them of my quest to find a signed copy of the book. They delivered my message to Mr. Hillenbrand who indicated that he was quite moved by my email. The book was no longer available but he had a copy he wanted to share with Jill. I was going to Cincinnati to spend Thanksgiving with Lori, so I made arrangements to pick up the book. The proprietor of The Bookshelf presented me with *I'm the Best*, which Mr. Hillenbrand had signed, "Merry, Merry, Merry Christmas to my friend, Jill! Happy Reading!" Accompanying the inscription was a small drawing of the scrappy little dog from the book, his bowl, and a tiny Christmas tree. A signed poster from Will's current book, *Sleep Big Bear, Sleep!*, had also been left for Jill.

I was thrilled with these gifts but another surprise was in store for me.

There was a cardboard display on the checkout counter for

*Stopping by the Woods on a Snowy Evening,* a children's book based on the poetry of Robert Frost, wonderfully illustrated by Susan Jeffers. One copy remained in the display. I did a double take. I bought it. I had given this book to Doug on the Christmas before the crash. Doug was a big fan of Robert Frost. In fact my wedding gift to him was a book of Robert Frost poems. (In 2015, when I spotted the same book on a wall display in another bookshop in Inlet, New York I got goose bumps, and felt Doug's presence.)

Christmas could not come quickly enough. It was so hard keeping this special gift from Jill. On Christmas morning I wanted to give Jill the impression that we could not find the book, so I didn't put it in her pile of presents. We waited a few minutes after the last gift was opened before bringing out the book and poster. It was an emotional moment for all of us.

Jill and I were so grateful to Mr. Hillenbrand for his kindness. We sent thank you notes to him.

That was not the end of this story. On St. Patrick's Day I received an email from him which included an illustration of a holiday egg. All my correspondence had previously been through the book-

store. I was hopeful that he had received our notes after Christmas, but I took advantage of this contact and sent another note to his email address thanking him again.

The following message came back:

*Jill with Hillenbrand gifts.*

Dear Karen,
I have the email (sent to the Bookshelf), your
letter and Jill's letter. I carry them with me in
my mini backpack. My backpack holds my idea jour-
nals, pencils and manuscripts of books yet to be
(and special letters).

It is also the place of my beloved copy of THE
TALES OF PETER RABBIT, read to me when I was 3
years old, by my Grandmother. She is long past,
yet I still hear her voice and feel the warmth
of her lap each time I go into Mr. McGregor's
garden. I was moved so deeply by your story (and
Jill's) that I can't put it into words...it
leaves me breathless. Your courage to move on and
rebuild all that is good in life is truly
inspirational.

Your friend in books,
Will

How touched I was that our letters were in such good company. I appreciated that he shared the personal story about his grandmother.

Another visit to Cincinnati brought Will and me together. We met in a small coffee shop in Madiera. I shared a bit of our story, and he told me about the journey leading to his award-winning work. The highlight of that meeting was a chance to actually see his backpack where he still kept our letters. It was such an honor to be given the opportunity to glance at drawings in his notebook—inspiration for his future books.

In 2013 while in the Kentucky area for my grandson Caden's Baptism, Lori's in-laws, Jessica, and I decided to stop at The Blue Marble Bookstore in Fort Thomas, Kentucky which is affiliated with the Bookshelf. As I walked into the shop I explained to the proprietor that I had bought copies of Will's books through the Bookshelf. Without saying a word he pointed to a corner of the shop, and, much to my surprise, there stood Will and his wife. It was wonderful to see them, and Will graciously posed with Jess and me for a picture.

Having always loved the beautiful illustrations in children's books, I do feel that fate had arranged for me to cross paths with this talented, kind gentleman on several occasions. Perhaps it also served to remind me that when it comes time to read the Robert Frost book to my grandchildren they will in some way hear their grandfather's voice reading the story, and feel the warmth of his lap.

Originally written 3/28/11 and updated in 2013

## SIMPLE PLEASURES

*"For in the dew of little things the heart finds its morning*
*and is refreshed."*
~ *Khalil Gibran*

It was the day after Christmas and already we were being weaned off the holiday.

The pile of presents that had made it impossible for me to step into my upstairs closet for several months had disappeared, and I hoped these gifts had brought pleasure to family and friends. Thanks to the efforts of my daughters who shared Christmas Day with me, the tumble of wrapping paper that flew off boxes was stuffed in bags and was already on the curb for garbage pickup. Jess had magically removed any hint of the chaos that cluttered my kitchen, following what seemed like my constant preparation of food during a twelve-hour period. Without distractions, I was left to reflect on the simple pleasures of Christmas Day, 2013.

As I emerged from the cobwebs of sleep Christmas morning, I snuggled under the warm covers and waited. Finally, the muffled sounds of voices reached my ears. These sounds are not only a part of the holiday season—they bring a smile to my face anytime one of my girls and their guys come home. Their voices wrap around me like a warm garment, and Doug's voice echoes through time.

When the girls returned for a visit, Doug would always be the first one down to the kitchen in the morning. They would have their special time to catch up, and Doug could enjoy guy talk with the boys—a luxury for a man living with five females. I like to be reminded of those days when I would catch a few more winks while listening to the murmur of their voices.

The girls insist that I adhere to family tradition—Christmas breakfast must include cinnamon buns and my cheese wreath. I planned this year to prepare these customary treats prior to the opening of gifts. My hopes of being well organized seemed doomed when I realized I had forgotten the refrigerated biscuits. Would the girls be denied their traditional cheese wreath? Kim and Jeff came to the rescue, locating an open convenient mart where biscuits sat ready to extend a Wielinski Christmas breakfast practice.

Tradition is such a big part of the Christmas holidays. I have often thought that as the girls got older they would not miss a tradition or two—mention that possibility and immediate cries fill the air. "We have to do that—it's tradition!"

Wielinski tradition allows only one person at a time to open a present. This practice earns glares and protest from the guys who think this process takes far too much time. We have scaled down gift giving, but pretty much adhere to this policy. This year's gift exchange only took about two hours—and that included a "half time" break for breakfast—not bad for eight participants.

Doug's presence seemed especially strong this Christmas. I gravitated to the Clarence Flea Market searching for unique gifts for my sons-in-law. I felt Doug's approval as I purchased two sturdy glass Iroquois Beer mugs for Jeff and Dan. Doug would have considered the mugs a good find—a reminder of my Schwab family history with the old Buffalo brewery. Many times during my shopping excursions I saw items I knew Doug would have enjoyed: his childhood favorite, Hopalong Cassidy, appeared on a metal shooting game, and several souvenirs from the Pan-American Exposition held in Buffalo in 1901 would have been welcome in his collection. I did purchase a small tip tray from the Exposition for my son-in-law, Dan, who enjoys historical items. Dan was also the recipient of two small volumes of Edgar Allan Poe writings. I had discovered those books in a summer visit to the flea market.

Of course, tradition still makes it necessary for me to hang stockings for the girls. When Jill revealed that Dan had not given her a stocking this year, I chuckled when he explained "I didn't have time to shop for knick-knacks this year." He really does have that right—from now on I will associate knick-knacks with Christmas stockings—what else would you call a fuzzy cat tape measure, small wooden cat, and Santa bottle stopper?

The spirit of Christmas does take on more meaning when a

little child enters the scene. Last Christmas, our greatest gift was my granddaughter's arrival at home. Lydia had spent four months in the hospital after her premature birth in August. This year she is a lively toddler who lives up to that title as she "toddles" around from place-to-place demonstrating her newly acquired walking abilities. As a grandmother, I am always amazed and convinced that Lydia is a brilliant child when she accomplishes all her firsts. I remind myself that these are natural steps in child development and that my own children went through the same process—yet, I do think she is special. My heart sings when she smiles at me, or approaches me with open arms. I scoop her up and not only I but Doug, too, embrace her.

Christmas Day continued in a leisurely fashion—gifts to admire, drinks to sip, snacks to nibble before the big pork and dumpling dinner. Then basketball games and bits and pieces of The Christmas Story on TV over and over again, and reminiscing about Christmases past.

I especially felt that feeling of peace, which seems to symbolize the spirit of Christmas, as Lydia lost her battle to stay awake and finally napped on her daddy's chest.

*Jeff and Lydia*

Simple pleasures—it doesn't get much better than that. My heart is refreshed.

12/31/13

# JANUARY 2010

*"Life is like riding a bicycle — in order to keep your balance, you must keep moving."*

*~ Albert Einstein*

It was time for both Kim and me to move on.

Kim and Jeff moved into their newly built home in Darien. I was excited and happy for them, but Kim's departure marked the beginning of my "empty nest" days. It would be the first time I ever lived by myself. There had always been someone to share everyday life with—parents, my sister, Doug, our girls. Now, there would be no one waiting at home.

Of course, I did have the cats. I wasn't talking to myself, I was talking to the cats. Belle resisted Mia's presence at first and did her share of growling and hissing. Luckily, Mia's mild-mannered disposition resulted in relatively few confrontations.

South Grove Street was finally ready for my moving day on January 9. The hardwood floors were ready; new doors for the garage were a big improvement; a new furnace produced heat that would keep me warm; wallpaper along with dog and cat border were removed from my bedroom; and my friend, Sue, and I had done some last minute painting in the spare bedroom. I was thankful that the "purple" color that appeared as we applied the paint turned into the anticipated periwinkle blue.

As I packed for the move I was once again forced to go through things of Doug's that surfaced from the site, the garage, and his office. It was odd what could set off a burst of emotion, such as tiny boxes of raisins and tins of orange cappuccino coffee.

The reality of living in the Buffalo area manifested itself, as several inches of snow fell the night before the big move. My cooperative landlord arranged for the back patio to be plowed in the dead of night so that the furniture movers would have an easier time of it.

I was thankful to the host of family and friends who arrived to help. Their cars were packed with remaining boxes as I said goodbye to Krause Road.

It was mind-boggling to decide where to place furniture and direct my work crew during the unpacking process. It would take me days to figure out where some things had ended up.

The house came to life as thanks and friendship spread through my new kitchen. Two crockpots of chili—mine and one from my new East Aurora friend Zoe—rewarded those kind people for all their hard work.

At the end of the day, when the concern of their escape had ceased, I let Belle and Mia out of their cages. Mia immediately explored her new surroundings. Belle on the other hand—not one to easily accept change—refused to emerge. Jeff finally coaxed her out. She remained glued to his side for a while and then retreated under the couch. It took her a few days to accept the new home.

Learning to live alone was an adjustment. Part of the problem was the emptiness of not having Doug or the girls around, and there was a new fear. What if something happened to me in the house? Who would know?

The rest of January progressed without any major incidents — the commute to work in Clarence was only a half hour on back roads, I became familiar with my new surroundings, and I slowly adjusted to living alone.

I hesitate at this point as I am not sure I should write the following—perhaps it is too personal. It could prove to be one of those times when you start to speak and someone hastily puts up a hand and in dismay retorts "I don't need to hear about that!" If

I am truthful, though, this involves an important aspect of what I lost after the crash.

At the end of January, I went to the gynecologist for my annual checkup. Lying on the examination table, in that oh so awkward straddle with feet in cold stirrups, reality hit me square in the face and brought tears to my eyes. Although totally professional, this was the first time anyone had touched that part of my body in almost a year. My painful loss of both Doug's tenderness and passion, along with the realization that such intimacy was probably something I would never experience again, came unexpectedly. It was a reaction I certainly did not anticipate beforehand.

I would think that other couples who have been together for over thirty years get into a rut sometimes, and Doug and I were no exception. We got our weekly coupling in and would be satisfied, but there were still those times when that special magic and excitement we felt in our younger days would suddenly emerge. In some instances, those moments exceeded earlier pleasures because of the history we had created together.

The visit to the gynecologist made me mourn the loss of that part of our relationship.

It was a balancing act—I needed to keep moving, accept change, weigh the bitter with the sweet, and not let life knock me down.

9/16/12

## LAND OF MAKE-BELIEVE

It is one of the "perks" of our marriage—waking up and feeling the warmth of Doug's body next to me. It is a very comforting sensation.

We have always shared a double bed, not a queen or king-sized one. There is a narrow space between us as the night begins but by morning that space has vanished. Doug is one of those people who does not budge during the night, while I am the restless sleeper and naturally gravitate toward him.

I blush as I write this, but there is something mellow and satisfying about morning intimacy. A dream-like quality surrounds it, and lingers as you slowly emerge and face the reality of the day. Doug will rise shortly and start his Saturday ritual. He'll head over to the grocery store for fresh hard rolls, thinly sliced Krakus ham, honey-roasted turkey, a new frozen pizza that catches his eye, and, if it's on sale, General Foods International Orange Cappuccino or French Vanilla instant coffee.

I'll go into the radio station for a couple of hours and he'll do odd jobs around the house.

Church in the afternoon, and then we'll meet Kim, Jeff, and whatever kids are in town at one of the local establishments for a glass or two of beer and dinner.

I always look forward to Saturdays.

When we were children, visiting the land of make believe was a favorite pastime. In the end, though, that imaginary journey came to an end when our mother's insistent voice told us it was time for supper or bed.

Reality calls me back from this departure into the land of make believe. It is a pillow I hug, and warmth comes from two small cats, nestled against my legs and back. I willingly accept the comfort they bring.

I encounter Doug in my dreams, although those visions are mostly vague and not remembered. One vision, shortly after the accident, remains vibrant. We were in the Long Street house and all the girls and their guys were home. The bedrooms were occupied, and for some reason Doug and I were sleeping in the hallway. I remember thinking to myself "I know he's dead, but I'm going to hold him one more night."

Getting through a Saturday is hard now. I escape to the land of make believe now and again to lessen the pain of losing Doug—a remedy for my loneliness, but only a temporary fix.

Looking back, those ordinary Saturdays were really quite extraordinary. Perhaps in time, I will feel that way again.

10/8/11

## An Interesting Turn of Events

My initiation into grandparenthood came in a fast and furious manner. I stood by Kim's side at Sisters Hospital in Buffalo when Lydia Frances Lipiarz arrived at twenty-five weeks gestation, weighing in at one pound, twelve ounces on August 4, 2012.

Due to complications, Lydia was transferred to Women and Children's Hospital a month after her birth. Although my visits usually coincided with her parents, Lydia and I had a chance to bond alone on an otherwise wet and gloomy Saturday.

She was inching her way toward her third month of life, and had recently "ounced" her way past the five-pound mark. To maintain a normal body temperature, she remained in an isolette. I slipped my arm through the porthole, and rubbed her little back and buns as she rested on her tummy. I traced her perfect ears and stroked the soft down on her head. This sweet baby is not only a manifestation of the love Kim and Jeff have for one another, but also for the love between Doug and me.

I approached a nurse in the newborn intensive care unit (NICU) and asked if I could hold Lydia. She noticed that my voice was husky and inquired, "Do you have a cold?"

"No," I replied, "I'm just emotional."

Lydia was swaddled papoose-style as I cradled her in my arms. I sang bits of "Lydia, the Tattoo Lady," and "You Are My Sunshine."

When I learned this baby girl would be named Lydia I kept thinking that I had once heard a song about "Lydia." It was a funny song, and I thought perhaps the Three Stooges had sung it. Finally, I decided to Google "songs with the name Lydia." I discovered that "Lydia, the Tattoo Lady" was actually first sung by Groucho Marx in the movie *At the Circus* in 1939. Reportedly it was one of Jim Henson's favorite songs. The first episode of The Muppet Show included a skit where Kermit the Frog sang about "Lydia," a pig festooned with a variety of tattoos that Jim Henson drew himself. Muppet performers also sang the song at his funeral.

"You Are My Sunshine," could be called a tradition. As a new mom I used to sing that to Kim while frantically trying to make her stop crying.

Lydia remained wide-eyed during my singing. I whispered to her about her cousin, Caden, her many aunts, and the pets who were waiting for her at home. We were together about forty-five minutes, and although she probably did not absorb much of my chatter it certainly soothed me.

As I left the hospital, I noticed it was almost four o'clock. I wondered if St. Louis Church downtown would be having a mass. When I had worked downtown I would often attend Good Friday services there. Doug and I would also attend mass there when we happened to be downtown.

Cars parked around the area and people scurrying into the church confirmed that there was indeed a four o'clock mass.

The grand Gothic style of the church is reminiscent of my childhood church, St. Mary of Sorrows. Granted our church was not as large as St. Louis, but it still contained beautiful stained glass windows, the main altar flanked by two smaller altars, marble columns, impressive hand carved woodwork, and life-sized statues of saints throughout.

These Gothic style structures are a thing of the past and a far cry from the modern, semi-in-the-round format churches of today. Sitting there was also different from participating in the mass while seated on my couch, starring at the television. Mass, especially Saturday mass, was difficult to attend after the crash. For one thing it was something Doug and I did each week together, and I found going was often emotional. It even made me feel panic stricken at times. So, a televised mass became another option to fulfill the Catholic requirement of mandatory Sunday mass.

The history of St. Louis church goes back over 150 years. Louis Stephen Le Couteulx de Chaumont, a Buffalo resident of noble French ancestry, felt there was a need for a Catholic Church in Buffalo. Originally called Lamb of God, the first parish was opened in 1832. Hand-hewn lumber from a forest on Delaware

Avenue was used to build the church. A new brick church was constructed in 1843 but destroyed by fire in 1885. The current Gothic structure was dedicated in 1889, on the Feast of St. Louis, and declared the Mother Church of the Diocese of Buffalo.

Does everyone's mind wander during a religious service? As this mass at historic St. Louis began, my mind certainly rambled all over the place—there was just so much to take in.

I noticed a woman three rows in front of me. She was hard to miss with a bright yellow sweater and green hat perched on her head. Throughout the mass, she would raise her arms and sway—lifting her eyes toward heaven in adoration and praise, filled with faith.

I would like to have her faith, but admit that there are times when doubt enters my mind. Faith and hope are difficult to maintain constantly—the virtue of charity is much easier to practice. Still, I do find peace at mass.

Not only was I watching this devout woman, but I was considering the three men two pews in front of me. I was stereotyping them as gay men whom I find interesting. More often than not they are involved in the arts, enjoy fine food and wine, and are friendly. Perhaps I should find some gay men for friends, I thought. At this point in my life I still crave relationships with men, and friendships with married men, or gay men, are safe. There is no need to worry about taking those relationships any farther, which I believe would not work for me.

See what I mean, such a wandering mind.

I was also trying to figure out what scenes were depicted on the stained glass windows. Some were obviously from the life of Christ, and I imagined others were scenes from the life of St. Louis. What was his story? Later I would do some investigating. I found a website called the "Catholic Encyclopedia." At the age of eleven, Louis, son of Louis VIII and Blanche of Castile, became a king following the death of his father. He married at age nineteen and fathered eleven children (eleven apparently an important number in his life). That fact alone—that he had eleven children—should have qualified him for sainthood.

His mother's remark, "I would rather see you dead at my feet than guilty of mortal sin," encouraged him to lead a good life. He spent time in prayer, fasting, and penance, and also was renowned for charity. Beggars were fed from his table. He washed their feet, ministered to the lepers, and founded hospitals and houses for the needy, including one for reformed prostitutes. In addition he led crusades, one of which resulted in his death.

Yes, some of the stained glass windows definitely depicted those crusades.

My attention was drawn back to the mass. I was disappointed that the priest did not use the beautiful wood carved pulpit, reached by climbing a spiral staircase. Father had some difficulty approaching the altar rail to receive the gifts at the Offertory, so obviously climbing those stairs was out of the question.

At the Consecration, the ringing of bells, performed when the priest elevates the Host and Chalice, helped refocus my wandering attention. At St. Louis, this was no ordinary tinkling of bells—these were gongs, loud and vibrating.

Apparently the celebrant had a more personal relationship with St. Louis—at one point, he prayed for St. Louie.

I confess that there was one other thought invading my mind during mass—Ulrich's Tavern.

Located at the corner of Ellicott and Virginia Streets, Ulrich's Tavern has the distinction of being Buffalo's oldest documented continuously operating tavern. It opened in the fall of 1868, and per their website "Ulrich's purpose for over 144 years has never changed—to provide a public house where one can enjoy food, drink and camaraderie."

Doug and I enjoyed evenings of that camaraderie on several occasions. One night we sat at the bar and laughed as we talked with the bartender and other patrons. The bartender—a hardy lass—assured Doug that a particular beer on draft would enhance his "performance." Unfortunately, I cannot recall if that was the case.

On another visit we shared a meal with our Long Street neighbor, Anita, and her friend, Dorothy. Anita, who would soon turn eighty, considered this a real treat and agreed that a glass or two of wine was a nice addition to the night out.

There is one special memory, though, that Ulrich's Tavern harbors within its historic walls.

A few months before the crash, Jess came for a weekend visit. She joined Kim, Jeff, Jill, and her friend, Annmarie, Doug and me for dinner at The Pearl Street Grill in downtown Buffalo. Doug and I decided to take all the kids to Ulrich's after dinner. The look on their faces, as we walked into that old, dark and dingy bar, clearly said, "What kind of place have you taken us to?" The spirits of many past revelers swirled around these young people, and soon they were infused with the camaraderie that lingers in every corner.

I am so glad that Jess took pictures to record that night. Happy faces live on in all the pictures—there was no hint of the sadness that would all too soon darken our lives. There is one of the sign above the men's room designating it as the "Used Beer Department." Several shots were taken of Jill inside the old phone booth, and my favorite picture captured Jill standing outside, arms spread out under the tavern sign, proclaiming in a mellow voice "I'm just loving life!"

*Jill at Ulrich's Tavern.*

An assortment of beer trays were caught on film—including several Doug had in our own collection. Breweries like Iroquois, Simon Pure, and Phoenix had connections to our families. I, especially, came from a long line of brewery workers—my Grandpa Schwab, my Dad, and one of my uncles all worked at the various breweries that were once a big part of the employment scene in Buffalo. Doug, too, had worked at Iroquois one summer. Even a small campaign picture of my great uncle, Mayor Francis X. Schwab was tacked up on a bar shelf.

I think of that night often since it was probably one of the last times so many of our girls and their guys were with Doug and me. It was what we loved to do on Saturday nights—church, dinner, and a visit to a favorite watering hole.

I had not visited Ulrich's since the accident. I really wanted to stop in, have a drink, and perhaps get a bite to eat. I wasn't sure I had the courage to walk into a bar by myself, and also wondered if I wanted to face the memories associated with Ulrich's.

Go for it, I told myself.

The bar stools were all empty. The owner was giving a few other patrons a history lesson about a speak-easy once located on the upper floor. I took a seat, checked out what was on tap (just like Doug would do), and selected a German lager. The bartender and waitress were friendly, easing my anxiety. As I waited for an order of German potato pancakes, I decided to send a text to Kim and a friend who I had coincidentally talked with about Ulrich's recently. Texting soothed my nervousness about sitting at the bar by myself—I did not feel quite so alone.

Great Uncle Frank still retained a place of honor on the bar shelf. Some renovations had been made, and the bar area seemed brighter, but the comfortable good times remained intact.

My stay at Ulrich's was not long, but I felt a sense of accomplishment. It is never easy visiting places that Doug and I had frequented—those first times are always the hardest. These small confrontations are big steps in moving on—not letting go completely of my past—just incorporating the past into the present.

What an interesting turn of events had developed on this Saturday. I ended up exploring the history of Buffalo, my own history, and the day had started with history in the making — Lydia.

11/5/12

# FEBRUARY 2010

---

*"Afer you have wept and grieved...cherish the functions
and the life you have left."*

~ *Morrie Schwartz*

I became reflective as the anniversary date approached. What were we doing those weeks before life took such an unimaginable turn?

When I looked at my calendar from February 2009, my eyes were drawn to the emptiness displayed on that page. There were no momentous occasions written down—just ordinary days, filled with the routine of daily life. How I wished I could remember every detail of those days, and recall every word Doug and I exchanged. There must have been laughs, cuddles, and kisses. Did I say, "I love you?" We didn't say it that often, but it was always implied.

I should remember more about those precious days. I do not. There was no way to avoid 3407 in the eleven days leading up to the anniversary.

The National Transportation and Safety Board would report their findings regarding the crash of Flight 3407 on February 2. Many of the family members, as well as my attorney, would travel to Washington, D. C. A live-feed of the proceedings would also be available at the Millennium Hotel which my brother-in-law, Billy, and I would attend.

The official report, NTSB Number: AAR-10-01, summarized the events of February 12, 2009:

Continental Connection flight 3407 was on an instrument

approach to Buffalo-Niagara International Airport, Buffalo, New York, when it crashed into a residence in Clarence Center, New York, about 5 nautical miles northeast of the airport. The 2 pilots, 2 flight attendants, and 45 passengers aboard the airplane were killed, one person on the ground was killed, and the airplane was destroyed by impact forces and a post-crash fire.

The National Transportation Safety Board determines that the probable cause of this accident was the captain's inappropriate response to the activation of the stick shaker, which led to an aerodynamic stall from which the airplane did not recover. Contributing to the accident were (1) the flight crew's failure to monitor airspeed in relation to the rising position of the low speed cue, (2) the flight crew's failure to adhere to sterile cockpit procedures, (3) the captain's failure to effectively manage the flight, and (4) Colgan Air's inadequate procedures for airspeed selection and management during approaches in icing conditions.

The safety issues discussed in this report focus on strategies to prevent flight crew monitoring failures, pilot professionalism, fatigue, remedial training, pilot training records, airspeed selection procedures, stall training, Federal Aviation Administration (FAA) oversight, flight operational quality assurance programs, use of personal portable electronic devices on the flight deck, the FAA's use of safety alerts for operators to remit safety-critical information, and weather information provided to pilots...

There were no surprises in this report—rumors of this hypothesis had surfaced soon after the crash.

Let's read between the lines: Flight 3407 crashed into the home of the Wielinski family, killing Douglas Wielinski, and the passengers and crew on that ill-fated flight. Those lost included: Beverly Eckert, crusader for her husband and all victims of the 9/11 tragedy; Elly Kausner, a 24 year-old aunt coming home to participate in her nephew's Valentine's Day school party; Lorin

Maurer, heading to the wedding of her boyfriend's brother, filled with happiness that she, too, had met the man she would spend her life with; Jennifer Neill, happy and content in her seventh month of pregnancy, as she felt her son kick within her; Donald, Dawn, and Shawn Mossop, anticipating a visit to Toronto along with Dawn's sister, Ferris Reid; Beth Ann Kushner and Maddy Loftus, young women on the threshold of life, who would never know the joy of marriage and children.

Where is it mentioned that two people escaped the wreckage within minutes of explosions that would send flames destroying what remained in their path?

The report does not mention the pain of family and friends waiting for the arrival of Flight 3407. They were escorted to a room, and sat in a dazed state, barely comprehending what had just happened. They waited, hoping for word of miraculous survivals, word which never came.

Where is the record of Kim approaching the chaos surrounding her home, seeing nothing but black smoke swirling from that spot? Where were her mother, father, and sister? Can the NTSB visualize the scene she encountered, or recognize the terror and helplessness felt by her out-of-town sisters, Lori and Jessica, as CNN news reports showed the flames and calamity unfolding on Long Street?

The tragic reality encountered by so many people was caused by carelessness—due to fatigue, lack of training, or saving a buck. Lives were shattered.

The contributing factors that led to the crash of Flight 3407 would be explored in a PBS Frontline special, airing on February 9, entitled "Flying Cheap." I was apprehensive about watching this program alone, and asked my friend Zoe to be my support that evening.

The opening scene recreated air traffic control's loss of 3407 on the radar scene—the beginning of a horrific night.

Karen Eckert, sister of Beverly Eckert, and Kevin Kuwik, boyfriend of Lorin Maurer, recounted how they heard the grim news: Karen watching a news report and Kevin from a State

Trooper's radio announcement.

Scott Maurer, Lorin's father; Kevin, Karen, and another sister of Beverly's, Susan Bourque, began the crusade for airline reform. Together with other 3407 family members they lobbied for safety reforms.

During this program, experts stated that the crash of Flight 3407 throws a spotlight on regional airline carriers, calling the crash "the watershed accident for this decade." The experts also cited "a decade of missed warning signs ... and corners cut on safety."

The program was hard to watch. Everything pointed to an accident that could have been prevented. It was especially hard to see the pain so clearly etched on the faces of the 3407 family members who shared their stories—including their reactions after watching an animated re-enactment of the crash during NTSB hearings in May, 2009.

I had trouble falling asleep that night.

The crash occurred on a Thursday, so Thursday, February 11, felt like the anniversary date to me. I worked that day, and I dreaded the evening. Before I left work I thanked my co-worker, Laura, for the support she had given me during this year. As another co-worker, Rae Ann, left early I decided to leave a message on her cell phone. An email I sent early the next morning explains how that went.

> Hope my emotional call last night didn't upset you. I thought I had control of my emotions, but obviously I did not (I paused mid-way through the message, sobbing and fighting to gain control.) Tears continue to come and go, but I wanted you to know that I'm OK. My co-workers are the best, and I wanted to let you guys know that.

Rae Ann replied:

> Karen, I have to admit I was a mess after I heard your message. I was afraid to call you because I didn't want to upset you anymore. There isn't a day that goes by that I don't think of you and

your family and how strong and loving you are despite this awful tragedy.

I found emotional release through writing as the clock ticked
toward 10:17 p.m.

I emailed my brother-in-law, Billy:

I know I've told you before, but as the first
anniversary approaches, I just want to make sure
you know how much I appreciate all your support
and help. The road I've traveled would have been
so difficult without you taking care of me, and
protecting me like a big brother. I also thank
Maureen for letting me monopolize so much of your
time. Thanks for being there for me.

I also thanked Phil, my attorney:

This is stuff I usually write in the middle of
the night, but on this Thursday—which feels more
and more like the anniversary date—I just wanted
to thank you and the firm for all your support,
guidance and help this past year. I know we have
a long road ahead of us, but I really appreciate
your guidance, understanding and especially patience in dealing with me as I face this mess. To
top it off, I really like all of you too!

My Long Street neighbors, Michele and Paul Beiter, were in my
thoughts. They had taken Jill and me into their care the night of
the crash.

Michele and Paul wrote:

We have been thinking of you and the girls, and
of course Doug, more than usual this week. We
are hoping that each little bit of time passing
brings healing to you all. Peace and prayers.

I replied:

> I am certainly thinking of you also. Tonight is
> going to be tough, since everything did happen
> on a Thursday night. Emotionally, I feel pretty
> drained already…I'm sure we will come to the site
> sometime this weekend…I still have to bring my-
> self to stand by the flag (which marked where
> Doug's body was recovered). I'll never be able to
> thank you and your girls for all your help that
> night. I know it could not have been easy for
> you, and I hope, as you say, time will continue
> to bring healing.

Jess arrived that evening, and Lori would arrive from Cincinnati in the morning. Jill stayed in North Carolina with Dan.

Jill sent an email on February 11 with instructions, "Read February 12." I honored that request, and as dawn broke through the darkness of night, I read her emotional message:

> Mama, Kim, Lori, Jess, Jeff & Chris:
>
> I wanted to send a little note to you since I was
> unable to come home this weekend. I am sorry that
> I can't be there. I hope you know that I really
> wanted to spend this weekend with you guys!
> This has been such a hard year, and it has not
> gotten any easier to deal...I still feel broken
> inside and am trying my best to continue each day,
> since I know Dad would have wanted me to live on.
> I know that he…and Spots as well...is looking and
> watching us every day and making sure that we stay
> safe. I have a hard time wondering why this all
> happened, and why to us? I know one thing—that
> we have been blessed with each other, and all
> the amazing people out there that care and love
> us. I have always felt that we have been such a
> close family, but this of course has brought us
> together even more.
> Mama, I am so happy we found each other that
> night. I always wonder what I would have done if

I had not found you...it scares me to think about it. You helped me survive in so many ways. So, thank you Mama! You help me stay strong, especially when I see you being strong for me.

I am so thankful to have three such amazing sisters in my life, and for everything you do for me. I know you guys all had such different experiences that night than mom and me. I can't imagine the pain and horror you all went through when you didn't know what was going on. I am sorry you had to suffer through that!

For Jeff and Chris. We are all so lucky to have you guys as part of our family, and wouldn't have been able to get through everything without your support and love.

Now that today marks the one-year date of the crash, I am glad to know that you guys are all together...there for each other. I will be okay... Dan is here helping me through it. I know today is going to be rough...I already felt the pain and emotions, when I wrote this on Feb. 11. As I sit here tonight watching the Sabres play the Hurricanes, it is hard not to think back to last year and going to the game with Dad. How I wish he was here today so much! I know, though, that he is always with us and keeping us safe, just like he was on Feb.12 when Mom and I had to get out.

I love you guys so much and like I said before, I couldn't have made it through this year without you. Stay strong, and let's keep making Dad proud!

Miss and love you all,
Jill

I replied:

Well, of course I'm crying now. I, too, am so thankful that we found each other that night. Panic sets in when I think about the 'what ifs' and how I would have felt if something had happened

```
to you. You can't dwell on the 'what ifs" or
'whys,' though. The reality is, we made it out
somehow and dad would want us to move on and en-
joy and love life. You hopefully know how proud
I am of what you have accomplished in this last
year, and although we'll miss you being with us
today, we'll talk—and cry—together on the phone.
It's comforting to know that we've always been a
close family, and will always stay that way. Love
you so much,
Mama
```

After that emotional exchange we went to mass. My pastor, Father Bob (who also married Lori and Chris) noted the significance of the day, and acknowledged us as he left the altar.

A large contingent of 3407's passengers' family and friends, along with members of the community, walked from Long Street to the Buffalo-Niagara International Airport. It was such a symbolic gesture—completing the journey of those lost that night. The families were included in my night of emotional release:

```
Just a quick note to let everyone know you will
be in my thoughts and prayers tomorrow. For those
who are walking tomorrow, the forecast looks good
and the large numbers should bring more exposure
to the necessity of changes to insure aviation
safety. I wish you a safe walk, and as you finish
your loved ones' journey may you find peace.
```

The girls and I did not join the walk. For us, there was no journey to complete. Doug was home.

We did attend a tribute to the first responders at the Clarence Town Hall that evening. Pictures taken that night and the weeks after the crash were shown. The girls and I held hands to ease the emotion we felt as we viewed the blazing inferno and its aftermath. We talked to several other family members, responders and officials, most of whom would assemble at the Zion Church in Clarence Center and proceed to Long Street for a vigil at 10:17.

I had no desire to commemorate the events of February 12, 2009 at the site surrounded by the pain of so many others. We drove back to East Aurora and got Jill on speaker phone. Tears were shed. We talked about that night, and then became silent at 10:17 pm— one year ago. That was the moment our lives changed forever. We remembered some good times with Doug and even shared some laughs. I think we made the right decision—being together with Jill, rather than in a large crowd of people on Long Street.

The following day Lori, Jess, and I visited the Long Street site. Kim emotionally did not feel prepared to make that journey yet, and would not do so until a few weeks before the dedication in June of 2012. I finally would approach the spot where Doug was found. We formed a circle around the tiny flag, cried and prayed. The Beiters came over to talk to us, and told us they lit a candle for Doug the night before as names of the deceased were read.

Before we left we tied a small note, encased in one of Doug's plastic sleeves for baseball cards to the flag:

*"Doug/Dad: You are greatly missed and loved. Karen, Kim, Lori, Jessica, and Jill. "*

We stopped at Doug's grave and spent some time at Kim and Jeff's house.

That night, I prepared Doug's favorite meal—Pigs in a Blanket. I had not made that dish since the crash and it tasted delicious. Lori's in-laws, Mary Fran and Roy, Jess' friend Nicole and her boyfriend, Shaun, joined our family in a celebration of Doug's life, capped off by his favorite dessert—cherry pie.

The Grove Street house was beginning to feel like a home now that my out-of-town girls and friends had shared time with me there.

The necessary glaucoma surgery could be delayed no longer. Surgery on my one eye took place on February 22. My friend Sue became my chauffer and caretaker for the next few days. To assure my girls that all went well, and infuse some humor into the day, Sue sent them a picture of me—eye patch in place and a pirate hat perched on my head. All that was missing was a parrot.

I would be confined to the house for the next week and a half. This incarceration allowed me to continue in earnest the task of writing thank you notes to many people who supported us after the crash. The process was slow. Not only did I have to limit the amount of eye strain, but there was an emotional toll of comprehending the kindness of so many people during the early days following the crash. Eventually I would send more than 600 of these handwritten expressions of thanks, and yet I feel some guilt that I should have written even more.

Guilt is an emotion that surfaces occasionally. I have heard that survivors often are overcome with guilt. But that's not the reason for my guilt. If anything, my survival colors the way I look at the crash. The miracle of survival encourages me to carry on. I survived for a reason. I may never realize the extent of that reason, but being allowed to remain on this earth for my girls would be a big part of it.

My guilt comes mainly from my lack of involvement with the 3407 families. I feel I should be more a part of their efforts in changing airline safety. The emails I send off to Washington officials in support of those efforts does not seem like much of a contribution.

There is also the guilt that I have not shared more of their grief. They have reached out and invited me to gatherings, but I remain emotionally capable of only exposing myself to their pain on a limited basis.

I suppose given my unique experience—being someone who not only lost a beloved husband, but also survived carnage and the loss of a home—no one would condemn my lack of association with them. The truth remains, though, that feelings of self-reproach do surface now and then.

During the last eleven months I have searched calendars and emails to recall the details of the year following the crash. The process has presented many revelations.

I have realized the power of motherhood and family. My need to protect my daughters and provide for their safety and happiness has been a driving force in survival following the months after the accident. That need gave me necessary goals—a future. Although our family bond was broken by the loss of Doug, it has managed to hold us together. How devastating his loss would have been to me without our girls, who are a constant reminder of his existence and love.

The kindness of others can be overwhelming. Consoling words, financial support, and a sincere desire to help my family endure such tragedy came from so many people. My faith in the human race has been renewed constantly.

I truly believe in the importance of humor. Although it may seem to others that humor has no place in such sadness I find it a life-saver. I am thankful my sense of humor was not crushed by the weight of despair. Humor has been a source of comfort, and has lifted us out of the depths of depression.

*Karen and Doug*

Doug will remain a constant presence in my life. I move on, but he is never far away.

In the days after the crash, I encountered

that pit of loss—the emptiness that surfaced from losing Doug. It made me recall the loneliness I felt before meeting him—the feeling of not being complete. How I hated that feeling, and how whole I felt when he entered my life. I wasn't sure I could endure that gnawing emptiness again.

Perhaps the most surprising revelation was the discovery that I am stronger—and tougher—than I ever imagined. I can survive, and part of my strength comes from all those years with Doug. He gave me the love and assurance that I am someone unique and special—after all, he chose me to share his life.

I have confronted the past, present, and future. I have woven a tapestry interlaced with threads of emotion. Constant memories woven together with the reality of life have produced a rich, varied, and intricately designed picture of who I am. It is definitely a work worth sharing with others.

10/20/12

# BOUND BY TRAGEDY

"I can't imagine what you've been through!"

It's something I have heard many times since the crash of Flight 3407 that killed Doug and destroyed our home. My escape and Jill's also seem unimaginable.

Gerri Pomponio doesn't have to try and imagine.

She and her daughter Jennifer lived through the crash of American Airlines Flight 587 into her home on November 12, 2001, killing five people on the ground, including Gerri's husband, Franco. She had attempted to contact us after the crash of Flight 3407.

We had not watched much of the 3407 crash coverage the day after our tragedy, but it was clear to me that I needed to let family and friends know that Jill, Kim, and I had survived. I felt comfortable giving a statement to Barbara Burns, a reporter for WBEN Radio, who is related to my sister-in-law.

Gerri heard that interview and contacted Barbara. She wanted me to know that she was there for us. I would not reach out to Gerri until the first anniversary of the crash approached. We exchanged emails:

> Gerri:
> I apologize for not getting in touch with you sooner, but having gone through similar circum-stances, I'm sure you know what a crazy year this has been!
>
> Please know that our family appreciated your efforts to reach us so quickly after the accident. I definitely want to talk to you, and promise to give you a call in the next few weeks. I know you can relate to our pain and the abrupt change in our lives.

Gerri responded:

> Hi Karen:
> You need not apologize. I am so happy to hear from

you. I have often thought of you and your family. I would definitely love to speak with you. While I hope that our communication will bring you some solace, be sure that it will be just as helpful to me. There aren't many people who truly understand the magnitude of this tragedy and the broken pieces that are left behind for us to pick up.

I was apprehensive about calling Gerri. I wasn't sure how I would react to her story, or whether I could tell her mine. It was March, 2010 before I mustered up the nerve to call. In the end we talked for almost an hour.

She explained that when she and her daughter heard of Flight 3407's crash it caused them to relive their own experience, and the longing they had to have someone to talk to at that time. They felt strongly that they needed us to know they were there for us.

Flight 587 had just taken off and was headed to the Dominican Republic when it crashed into the Belle Harbor neighborhood. Gerri and Jennifer were in a downstairs bathroom, hastily trying to get ready for a doctor's appointment and then basketball practice. At the impact of the crash Gerri thought her hair blower had blown a fuse and caused an explosion. She quickly realized that wasn't the case, and looking out the bathroom door found that her house was gone. The plane had struck the front of her home, where her husband, Franco, was sleeping after working the night shift. Unable to reach him they escaped through the backyard by breaking a hole in a fence.

"It's something you don't get over," she said.

Jill and I could not just walk out of a door to escape. We needed to push and crawl our way out of the wreckage around us. Like them, though, we ran for safety.

According to Gerri "people said the right things" after the crash. "Call me if you need anything," they would say, but the reality was that they didn't call. "It's difficult to make a call and ask for help, and when you don't people assume you can handle things on your own."

When her brother became seriously ill she, too, told him

"Call me if you need anything." She quickly recalled her own life lesson and instead of waiting for his call picked up the phone and told him she was ready to assist him.

Life can change in an instant, and I now try not to "put off" doing things. We all say "I'll call you," or "We'll get together." I make the extra effort to actually do it. So many reached out to us in our time of need, and if I can pay back someone who needs assistance I try to do so.

About two years after her tragedy, Gerri had her emotional crash and sought professional help.

This was not good news to me. I already felt emotionally drained. Could I possibly feel worse? I have had professional help from the start. I balked at the thought that I needed assistance. I am not one to hold feelings in. I do not repress feelings but express them to my friends, or anyone who will listen. I have to admit, though, that I find solace in going to a psychologist. I can tell her anything.

As my first anniversary passed, I already knew what she meant about "crashing." The almost constant concern of family, friends, and attorneys slowly diminished to a trickle. It took some getting used to, and I could certainly understand that everyone was making an effort to move on. It was a noticeable change.

Perhaps the process of retrieving items from crash sites has improved in the eight years between our tragedies. Gerri has very little from her home. Of course, this could also be due to the size of the planes. Two hundred fifty people were on Flight 587 compared to fifty on Flight 3407. Although it is emotional to sift through the remains from our site, there is so much meaning associated with what did survive. In the long run, it brings great comfort.

We also have all the things from the untouched garage crammed in rental storage sheds. Facing the fact that I will at some point have to sort through all of that is a daunting task, but I know a treasure of memories await me when I start.

One of the biggest differences between Gerri's story and mine is the fact that she does not have a connection with the family members of those killed on the plane. That is something that I have had great difficulty in accepting. It is true that we all lost loved ones that night, but their situation is so different from mine. Their loved ones were together and had purchased tickets for their journey. Doug was alone and supposedly safe in his home. As time goes on, I find it easier to be with the families, but there is still the difficulty of feeling—and seeing their pain while dealing with my own.

Gerri did not want a memorial on the site of her home and the remembrance of Flight 587 was not erected on the area where the homes were destroyed. New homes are now on those sites.

Although what will be built on the Long Street site has not been my sole decision, I feel a responsibility to make the memorial something that will satisfy both the families of 3407 and the neighbors of Long Street. It weighs heavy on my heart. I have to accept that it will not satisfy everyone.

During that second year, I often thought of Gerri. The year after the crash there was so much to deal with: finding a new home and furnishing it; sifting through what remained from the site; hunting for all that lost paperwork and trying to figure out how to replace missing documents: driver's licenses, birth and marriage certificates, passports, and social security cards. I had been so busy I truly think I could not totally mourn Doug. How to live without him was really magnified in that second year.

I feel Doug is often the forgotten victim of Flight 3407, but Erik Brady from USA Today helped keep Doug from being remembered only as the "one on the ground." His article was a tribute to Doug's life and something I will always be grateful for.

I was curious how Gerri managed to get through the process of a lawsuit, one that took her seven years to resolve. I was amazed that it was settled shortly before they were scheduled to go to court.

I have yet to be "deposed" by the defense, but I already find the legal process to be a cold experience. We are currently in a "discovery" phase and are required to basically dissect Doug's life. I hate it. I have had to provide details on how he ate, vacationed, and spent money in the years from 2005 through 2009. The girls and I have had to detail how he supported us and provided guidance. I almost had to laugh when I saw one of the questions I had to supply an answer to: "Where did the decedent live at the time of death and where does he live now?" Really? Do I answer, "Heaven, I hope" or do I put down the cemetery lot number!

After that contact in February, 2010, I did not correspond with Gerri until August of 2011. I think the discovery process made me want to see how she handled the humiliating feelings it produces. She replied that "it was a long and difficult process," and "draining."

As I write this, she is approaching the tenth anniversary of the crash of Flight 587 and is planning a special mass and gathering of Franco's family and friends to enjoy a meal and celebrate his life. We had a similar celebration of Doug's life on the second anniversary of his death. It was a heartwarming experience, and I hope her gathering will generate the same feeling.

It was surprising to learn that Franco and his son, Michael, who was at college at the time of their tragedy, were sports memorabilia collectors. All was lost in the crash.

I related to Gerri the therapy I have found in joining a local writing class. It has given me the opportunity, or perhaps I should say inspiration, to write about my experiences since the crash. It's true that sometimes I feel drained after writing these stories, but expressing those feelings is a form of release. In particular, a story about my experiences with the insurance adjuster allowed me to finally mourn the loss of our home. I hoped it wouldn't be construed as a lament of "items" lost. The loss of life that night far outweighs the loss of possessions. Rather, I hoped it would be viewed as a tribute to family memories associated with those possessions.

Gerri is also writing a diary, but says her entries "are not always consistent."

Sometime in the future, I know I will meet Gerri. Our tragedies bind us together. We share similarities and yet there are differences. The bottom line is that we lost husbands we loved, and we are survivors.

10/11/11

## SHARING A MEAL

Over the years, our family always managed to find time to share a daily meal. Despite crazy schedules carting four daughters to a variety of practices and games, somehow the family gathered for that meal. When my dad, a man whose dinner was promptly served at five o'clock p.m. came to live with us, he would often come into the kitchen and ask, "Are we eating tonight?" It could be at home or in a restaurant but eventually we came together to share the events that had shaped our day.

Now that I'm on my own, those times are few and far between. But on a snowy Saturday I found the feeling of togetherness that brought my family to the table could be felt in other ways.

They came to celebrate the life of Doug on the second anniversary of his death—people who had touched, or been touched by him. There were two of his brothers and his sister; three of our daughters, one with a husband and one with a fiancé; neighbors who still live on Long Street and neighbors from our previous home on Everwood Court; two of Doug's co-workers, and friends who had originally introduced us.

More than twenty people were packed into my tiny house, and the majority found themselves around the kitchen table. Why do people always seem to end up in the kitchen? I'd like to think that it was because of the Wielinski chili that was served based on my mother-in-law's recipe that fed nine children. Realistically, I think people gravitate to the kitchen because of the comfort that food seems to bring us.

There were no fancy plates or bowls but richness filled the air as these friends and family members captured our hearts with memories of Doug.

One story was about my friend's husband, Gene, a baseball coach, who encouraged my sister and me to attend a game and "meet a couple of guys." I kept my eye on the curly-haired catcher throughout the game, hoping he was one of those guys. "If he's one, "I told my sister, "he's mine!" My future husband never believed that story.

One of Doug's brothers brought photos capturing many moments of his life: baby pictures; the high school senior picture; a college photo where he resembled George Harrison (incidentally, always my favorite Beatle!); the young man, barely graduated from college, in an Army uniform heading to Vietnam; and some happy wedding pictures.

*College years*

The Everwood Court neighbors recalled how they thought Doug, in beat up shorts and a sweatshirt dotted with holes, was the groundskeeper the first time they met him. They came to the conclusion that his casual appearance and friendliness were an indication that they had picked the right house with a good neighbor.

Our 80-year-old Long Street neighbor, Anita, recalled how Doug had surprised her one birthday with a bottle of wine and pizza, and how one summer he announced to her that he would paint her garage—a project that came to involve our whole family.

This gathering was the first time since the crash I had spent considerable time with the Long Street neighbors. I certainly had seen and talked to them over the last two years, but gathered around the kitchen table we had the opportunity to not only reminisce about Doug but also discuss the aftermath of the crash.

They too are survivors of a horrific night. I occasionally go to the Long Street site, but how painful must it be for them to see that vacant lot every day.

Yet, here we all were together to celebrate a life well lived. That gathering brought immeasurable comfort and it strengthened a bond, which like the family meal, makes it easier to celebrate and face each new day.

2/16/11

## The Essence of the Man

My psychologist told me that following their initial grief, people often reach a point where they begin to fear that they will forget their loved one. Their face, voice, essence fades.

In this day and age, it is easy to refresh your memory. I can hear Doug's voice by listening to his old work voice mail recording, or watch a clip from a television news report. There is also a barely visible VHS tape, but yet the audio can transport me back to a Christmas morning long ago.

I see him in my girls and occasionally in my dreams. I bask in the warmth of kind words from friends.

On the second anniversary of the crash, I invited family and friends to gather and celebrate Doug's life. If possible, I asked them to bring a letter describing a special memory of Doug.

The response was heartwarming, and I found comfort in those remembrances.

Doug's boss from Luvata, Todd Heusner, recalled a 2008 sales meeting held in Lewiston. Bad weather prevented a planned afternoon of fishing or golf for "fun and bonding." Todd wrote:

Bowling seemed a good option. Everyone shows up at the alley in Lewiston for a few throws and longnecks. Most of the group hasn't bowled in years, and of course nobody has their own equipment, or if they did, they decided not to make the effort to bring it. Not Doug, he must have made the trip back home...he walks in with this bowling bag from another era, which captured some attention from the group...Out comes the ball, which is obviously very old, but what the hell, a ball is a ball. Then come the shoes. He pulls out these shoes that had probably been fit to retire in the 50s.

Of course, Doug took some ribbing about his antiques, but being a true historian, he tells the history of these treasures. Turns out the equipment was handed down from a brother (or two?) to Doug as a teenager. He obviously had fond memories of the circumstances of how it ended up with him. Why in the world would you ever get rid of this stuff? In his mind, it was perfectly functional, and you could tell by the conviction he had in telling us that it represented something very important and powerful to him. I remember the bowling bag as a symbol of what Doug was about—love and conviction to family and friends, and the ability to treasure history and connect it to significant events in his life.

I smiled reading that recollection. Doug probably did not have to return home to retrieve the bowling equipment. Ever prepared—he kept that equipment in his car trunk along with a small canvas bag filled with some golf clubs, just in case the opportunity arose.

I have told the story before regarding Eric and Kathy Southard, who lived next door to us on Everwood Court. When they were inspecting their prospective new home with the real estate agent they saw Doug raking leaves and dragging them to the curb. They assumed he was the groundskeeper. Kathy wrote:

We knew right after we met him that we had found the right house, because our new neighbor was so friendly and down to earth…Doug always seemed like a big brother… when we had our first disaster, he came over to help put a new sump pump in. He showed much interest in our children…he learned our son, Tom, liked astronauts and the history of the Space Race. Doug quickly went inside and returned with a plastic covered "Life" magazine from July 1969 with Neil Armstrong on the cover. It remains a treasured gift. When he found out…a distant cousin briefly played for the Sabres, Doug went on a mission to find his hockey card. He discovered that Eric's stepdad was from Lockport and was the former sports editor for the Lockport paper. Doug quickly produced some memorabilia from the 1960s for him. These 'things' he shared were not really 'things;' they were and will remain symbols of

Doug's sincere interest in and generosity toward others. One of the most important things about Doug is that he was a good neighbor and friend…He was truly interested in others, and interesting to others. We miss him and are honored to have known him.

My friend, Cindy Boudreau, and her husband, Gene, played an important role in Doug and my story. At this celebration of Doug's life Cindy wrote:

Throughout the years since we've known both you and Doug, I recall pleasant memories of first introductions, softball games, your beautiful wedding, your first home, and of course, the birth of your girls. To say that marriage unites two beautiful people is an understatement, since you are living proof that Doug lives on through you and everything you do. Even though we come to a marriage as two separate individuals, through the years we begin to take on each other's personalities and mannerisms. Doug had a wonderful light in his eyes that I will never forget, a soft chuckle when he laughed, and a wonderful sense of humor. Family was his number one priority and he had a gift for storytelling. Karen, I see all those wonderful qualities in you!

Doug had a way of making me feel that sharing his latest treasure and the story that went with it was 'just between us'. He never bragged about owning anything— it was as if he felt he was the caretaker of his remarkable finds, lovingly organizing and displaying things in such a way that showed respect for their previous owners. Karen, there is no higher compliment to Doug's memory than to say that you embody all of his most wonderful traits. His spirit lives on through you and your children. I will continue to smile each time I think of him. I like remembering Doug as a "caretaker" of his collectibles. Although he hoped selling some of these collectibles would make retirement or college debts easier to manage in the future, he primarily loved to preserve and share the history of what he collected with others. In some ways, he was more a historian than a collector.

Our Long Street neighbor, Michele Beiter, described that special essence that made Doug who he was. She wrote:

I guess the surprising thing about life is that when you look back, you realize how many "touches" someone brought to your world. Once that person passes, the importance of the "touches" are amplified as you realize that it is the essence of the person that is important, endearing, noteworthy and what remains with you forever.

To me, Doug was zealous, interesting, warm hearted and intense, with more ideas than could be accomplished by one man…so he commandeered help from his family. His interests were many—not fleeting, but truly something he would get lost in. This was apparent when he brought me in for a "Tour" of some of his treasured artifacts. I was impressed with the depth of his knowledge of history and the care he took to preserve it…to bring it to life!

He gave of himself freely—we can all recount many of these occasions in our short time we knew him as a Long Street neighbor…And so it is the essence of his being—his zest, intensity, warm-heartedness—that comes to mind as I think of Doug. And so those qualities are reflected on; we remember to carry them on through our own actions.

Lives are important. The spirit of a person stays with us. I have perfect pictures of Doug in my mind—his smile, his great hair, his intensity.

Michele's husband, Paul, wrote:

Doug and I had much in common: our education, a gaggle of daughters and a love of working around the house. I liked watching him cut the grass. He would often dress in shorts and work boots, but always pushed the mower at breakneck speed.

I went to talk to him one day about a project he was working on. I asked him why he had not asked me for help. He lit right up! "Boyfriends!" he exclaimed. "The best thing going, just wait and you will see."

He went on to say that was the advantage of all daughters. Doug always seemed to look at the positive.

I enjoyed talking with him. He would drop what he was doing and seemed to give me his undivided attention. I was especially impressed by his generosity. He would look out for Anita (neighbor across the street) and offer assistance. Simply wonderful. I just need to remember Doug.

It is easy to remember Doug. So many people could see the qualities that I saw in him—qualities that made me want to share my life with him. I was a lucky woman, he saw something in me too.

I miss the essence of the man—those little touches: his hand entwined with mine, the cuddle in the early morning or late evening, a tender kiss or mischievous smile. I miss being loved.

1/8/13

# PART TWO

## THE 3407 FAMILIES

# FEBRUARY 2013

The bin has been opened several times. I flip through a stack of newspaper clippings until I find The Buffalo News, February 14, 2009, and February 12, 2010.

I turn the pages until I come to condensed biographies of the fifty-one lives lost when Flight 3407 crashed into our home on Long Street on February 12, 2009. Their life histories were compressed into a few short paragraphs. They all left behind family and friends who grieved for their loss.

I repeat the ritual of reading these brief narratives whenever I will be meeting those who were left to mourn. These occasions have been limited. It is difficult to see their pain.

Over the years a contingent of family members has travelled to Washington, D.C. to urge "one level of safety" between regional and major airline carriers. As a result of their efforts, The Airline Safety and FAA Extension Act of 2010 was passed by voice vote in the House, by unanimous consent in the Senate, and signed into law by President Obama in August, 2010. Key elements of the law were new regulations dealing with pilot fatigue and qualifications; crew member training; safety management systems; requiring all airlines to invest in the best practice accident prevention programs; and the creation of a new electronic pilot records database to allow for better screening of pilot applicants.

The biggest accomplishments so far are the new regulations on pilot flight and duty time limitations addressing pilot fatigue. The Department of Transportation (DOT) also issued guidance and enforced the ticket disclosure provision that requires all travel agents and websites to identify when regional carriers are operating a flight.

2013 was an important year, as FAA and DOT were targeted to release the new regulation on pilot qualifications by August 1 and the new regulation on crew member training by October. Originally, the latter was to be completed in August of 2011.

Kevin Kuwik, one of the 3407 families' unrelenting leaders in this quest for safety, asked family members to seriously consider meeting in Washington on the fourth anniversary of the crash to "reiterate our mission—REGIONAL AIRLINE SAFETY... COMPLACENCY IS THE ENEMY. Our goal is to continue to maintain awareness of this issue so that no other families have to suffer as we have."

I always supported that goal, and although I participated in email campaigns to deliver that message I felt guilt; I should be doing more.

The time finally seemed right to join the group in Washington. Would I be able to handle my own grief on this anniversary, as well as the grief of family members I would meet?

A posting on Facebook offered some resolution to that question. It appeared in The New York Times on December 25, 2012, following the senseless murders in Newtown, Connecticut. Writer Maureen Dowd asked, "Why, God?"

My own faith was shaken by the loss of children and adults in that tragedy, and I found some comfort in the author's story of Father Kevin O'Neil and his gift to "lighten the darkness around the dying and those close to them."

His words also reminded me of my limited relationship with the 3407 families. Father O'Neil said:

> I have never found it easy to be with people who suffer, to enter into the chaos of others. Yet every time I have done so, it has been a gift to me, better than the wrapped and ribboned packages. I am pulled out of myself to be love's presence to someone else, even as they are love's presence to me. I will never satisfactorily answer the question, "Why?" because no matter what response I give, it will always fall short. What I do know is that an

unconditionally loving presence soothes broken hearts, binds up wounds, and renews us in life. This is a gift that we can all give, particularly to the suffering. When that gift is given, God's love is present.

Those words encouraged me. Now I had an opportunity to console and be consoled. It was time for me to jump the hurdle of guilt.

Family members began to arrive in Washington on the Monday before the anniversary. I met Susan and Bill Bourque and Justine Krasuski for dinner. Susan's sister, Beverly Eckert, was a passenger on Flight 3407, as was Justine's husband, Jerry.

Susan and Bill live a short distance from my home in East Aurora, and we occasionally meet while I am walking. Susan and I also had a long visit shortly after the accident when I discovered pages from Beverly's Sacred Heart High School yearbook among the items given to us from the Long Street site.

During dinner I mentioned to Susan how unbelievable it was that her family had to suffer the loss of Beverly, as well as the death of Beverly's husband, Sean Rooney, who was lost in the destruction of the Twin Towers on 9/11. She explained how close the two couples were, and the emotional pain they had endured following Sean's death.

Shortly after that conversation, I noticed Susan holding a pair of salt and pepper shakers on the table. They were silver, very modern and sleek in design. She looked at me quietly and simply said, "The Twin Towers." A chill ran down my spine, and I could only offer my hand on hers as a form of comfort. I, too, know how an unexpected item or sound can trigger a remembrance of the crash and our loved ones.

Just weeks before the Washington trip, I had pulled another box of retrieved items from my garage and found a pair of snowmobile boots and a pair of sneakers. They belonged to my daughters. The box was in the back of my SUV for delivery to Kim. I forgot to drop it off and the box remained on that back seat for over a week.

As I left work one night, I opened the back door to throw a bag in. Suddenly, my eyes were drawn to three words written on the side of the box — BACK OF PLANE. How many times did I handle that box, and yet I never noticed the writing? Considering where the plane had crashed it made sense that these items, in a back hall closet, could somehow end up inside the plane. Yet, I was unnerved by that image. I could barely drive home, and actually had to pull over at one point to compose myself.

We are ripped away from reality and transported to the past in seconds. I love a photo of my grandson, Caden, in which his sweet face looks at the camera with a sad or tired expression. I looked at that picture and smiled so many times before I noticed a framed poster in the background. A 3407 poster hung on the wall. Caden's sad look, along with the poster now tugs at my heart. He, too, will feel the pain of our tragedy.

*Caden*

Justine and I have worked together on the 3407 Foundation Board. As we talked that evening, we both admitted that neither of us could summon the courage to board an airplane. Justine and Jerry loved travelling to Las Vegas and were even considering purchasing a condo in that city. She now has no desire to return.

I shuddered when Justine told me they recovered "a piece of Jerry's thigh, teeth fragments, and part of his jacket shoulder."

That is all.

My shocking revelation came three months after the crash when I was informed that Doug's legs had been identified. I was not originally told that they had been severed. Justine's remark now makes me wonder what exactly rested in Doug's coffin. Do I really want—or need to know?

I already had much to contemplate as I walked back to my hotel.

February 12, 2013, dawned, and with it the realization that it was now four years since fate stepped into our lives in a horrendous manner.

It was still dark when I hailed a cab and headed over to St. Peter's Catholic Church. Ken Mellett, father of guitarist Coleman Mellett, who was killed on Flight 3407, had arranged this gathering, and explained in an email:

> We have traditionally started February 12th at St. Peter's on Capitol Hill. We are close friends of the Pastor Father William Byrne. Before Father Bill was a priest, he was a grammar school teacher and Coley was one of his students. Mary Ellen (Ken's wife) and Father Bill were faculty members on the same small school staff. St. Peter's is where we held the service for Coley after the accident…Father Bill has encouraged us to invite all of the families to attend the service…all denominations are welcome.

About twenty-five family members gathered and willingly accepted Father Byrne's blessing, not only for peace on this anniversary date, but for strength enabling us to relay our message to those we would meet during this long day.

After a short walk to the House of Representatives we easily passed through security. We put bags and coats on a conveyor belt to be scanned, and walked through the security gate. I was surprised that our IDs were not checked, nor did we have to say where we were going or how long we would be there.

We seemed to be in the belly of the building and passed through a series of tunnels before reaching the Longworth building cafeteria. We quickly grabbed breakfast and listened intently to Kevin as he outlined the itinerary for the day. Between 9:00 and 11:30 a.m., fifty of us would break up into groups and go door-to-door taking our message to the congressional offices.

My head was spinning and I happily attached myself to Terry Maurer. Terry and her husband, Scott, are veterans of these Washington trips. They lost their daughter, Lorin, who was Kevin Kuwik's girlfriend. Along with Kevin, Scott is a tireless leader in this safety quest. By the end of the day I would tell Terry and Scott that I felt they had adopted me during my virgin voyage on Capitol Hill.

It was interesting to go behind the scene and be allowed to enter the congressional offices staffed by enthusiastic, and no doubt idealistic, interns. Their reception toward us ran hot and cold.

Terry and I would identify ourselves as members of the Flight 3407 families, point out that it was the fourth anniversary of that crash, and ask for the name or business card of the representative's transportation staffer. We asked for their continued support in working to complete the objectives of the law passed in 2010. We also distributed fliers indicating the special requirements that still needed to be implemented, and told them about our loved one.

We visited about 30 offices that morning. Each time our stories about our loved ones were the same. I would introduce them to Doug: "This is my husband, Doug, who unfortunately was killed when Flight 3407 crashed into our home. My daughter, Jill, and I were also in the house, and somehow miraculously survived."

Terry would relate Lorin's story: "This is my daughter, Lorin. She was thirty years old, had no connections to Buffalo but was on her way to her boyfriend's brother's Valentine's Day wedding. She never made it. The wedding still took place, but you

can imagine the pain of that family as they celebrated one son's joy and another son's sorrow."

The repetition of these comments never diminished the pain or effort it took us to relay that information.

Every now and then, Terry would come out of an office and say: "I think I got to that one."

At 11:30, staffers from Congressman Chris Collins' office escorted us through the maze of tunnels to the Capitol building. Entrance into the Capitol entailed more security inspection checks for everyone in our group before our arrival.

For the press conference at noon we entered a room filled with reporters adjusting their lights, cameras, and microphones. Kevin Kuwik, Scott Maurer, and Karen Eckert would speak on behalf of the families. Kevin compared our group's fight against the airlines to an underdog basketball team, like Buffalo's Canisius College taking on Duke: "It's halftime and Duke has the momentum, but we're not giving up." Scott looked into the cameras and directed his comments to President Obama, asking him to push implementation of the bill he signed back in 2010. It was a promise the president gave the families at the time he signed the bill into law.

New York State politicians extended their support: Senators Chuck Schumer and Kirsten Gillibrand along with Congressmen Tom Reed, Brian Higgins, Louise Slaughter, and Chris Collins.

Senator Schumer, a supporter of the families since the beginning of their fight, indicated that his office had spoken with the FAA that morning and was assured that the deadlines of August

1 and October 1 would be met.

I saw Jerry Zremski among the reporters. Jerry is the Washington correspondent for The Buffalo News, who covered the Long Street dedication. I appreciated Jerry's touching stories about the dedication, and he also connected me with Joe Popiolkowski, also of The Buffalo News. Joe provided me with a DVD of my dedication speech. I was happy to take Jerry and Joe to dinner last fall to thank them for all their efforts in making the dedication a memorable occasion.

As Senator Schumer was concluding his remarks he acknowledged Jerry, and informed us that despite the fact that Jerry's mother had passed away only the day before he was committed to covering the fourth anniversary of the crash.

Jerry sat by himself, his sorrow clearly visible. Following the Press Conference I approached him, offered my condolences, and gave him a hug. I faced yet another layer of pain on this anniversary.

There was no time for lunch. Terry and I rushed over to the Senate offices.

We were joined by Tammy Ganey, whose aunt and uncle, Ron and Linda Davidson, were on Flight 3407. Tammy's cousins have struggled with the loss of their parents. The Davidsons were the go-to people, the ones who kept everything in prospective, the family stabilizers. They are loved and missed by their immediate and extended family.

The Senate offices were larger than those of the Congress. They gave me the illusion of walking into a cozy den. We stopped at the office of a Georgia senator and were greeted with, of course, a bowl of peanuts.

Earlier in the day Terry had mentioned that many of the offices featured edible products from the senator's home state. She had high hopes that we would encounter a few bowls of chocolates in our trek. Pennsylvania would certainly have some Hershey treats, wouldn't they?

Since we had skipped lunch we enthusiastically asked the interns if we could have a few bags of peanuts. The young men sympathized with us. They invited us to sit down, offered us a cold drink, and chatted with us while we lunched.

At 2:30, we finally emerged from the confines of the political jungle we had traversed all day and piled in cabs for our meeting at the FAA.

We again went through security, presented our identification, and signed in. There was time to sit and relax a bit while we waited for all the family members to arrive and clear security. Tammy and I shared a bench and I decided to check my phone messages.

I was touched by a text from Jill: "Stopped at the cemetery and let Dad know what great things you are doing today."

The vision of Jill speaking with her dad by his grave threatened to unleash repressed tears. They lingered on the brink of my eyelids, and tumbled over when I also read an email from a friend who until now seemed oblivious to the reason I was in Washington. The message was simple:

    You are in my thoughts and prayers today, and
    always.

It was meltdown time. Tammy consoled me, as did Marilyn Kausner, who had lost her twenty-four-year old daughter, Elly. "Sometimes I just want to remember Elly for who she was, why I loved her, not dwell on her death. " Marilyn said. That applied to all of us, I thought.

We all knew this was an important meeting. Officially it was a "Briefing for the Families of Continental Flight 3407," and summarized the FAA's progress on The Airline Safety and Federal Aviation Administration Extension Act of 2010. Handouts documented accomplishments and further action needed.

Family members objected to the referral of "cost analysis studies."

"Can you put a value on my son's life?" a grieving father asked.

We were confused when told the training provision of the bill, now scheduled for implementation by October 1, 2013, could possibly be delayed until July, 2014. Hadn't Senator Schumer said that his office spoke with the FAA that very morning and was assured that the October deadline would be met? "Some misunderstanding," we were told. The meeting ended on discord.

Tammy and I opted to walk rather than take a cab back to the congressional buildings. The twenty-minute journey helped lessen the doubts we felt regarding this latest state of affairs. It also gave us time to become more acquainted. Tammy lives in the DC area and indicated points of interest along the way. If we had had more time it would have been fun to explore the city with her.

Our group assembled again for a meeting with Representative Frank LoBiondo of New Jersey, who is the new aviation chairman, and Representative Rick Larsen of Washington, one of the ranking members of the aviation sub-committee. Kevin asked Cindi Saltzgiver and me to talk about our loved ones and our lives since the crash.

Cindi's daughter was a business woman active in the bottled water industry. She was a loving wife and mother to two small daughters. She also volunteered her time and energies to those in need.

I explained to the representatives how the crash affected my family on so many levels: losing a beloved husband and father, dealing with the destruction of our home, and Jill's and my survival. I told them of Doug's many attributes, and stressed that "over the last four years, we have fought to rebuild shattered lives. We experienced bittersweet milestones—four daughters married without their dad beside them, and two beautiful grandchildren born, who will only know their grandpa through the words of Grandma, Mom, Dad, aunts and by looking at tattered photos recovered from the crash site. The pain never seems to subside. We ask why did this tragedy happen, but I am here today to ask, "Why is it taking so long to implement changes to make one level of safety a reality?" I kept my emotions at bay, but it was not easy. Those feelings would peak at the remembrance service at 5:30.

The significance of the date was apparent all day, but

*3407 family members personally distributed this flyer to lawmakers on Capitol Hill.*

culminated at the service. We gathered to remember and commemorate the fourth anniversary of Flight 3407. I was reminded why I never had any desire to join the families on their Long Street vigils on the anniversary date. For one thing, I did not want to return to the site at the exact time of the crash as I feared it would intensify recollections of that night. More importantly, I did not want to see the pain of the family members. Their pain has not diminished in four years. Their faces were a canvas outlining their anguish, raw and filled with grief.

Kevin Kuwik sat near me, heartbreak etched on his face. I could barely look at him. It broke my heart too.

Behind me, I heard a woman sobbing.

I was thankful the service was brief. The now familiar poster of our loved ones faced us, as one by one fifty-one names were read by Congressmen Collins and Higgins, National Transportation Safety Board (NTSB) Chairman Deborah Hersman and Senator Schumer. Each family member placed a red rose in front of the podium as the poignant song, "Because I Love You" by Jewel played in the background. My own tears joined those around me.

As the service concluded, I went to Kevin and hugged him. I could not help but wonder if the tears that found their source on Long Street will ever diminish and finally be completely exhausted. I am afraid the answer is no.

It had been a long day, and we definitely needed to unwind. We met at a pub with great atmosphere in Georgetown. A large back room was reserved for our group and we gathered around tables set up in a U shape.

It was not planned but I ended up sitting with Terry and Scott Maurer, my "adoptive family." The conversation flowed easily, perhaps aided by two very large cosmos on my part.

They told me more about Lorin, a girl who co-workers said could brighten their day with a mere smile. No words necessary. Scott told me how running had been a big part of Lorin's life and he now threw himself into that exercise to have that additional connection with her. They developed relationships with the 3407 family members outside of the Washington trips. Several of the 3407 ladies were welcomed by the Maurers in their South Carolina home, and Terry also participated in the women's retreats organized after the crash.

I shared Jill's and my experiences that fateful night of the crash. Was it wrong to tell a story of survival when they suffered such a loss?

I did make a confession to the Maurers. I remain jealous of couples like them—those who have been together for years and continue to have the opportunity to grow old together.

For many of us, this anniversary marked the first time we were not with family for the commemoration of the crash.

I was concerned about how my girls would handle this separation. I stepped out into the bustling Georgetown nightlife, as time crept toward that dreaded 10:17 remembrance, and called each of my girls. Their strength would sustain them.

I shared a cab with Terry and Scott back to their hotel. Although I felt I would be safe walking ten minutes back to my hotel they insisted that Scott escort me. We reflected again on the events of a busy day, and the amazing fact that Scott has made over fifty visits to Washington in the last four years. He told me: "Through the years, Lorin and our son led us on many adventures, especially with their involvement in swimming. We feel that Lorin continues to lead us to places and experiences we could have never imagined."

Physical and mental exhaustion brought instant sleep that night.

Wednesday morning we continued our lobbying efforts, focusing on those representatives connected with the aviation sub-committee.

I also received a lesson on the persistence of lobbyists.

Congressman William Shuster, the House Committee on Transportation and Infrastructure chairman, was not supportive of the families' efforts. Once, Kevin Kuwik's mother, Karen —coming out of a rest room—caught sight of the Congressman and led him by the arm to a group of families in the cafeteria. It seemed ironic that he would become the chairman of the transportation committee. Scott and Kevin attempted to arrange a meeting with him during this anniversary visit to no avail. They did learn however, that Wednesday morning he would be holding a closed meeting. Clad in our signature red, we congregated in the hall. Scott positioned us at any door he thought the congressman would enter. Suddenly, Congressman Shuster came out of the elevator and was immediately besieged by our group—some pushing their flyers toward him. He quickly entered another door but not before those flyers were in his hand. He learned that the 3407 families were still a force to be reckoned with.

Senator Schumer requested one more meeting with us. He was livid about the statements made to us at the FAA. He had contacted FAA Administrator Michael Huerta. Early the next morning, Mr. Huerta sent a letter to Senators Schumer and Gillibrand. Senator Schumer tossed a manila folder on the table and said, "There's a copy for everyone."

As you know, I met yesterday with the Families of Flight 3407...our staff provided the families with a handout containing misinformation, and for that I am deeply sorry. I would like to take this opportunity to correct the record and reaffirm our commitment to completing our work on these significant safety rulemakings.

We handed out a document that erroneously indicated that the Flight Crew Member Training Rule may be published in 2014. That is not the case. Let me be clear: we are doing everything in our power to move forward with all the important safety initiatives outlined under the Act. Specifically, I am committed to completing our work on the pilot qualifications rule by August of this year and the Flight Crew Member training rule by October of this year.

This news generated applause, and seemed to be the fitting end to our anniversary visit.

My days in Washington had provided insight into the function of government and lawmaking. I also gained insight into the true meaning of dedication to a cause. I always respected those who gave their time and effort to improve air safety, but I was amazed at the number of times they made these visits and the personal cost they incurred.

We definitely share similar feelings of loss and frustration, and continue to struggle as we adjust to our new lives. Still I can never feel completely one with them. They are the "Families of Flight 3407." My girls and I are the family of "one on the ground." Their loved ones all bought tickets for Flight 3407, entered that plane together, and in those terrifying last moments I have no doubt that those who sat together were holding each other's hands at the end.

Doug was alone at the end and probably did not even have time to shout out my name.

The journey gave me new understanding of these differences, but I also am thankful for the love and support the families have always given me.

As Father O'Neil said: "Loving presence soothes broken

hearts, binds up wounds and renews us in life."

I have been fortunate. There are many who provide me with that loving presence.

Those bins full of newspaper clippings are closed for now, but will no doubt be opened again.

2/27/13

# NEVER SAY NEVER

I was adamant. There is no way I would do that!

Every year I was invited to attend a ladies' retreat with women whose lives had drastically changed following the crash of Flight 3407. What an emotional weekend that must be. Why would anyone want to subject themselves to such pain?

Yet, on a sunny Saturday in April 2013, there I was driving toward Findley, New York to join those ladies. Never say never.

I had received an email from Susan Bourque who lost her sister, Beverly Eckert, on Flight 3407. Our paths have crossed on several occasions, including a trip to Washington, DC on the fourth anniversary back in February 2013.

This year the ladies' retreat would be held April 25 to 28. Susan emailed:

> I am thinking of driving down for one day and maybe one overnight. Ruthann Stilwell, who is organizing the thing said there should be plenty of room and urged me to come. I thought I would check and see if you were interested in going for the shorter time. They have some serious discussions, but most of the time it is about company and companionship, eating and drinking.

After some consideration, I decided to go. Terry Maurer, whose daughter was on Flight 3407, would be coming from South Carolina. She and I had spent considerable time together during the D.C. visit. They had made it easier for me to follow where they led. It would be nice to see Terry again, and she had strongly recommended attending these retreats. Emotionally I thought I would be able to endure one day and night with the group.

Findley is located close to the New York/Pennsylvania border in beautiful Chautauqua County. Vineyards dot the landscape, and it is close to the mountains that provide accessibility to winter skiing at the large resort of Peek 'n Peak. Spring blossoms were in full bloom, and warm temperatures suggested that our long, cold winter was at last a memory.

A large barn converted into a bed and breakfast called A Needle in a Haystack, had been chosen for the retreat. The location was a haven for quilters, and examples of their intricate artwork hung on walls and covered the beds. Each room was named for cows who previously lived in the barn. Bessie, Daisy, and Blackie were a few of the bovines memorialized.

Susan and I found the ladies forming a circle in a room, obviously equipped with long tables and supplies for visiting quilters. A list of possible questions that could be discussed during the weekend had previously been sent to me including:

*The thing I most regret we never shared is…*

That could be easily answered: the girls' weddings, the birth of our grandchildren.

*I miss you when…*

I wake up and you are not there, I force myself to attend events alone, I see a flea market, I hold Caden and Lydia, the girls have questions or problems—the list could go on and on.

*I smile every time I think of…*

Our last words, your excitement when making a collectible "find," Saturday morning runs to the grocery store for hard rolls, the curls down the back of your neck.

That morning there was only time for a brief discussion of when we missed our loved one.

I was happy to see that the serious side of the weekend had ended for the moment. Maybe this would not be so difficult.

I joined several of the ladies for a shopping excursion in the little town, and let the beauty of Lake Findley and the awakening of spring lift my spirits.

The entire group met at Peek'n Peak for lunch. Although the resort had opened in the 1960s, the décor had a 1940s vibe. I could picture wartime heroes returning with their sweethearts, sipping gimlets or whiskey sours while listening to the big bands.

A few of us decided to make the rounds of nearby wineries while others soaked up the sun on the B&B's deck.

One fact was becoming clear—the aftermath of the crash of Flight 3407 had changed the lives of many. A ripple effect of sorrow continues, and in some instances brings additional pain. I was being introduced to some unbelievable stories of relationships and even personalities changed drastically by the crash. These are personal stories which I have no right to relay. It is almost impossible to comprehend what these family members endured.

As evening approached, we gathered around an outside fire pit. The ladies asked if I would share my experience with them. "We were so engrossed with our own sorrow, that we did not even consider yours," one told me.

Along with revealing my family's experiences that night, I brought a few of my writings, which I hoped would help them understand my relationship with Doug, my own fears, and how I perceived their sorrow. Darkness was descending quickly and I inched closer to the fire for light.

First I read "Land of Make Believe," a short essay about Saturdays with Doug. I started crying before I even began. How was I going to be able to do this? They were patient, and I knew they, too, experience that same void which seems to only deepen after losing a loved one.

I was not prepared for the emotions my poem "Sounds" unleashed, as I described things I heard the night of the crash, and sounds that continue to reverberate in my mind. Their crying was a backdrop for this recital. By the time I finished, my tears joined them.

"You wrote that?" several asked me.

I was humbled by their praise.

Finally, I shared some of my reflections on my first trip to DC with them in February. They were touched by my observations and the ability to put the feelings into words.

I was not sure whether I shook from the dropping temperatures or from emotion. It was a memorable evening for me as a writer, wife, and survivor.

When Susan and I left the next morning I had no regrets about my decision to go. As much as I have resisted being a part of their lives I find I am continually drawn to them.

It seems I cannot refuse the support and friendship they offer.

7/28/13

*Women of 3407 Retreat*

# SOUNDS

*by Karen Wielinski*

Distant droning
Plane engine
A sound so often passing by
Then unrecognizable
Low and crashing close behind.

Thundering vibrations
Rent the stillness of the night
No lightning gave a warning
Of the unwelcome intruder
Entering our lives

Crashing walls
Harbor of safety no more
Secured fortress shattered
Safety is an illusion
You cannot hide from reality

Silence. . .
All is still
A hush surrounds me
Is this the death that I often feared
Survival whispers, "Not yet"

A daughter's cry
Lustily you announced your arrival
As you emerged from my womb
Now your cry greets my emergence
The sweetest sound—despite carnage all around

Moments gone
Memories far from faded
Visions hasten to return
Constant apprehension never lessened
Phantoms so reluctant to depart

Howling, whistling wind
Eerie cries of those lost
Lamenting their departure
Reminding those left behind
Remember me

Creaking boards
Straining from the weight
Of such heavy hearts
Chills coursing down the spine
Anticipation of sorrows soon released

Scrapping snowplow
Distant moans unleashed
Vibrato raising
Creeping closer, closer
Please be on your way

Beating heart
Adrenaline has reached its peak
Remembrance heightens fear
Could fate be callous
To repeat an act so cruel

Escaping breath
Release oppression trapped inside
Take your place beside those cries
Mingle with the spirits retained
Those who left without good-byes

3/13/13

# PLANES

"We are going to live in Japan for a year and a half," Lori announced.

Chills ran up my spine as I lamented the distance that would separate us, but also because I knew this meant I would have to find the courage to get on a plane again. Since the crash of Flight 3407 I did not even consider boarding a plane. As the months passed, Lori wanted me to experience the sights and sounds of Japan. I knew I should take advantage of this opportunity to travel. Lori and her family would be visiting the States in April, 2014 and I could accompany them back to Japan. Heart pounding, I Skyped with Lori and watched as Chris punched my reservation into his computer. I had made the commitment.

I printed out my itinerary, but did not scrutinize the details—I did not want to think about the flights until absolutely necessary. Before my trip, a friend requested my flight numbers and times of departure as she wanted to track my progress. Information in hand, I began to leave a message on her answering machine.

"We leave from Rochester on April 10 at 9:45 a. m. on Flight number...oh no, I can't believe it...Flight 3470...this is freaking me out..."

The fact that my first flight in over five years would contain those numbers seemed impossible.

My nerves were definitely on edge as I stepped onto that plane heading to Detroit. It comforted me to have Lori and Caden sitting next to me, as did repeating over and over, "help oh Mary now 'tis time, help oh dearest mother mine," as we taxied down the runway and lifted off for a fifty-two minute flight. That time was also a coincidence, as Flight 3407's journey had been scheduled to take approximately 50 minutes. As we approached

Detroit tears welled in my eyes. I thought of those souls on ill-fated Flight 3407, but I was also relieved that I had been able to board this airplane.

We had a four-hour delay before continuing on the next leg of our journey—a flight that would last twelve and a half hours. As we ate lunch in one of the airport restaurants, I glanced to my right toward the gate area. The nose of a huge jet stared back at me. "Is that the plane we will be taking?" I tentatively asked. Chris confirmed that fact. Good Lord.

Later, we boarded this massive plane and ascended steps leading to the Business Elite section. Individual "pods" awaited our arrival—I had never seen anything like it. Departure seemed to come quickly, and I was once again reciting my prayers to Mary. As long as I did not think about the 350 people who were on board or the altitude we had reached, a constant supply of movies, food, and wine eased my apprehension. Despite the fact that I could flatten my seat into a bed position I could not sleep. This did not seem to be a problem for the other passengers. I refrained from turning on my light to avoid disturbing their slumber. Our final descent seemed to take forever, but I did open my window shade and was amazed at the mountainous landscape and water speckled with small fishing boats. I had arrived in Japan.

I enjoyed the beauty and spectacle of Japan over the next two weeks. I tried not to think about the return journey I would have to make on my own.

Lori and Caden joined me on the hour and a half combination subway and train ride back to the airport. Lori, who had served as my guide for this adventure, gave me final instructions and directions, and for the first time in weeks I was on my own.

Mary was at my side once again as I bid Japan farewell. Daylight had accompanied us on the trip to Japan but a shroud of darkness enveloped us during this flight. Even so, I could not sleep. The flight was bumpy and I sidestepped fear by once again watching every movie I had missed in the last few years. Time dragged even on this shorter eleven and a half-hour trip. Once on U.S. soil again, and successfully through immigration and customs, I looked ahead with apprehension to the final leg of my journey from Detroit to Buffalo. That short flight would be the most difficult.

To my dismay I found my seat, 1A, almost on top of the cockpit. As others boarded the jet I found myself looking into the cockpit—pilots preparing for flight—instrument panel clearly in view. The animation that included Flight 3407's panels flashed before my mind. It was difficult to wipe that vision away. Panic silently crept into every fiber of my being. *How could I sit here?* There was still time for me to bolt from the plane. My cousin lived in Ann Arbor. I could call her, spend the night, and rent a car tomorrow morning. No, I had to face this.

All doors were secured and we began to taxi for takeoff. I was so close to the cockpit I could actually hear the pilots talking. *Are they supposed to be talking now?* I closed my eyes and started my litany of prayers. I could feel the ascent, and although there was some shaking and mysterious whistling the plane settled into a comfortable stride. My fear subsided and I raised my window shade to view massive Lake Erie still dotted with ice floes. We would be in the air a relatively short time—35 minutes—but I realized the flight path would take us directly over Clarence Center, and possibly Long Street. Again my thoughts rested on those passengers of Flight 3407. Looking at houses lined up securely on the streets below I could not comprehend how, without warning, one could possibly be struck by a falling plane. Yet, I knew that was exactly what had happened to us. I wished and prayed it would never happen to anyone else again.

Home. It is wonderful to travel, but what comfort returning home provides. Even with memories to savor I was ready to return to the familiar surroundings of home, family, and friends. I had jumped yet another hurdle and proven to myself that I could fly again. Yet, I came to the realization that no matter how much time passes, I will never enter a plane without thinking of those passengers on Flight 3407—most looking forward to their return home, others enthusiastically anticipating meeting friends and family. I am filled with such sadness for their loss, and for the loss of my loving home and husband.

4/30/14

# EXPRESSIONS

---

The empty hall loomed before me. A series of closed doors did not seem welcoming but the colorful flags that flanked them did indicate that the offices on the other side of those doors were open for business. I still was a bit reluctant to turn those door knobs. What would I encounter?

In April of 2015 I was once again in Washington, D.C. with the Families of Continental Flight 3407 crusading for "one level of safety" for regional and mainline carriers. Despite the success of the families in promoting the passage of the Air Safety Law (P. L. 111-216), the current 114th Congress would be deliberating Federal Aviation Agency reauthorization in 2015. The enhanced screening and qualification requirements for regional airline first officers could be scrutinized. The buzz around Capitol Hill was that airline lobbyists would like to see those requirements pared down.

The families knew it was time to present themselves again to old supporters and to introduce themselves to newly elected officials. Although this was only my third time, many of the members of our group had been on this journey more than seventy times in the last six years. Again I was accompanied by one or two other members of our group for the morning rounds in the Senate. In the afternoon, we split up to take our message to a greater number of congressional leaders, so I had to face the afternoon on my own.

I still was unfamiliar with the vast world that exists on Capitol Hill. I prefer to follow and not lead, but I swallowed the lump of fear that threatened to immobilize me and carried on. I managed to weave my way through the underground passages concealed beneath the magnificent Capitol—a maze of tunnels, escalators, stairs, and elevators. That afternoon I apprehensively opened sixteen office doors. I told my story sixteen times, mostly to young interns and junior staffers. These energetic, optimistic twenty-somethings probably deal with lobbyists and constituents on a daily basis. I could tell many of their reactions were standard.

"I'll certainly bring this to the representative's attention," was a typical response.There were, however, some who registered an expression of shock when I said: "The plane landed on my house and killed my husband. My daughter and I escaped from the rubble."

I had seen a similar expression earlier that morning as I was introduced to one senator. As we spoke, he inquired if I had a loved one on Flight 3407, and his reaction to my story was clearly etched on his face. At one point, he leaned toward me and stated, "I want to share something with you." He told me how he had a personal connection to another plane crash years ago. I am sure an expression of shock registered on my own face.

There were many occasions during this three-day trip when my expressions easily revealed my emotions. Even after six years, I continually learn new heartbreaking stories about those whose lives were changed forever by the crash of Flight 3407.

In Newark, Flight 3407 sat on the tarmac after a delay in take-off. The captain announced that passengers could use their cell phones during this time. Justine Krasuski heard from her husband Jerry just as she was entering the Buffalo airport to pick him up. Because of the delay in his arrival, she returned home. Later, her friend called to ask if he had arrived.

Justine said, "No."

"Turn on your TV," her friend said.

Like many of the family members, at first she was not concerned because she knew Jerry was travelling on Continental. This crash involved a Colgan flight. Feelings of relief gave way to denial and finally horror for her and many others awaiting the arrival of their loved ones.

Jennifer West sat watching television in her Clarence Center home not far from Long Street. Her husband Ernie was flying home from a business trip. She heard what she now believes was the crash, followed by sirens, and recalled thinking that something bad must have happened. She hoped the noise would not wake up her daughter, Summer, who was sleeping in her crib upstairs. Jennifer's mom called around 11:30 to ask what airline Ernie was on. Jennifer assumed it was United, which he often travelled on. Why was she asking? Her mom hesitated, but finally told Jennifer that a Colgan flight had crashed.

"I felt in my gut that he was gone," Jennifer recalled. "I fell to my knees, crying hysterically." She placed a chair in front of a window by her front door and continued to leave messages on Ernie's cell phone.

"I was crying and bargaining to God, anything I could think of to bring him home safely. I just kept repeating the mantra, please pull in the driveway, please pull in the driveway." Although Jennifer's family kept calling an 800 number set up by the airlines to assist families, they did not receive confirmation that Ernie was on Flight 3407 until late afternoon the next day.

Now on this particular April day on the Hill, Jennifer West's flight home was scheduled for 10:30 p.m. She was concerned about the possibility of encountering bad weather in Buffalo and struggled with whether or not she should switch to an earlier flight. "I can't do it," she lamented. "Ernie changed his flight to come home earlier. What if something happens again?"

I had driven to DC with Ping Wang. Her husband Larry Guo Zhaofang was returning home from a visit with his parents in Beijing for the Chinese New Year. During our drive, and at the congressional meetings we attended, Ping expressed that they were living the American Dream. They had come to the United

States for graduate work, obtained jobs in technology and research, and become American citizens. Their son was born here. "Our little family was destroyed," she told me. "I have no family here."

Perhaps the most chilling story was from Aaron Davidson who lost both his mother and father, Ronald and Linda Davidson, on Flight 3407. At the time of the crash, Aaron was a Marine stationed in Iraq. His commander relayed the terrible news, and Aaron immediately began the heartbreaking trip to Buffalo. After memorial services for his parents, he returned to Iraq to finish his tour—seven months. "I was in a daze during the remainder of that tour," he said. "I lived in a fog. If I did not have my wife and children to return home to, I could not have borne it."

As for the widows of Flight 3407, they all express one common feeling in the aftermath of the tragedy—loneliness. Their faces convey heart-rending sorrow that is evident to me every time we are together. Originally, I was afraid to expose myself to their grief. Now I can take comfort in knowing that my sorrow is normal. Such emotion is not mine alone. We can admit that the state of being alone is not a welcome one.

We try to combat that feeling—we bravely walk through halls trying to convince senators and congressman that we need their support. We cherish time spent with our children and grandchildren. We pursue new interests while clinging to memories of our husbands.

Our expressions, though, will sometimes expose the fact that we are alone. Accepting that as reality is hard. Even more frightening is the realization that I am beginning to accept that fact.

2/7/1

# PART THREE

## 6038 LONG STREET

# THE BLOCK PARTY

"Come on, Karen. You can do this." It is not unusual for me to talk to myself. Living alone tends to make you do that, although sometimes I tell myself I'm really talking to my cats.

I turned down the street and pulled into a parking space. Stepping out of my SUV, I took a deep breath and hoped my legs would carry me. Canvas chair flung over my shoulder and broccoli salad secured in my arms, I walked down Long Street.

It was a route I had not taken in over two years. A warm summer day in August, 2011 marked the annual Long Street Block Party. I can only recall going to one such party when we lived there. After February 12, 2009, it became an annual gathering. Although I had been invited before, this was the first time I would make an appearance. It was time to face this particular demon.

Obviously, this event had been weighing on my mind. I had been with Kim and Jeff earlier in the day at a car show in East Aurora when I did something I had not done since the crash. As I was signing a petition for the local volunteer firemen, I started writing the Long Street address. I could not believe I did that. Without any conscious realization our minds can sometimes control our actions.

A neighbor from a few doors over and across from 6038 was the first to greet me. We hugged, and some of my apprehension eased. After the crash, I learned her sister-in-law's brother had worked with me at National Gypsum back in the 1970s. He stills asks her for updates on how I am doing.

Our diagonal neighbors, Cheryl and John Stephens, arrived. Another big hug came my way. We had shared a spontaneous Christmas dinner with them one time. Cheryl had stopped over in the morning with some of her delicious cookies, and since they had no other plans for the day we shared Christmas dinner. It had been a good holiday "gift." They had also joined us in February 2011 on the second anniversary of the crash when we gathered to celebrate Doug's life.

The rest of my immediate neighbors had not yet arrived, so I said hello to those folks who lived at the end of Long Street. I never really knew them. Their faces were more familiar from meetings with the residents after the crash.

Paul and Michele Beiter walked down the street with their three girls. I was amazed how the girls had grown. Their oldest would be a high school freshman in the fall. Because they took us into their home the night of the crash this family will always hold a special place in my heart.

They, too, had gathered with us on that second anniversary, and shared their kind remembrances of Doug. Michele was part of the Remember 3407 Foundation, and worked with me and other committee members to commemorate the crash and honor those who died that fateful night. Paul voluntarily kept the grass cut on the empty 6038 site for two summers.

I talked with our next door neighbors, Joe and Nicole McGreevy. Both are teachers and I occasionally would see them at school. We have had several meetings since the crash. Rightfully so, they were concerned about what type of memorial would sit next to their house. Rumors seemed to be a constant, and they feared some sort of large monument would be erected. I assured them that it would remain a reserved, park-like setting—something our family had wanted since the beginning.

On one visit to their home, they had presented me with a wall clock fashioned from a tree trunk from the site. A local craftsman had worked with them to create it. "I will not leave you comfortless," he had chiseled into the wood, and "I will be with you always."

That's when I gave them a small-framed, mounted print of "The Painter's Honeymoon" by Frederick Lord Leighton. Doug and I had seen the original painting while visiting the Museum of Art in Boston during a visit in May, 2008. I was drawn to the portrait. The young man had dark curly hair while this bride was fair. I thought of Doug and me, but I also could associate it with the young newlyweds who had recently moved next door to us. I bought two note cards of the painting, with the intention of giving one to Joe and Nicole. The second copy I took to work and pinned to my cubicle wall. After the crash I decided to give the young couple that copy. The other had been lost. I found a poster of the print, which now hangs in my new house, providing happy memories of the Boston trip and remembrances of good neighbors. During that visit Nicole also gave me a small plastic bag filled with puzzle pieces she had found on her front lawn. She hoped that the charred, black pieces would be from the Bisons puzzle that had been on our dining room table.

Her story about the crash was unbelievable. She and her father had been sitting on a couch, their backs to our driveway. They were within inches of the destruction. She told me that in her shock all she could keep thinking over and over again was: Do the Wielinskis know that this has happened to their house?

"I find that incomprehensible," she said with a small shake of her head.

Everyone had brought a dish to share at the block party. Along with hot dogs and fried chicken, there was plenty of food. Conversation came easily with my old neighbors, alleviating my qualms about being with them again. The time went quickly, and I soon was walking back down Long Street towards my SUV which was parked across from what had once been my home.

Orange flags dotted the landscape of the site. They had been on it for some time, but until Paul mentioned it I had not realized that they represented the outline of what would be erected on the land. I made a sudden decision to walk between the flags marking a future path that would eventually lead to a stone bench.

As I gingerly picked my way along, I glanced to the right. It was no longer there. Just before the first anniversary of the crash, Michele had mentioned to me at a foundation meeting that someone had placed an American flag on the site. I remember being surprised that this could be done without my knowledge. Any confusion I had about the placement quickly vanished as I realized what it represented. My brother-in-law mentioned to me that he had requested the coroner to show him where Doug's body was found. That flag identified the location. When I first drove over to see it I could not physically walk over to the spot, and I did not find the courage to step over to the flag until the day after the first anniversary of the crash. The flag remained there for over a year. Now it was gone.

I had avoided stepping onto the property as much as possible, and the lot without the house seemed larger than I remembered. I tried to imagine what would take the place of our home. I knew that a bench would face the street and give a view of a tree planted in Doug's memory. Plaques would honor the lives not only lost but lives changed forever by the crash. A home thriving with life and love had vanished completely, and now my vision of it continued to fade when I was confronted with the empty lot. It was time to leave.

When I got back to the car I realized that I had not felt Doug's presence at the site. I know that many of the family members do feel the presence of their loved ones there. I find Doug's presence more in my girls and the people, places, and things that he loved. That day I did not cry when I stood on the site. I cried when I left. I cried for Doug and our lost life as a family.

I sat in my SUV to compose myself before driving to my new home, my new life. Cheryl noticed me and hurried down her porch steps. "You were over there a long time. Are you OK?"

Many good and caring people live on Long Street. That is why the plaque on the site would not only honor "lives lost and homes changed," but also the survival of Long Street, "still a thriving neighborhood."

9/9/11

# Edge of the Undertow

I was shocked at my reaction.

One of the Flight 3407 family members had gone to the Long Street site and posted a video online showing the memorial construction progress. It was a nice gesture on his part and would bring the other families up-to-date. So why did I feel threatened? Forty-nine other families lost their loved ones when Flight 3407 crashed into 6038 Long Street on February 12, 2009. They had a right to share possession of the site.

A feeling of tremendous loss came over me. I stood at the edge of the undertow.

The realization hit me—suddenly and hard—that this piece of land where my life and home had existed would soon belong to others. That fact ripped at my heart and I sobbed. I never imagined that losing that piece of land would be so difficult to accept.

Retaining ownership of the property seemed essential if I were to have control over what would be developed on the site. Once the project was completed, I was hopeful that the Town of Clarence would accept ownership. I wanted that exchange to transpire and did not want my children or me to hold the responsibility of ownership on a permanent basis, so why this sudden lament? The goal of handing over guardianship of the tragic site seemed within reach, I was moving toward the shore.

The pull of the undertow was strong. I wasn't sure I was ready for this closure—the final goodbye to our home and the life Doug, the girls, and I had experienced there. My tears also flowed because I was ashamed that I wasn't ready to share this piece of property with the other families. Children hang on to their possessions and adamantly say: "No, I won't share!" I felt like a selfish child.

I needed to move away from the undertow. I needed to allow my feelings to sweep me back from the pulling force that wanted to retain possession, or step to the side and remove myself from the edge accepting the possibilities—and freedom—sharing would bring.

My psychologist provided some clarity in sorting through these feelings.

"I suspected that you would experience another layer to your grief regarding the land," she said. "Allowing this memorial to be there is the final piece to officially give up your home. You no longer will have the rights to privacy on that spot and to monitor the coming and going of people. That is a big deal."

As with any undertow I must stay calm and not panic. I do not have to drown in this sea of emotions. I am determined to emerge intact, reach the shore, and accept another change.

2/3/12

Author's Note: A few days before the sixth anniversary of the crash in 2015, I was finally able to transfer 6038 Long Street to the Town of Clarence. I felt remorse, but also relief.

# CELEBRATION OF LIFE

**June 3, 2012 3:09 p.m.**

I finally have time to collect my thoughts and reflect on yesterday's dedication of the Long Street Memorial—what an amazing day.

The wet start of the day was a mess for the morning 5k run. I love a picture of the kids and me taken just before the race. The sky in the background is dark and ominous. The intermittent rain did not dampen our spirits though. My friend Sue, who is always ready to lend support, walked with me as we passed placards lining the route, honoring those who perished the night Flight 3407 crashed into our home. I lightly kissed my fingers and placed them on Doug's picture.

The skies opened as we reached the finish line, and we were drenched.

Sue offered her home for much needed drying off and touch-ups before the afternoon dedication. As I emerged from my car at her home two thoughts went through my mind. If this weather was not so ridiculous to make me shrug and laugh, I would burst into tears. I also had to ask myself why we had ended up with such a cold, rainy day. My thoughts and prayers were answered almost immediately as the clouds parted and there was a hint of blue sky and traces of sun.

The girls and I arrived at the Long Street site around 12:30, and the Wielinski family members assembled. Billy suggested that we gather around the red maple that symbolized Doug and the former location of our home. The extended family held hands as Billy expressed sentiments about this dedication, and we paused in silence to recall our own memories. It was a good thing to do before the crowd appeared.

To me the day almost felt like a wake, with people coming to pay their respects and remember those lost.

*Dedication Day—pictured left to right: Kim, Jill, Karen, Lori and Jess.*

So many kind people came and I wanted to hug them all: my cousins, friends both old and new. One woman identified herself as an old classmate from elementary and high school. I recognized her the minute she said her name. Several members of the creative writing class came. I appreciated their support. They know so much of the history that went into the creation of the memorial that I have shared in my writings. My neighbors from Long Street and from South Grove Street attended. The presence of my young South Grove neighbors, including those who brought their small children, was especially touching to me. Members of the Sheriff's department, 3407 family members, my attorney and his family, and politicians greeted us.

Senator Charles Schumer was introduced to me and was so personable. He asked me to show him the markers and wanted to be introduced to Kim, Lori, Jessica, and Jill. He stood with me during the whole dedication.

*Karen with Senator Chuck Schumer by her side during the Long Street Memorial dedication.*   Photographer Sharon Cantillon/The Buffalo News

It was a beautiful program, which included two poignant songs performed by Sara Delling: "Never Alone" (Lady Antebellum) and "Be Still" (The Fray), which offered hope that our loved ones continue to surround us with their love.

The program called for Mike Powers, our 3407 foundation president, to speak before me. He had to fight back tears and I thought: *If he's that emotional, how am I supposed to make it through my speech?*

I cannot recall exactly when my dedication speech had begun to form in my mind. If I remember correctly, I began mulling over what I wanted to express on one of my walks through East Aurora. In April, I finally realized these thoughts had to be transferred to paper. The first draft was finished on April 18.

I sent the draft to Rick Ohler, leader of the creative writing group. He had been instrumental in helping me venture into writing and I valued his opinion. He recommended a few commas and grammatical corrections, but he called it "beautiful" and "perfect." My confidence level increased.

The moment of truth arrived. I have never been too successful in expressing my feelings about the crash in public. I truly wanted to be successful at this dedication. I would feel like I had let so many people down and would also be disappointed in myself if I completely broke down.

I started out with the remark that I had to take my glasses off to read, thus making the audience a blur which would hopefully help me get through the speech. That and my remark about Doug saying, "you're the Salutatorian, you should know the answer to that" resulted in laughs, which I was thankful for. After giving my thank yous to all those who made the day possible, I arrived at the hard part as I tried to explain my emotions. I did have to pause several times but I got through it.

Senator Schumer, along with Congressman Brian Higgins and Congresswoman Kathy Hochul, gave touching speeches. It was somber when all the names of those lost were read, and balloons floating into the air symbolized the release of silent prayers rising. During the final song Sue came over to hug me. My girls had not joined the dignitaries surrounding me and stayed with the assembled crowd. I couldn't keep myself from them any longer. I walked over to them and Billy for tearful hugs.

We lingered at the site until almost everyone was gone.

Again, it may sound strange but perhaps this was a necessary wake—greeting many people who came to pay their respects, saying a final good-bye, especially to our Long Street home, but also remembering Doug and all those who perished that night. Isn't that what a wake is—a remembrance and celebration of life? I feel it was also a celebration of survival and determination to carry on, not only for Jill and me but for all the families affected by the crash.

To soothe the emotions that accompanied the day, the girls, their guys, and I had a late lunch at Brennan's Bowery Bar in Clarence. I can never enter that establishment without thinking of Doug. It was one of our regular spots, and also was the site of the luncheon after his funeral mass and burial. At that time, I stood and asked everyone to raise a glass in celebration of Doug's life. We did the same this day.

I admit that two martinis, the feeling of accomplishment in seeing the vision of the memorial become a reality, and the relief of getting through my speech mellowed me.

Jill drove us back to East Aurora, and we stopped to indulge in a cupcake. Although at first hesitant, the girls agreed to my request that I walk home through the village. I needed the twenty minutes or so to reflect on the events of the day.

The questions started on the day after the crash. What will be done with the site? Will you rebuild? Will a memorial be built? At that time it was too early to even contemplate answers. Pros and cons came from all quarters, and the debates caused me heartache. Real discussion of the Long Street Memorial began back in the fall of 2009, and it was not until the late fall of 2011 that construction actually started.

Now it was done, and what an amazing dedication it had been.

When I came home, I discovered that a friend who was unable to attend the dedication had sent an email at 1:29 pm on that Saturday, June 2, offering support and congratulations on the successful completion of the memorial. The thoughtful timing of that correspondence, one minute before the official start of the dedication, added a few more grateful tears to my day.

Jerry Zremski, a Washington reporter for *The Buffalo News*, did a wonderful job writing about the dedication in the Sunday edition. I was absolutely thrilled that he quoted parts of my speech and even the headline for his article referred to my words, "symbol of love" and "celebration of life." Jerry had called me on the Friday before the dedication and wanted to ask a few questions. He mentioned he would be going over to the Long Street site shortly. Since I was still in Clarence I told him I would meet him there. Perched under umbrellas, we spoke for a good half-hour or so. I was happy to meet him as he has been very involved with the 3407 families and their work in Washington for air safety.

I woke early this morning in anticipation of delivery of *The*

*Buffalo News.* At 5:19 am, I texted Jerry:

> Story is wonderful. Thanks for using some lines from my speech. Our family often feels forgotten in the 3407 story. Thanks for making us such a wonderful part of your story.

Jerry responded:

> Your speech was wonderful! It would have been hard to not write a great story, given what an emotional day it was. Thanks for your help!

Some very touching shots appear in the photo gallery on-line. My heart broke to see the ones of my girls, especially one of Jill— her emotions are so vividly displayed on her face. I did not realize that she had not been back to the site since our visit days after the crash. How much harder attendance at the dedication had to have been for her.

My mood swings throughout the process of making the Long Street memorial a reality ran the gambit of every sorrow and happiness imaginable. In the end, the setting reflects love and respect for everyone affected by the tragedy.

6/3/12

Author's Note: Since the dedication, I have taken friends to visit the memorial. We walk down the path treading on the 51 markers representing those lost that night. We pause to view the stone showing our home at 6038 Long Street, "Remembering the Wielinski home and the endurance of Long Street." I point out the indentations in the pathway that outline the rooms of the house. Together we sit on the stone bench, facing the site where our home once stood and where Doug had joined 50 others as they passed from this life. It seems fitting and feels good to share these moments.

*6038 Long Street Memorial site*

# Long Street Dedication Speech

Given by Karen Wielinski on June 2, 2012

I'm reminded of another time I stood before an audience, as a scrawny seventeen-year-old giving the Salutatorian address at my graduation from Bishop McMahon High School in 1969.

Doug would always kid me about that. When I'd ask him a question, he'd reply: "Well you were the Salutatorian, you should know that."

The theme of my speech centered on a sociologist who believed in the theory that we assimilate characteristics of the people we meet in life.

In the last three years my life has been touched by so many people, and their support, care, and efforts have been instrumental in bringing us here today. I am thankful for the hundreds of people who reached out to our family and their generosity has also helped create this memorial.

I need to recognize Lori Adams and the memorial committee members who gathered and sorted through suggestions for this site, along with the 3407 Foundation board members who worked to implement the design, and our Foundation President Mike Powers who provided much-needed guidance.

My brother-in-law, Bill Wielinski, has been my rock—my defender against anyone who does not have my best interests at heart. He was instrumental in arranging for the University at Buffalo's Architectural Department's involvement. Our designer, Joe D'Anglio, somehow managed to take our vision and make it a reality.

In learning about the passengers on Flight 3407, I take comfort in knowing that Doug left this life in the company of some amazing people. I also find comfort as I walk down this path and see indentations revealing the outline of 6038 Long Street.

We come here today to remember. I come as a wife who lost a much loved husband and friend; I come as a homeowner, who continues to deal with the loss of a home and who still clings to the happy memories shared with family, friends, and neighbors; I come as a mother, who will always be grateful for reuniting with my daughter that night; and I come as a survivor, who will never completely be able to comprehend how I emerged from the rubble.

Each life lost that night is remembered in the pavers we walk on. The site that was the location of their death has been transformed into one celebrating life. It is also a symbol of love that enables us to keep their spirits alive and let even those who never met them know them through our words and actions.

Puzzles have figured predominately in the Wielinski family story. When making a puzzle, we become frustrated when a piece is lost—it diminishes the final picture.

The 3407 families have lost precious pieces of their lives, and yet we have taken steps to find ways to add to the beauty of our puzzle.

I'll close today just as I did from the stage at Kleinhans Music Hall in 1969: thank you for being a part of my life. You are a part of me.

# A CHANGE OF HEART

*"Miracles — they keep reality from paralyzing you."*

~ Jodi Picoult

I had waited all evening for this feeling. He was there with me, trudging through snow up to our knees.

Why did I want to return to 6038 Long Street at the exact time of the crash—10:17 pm? I always swore I would never return on an anniversary at the exact time when fate snatched my contented life from me and took the man who had filled my life with love and discovery. Others had lost loved ones that night, but Jill and I were the miracles of Flight 3407. We had emerged from the destruction. Fear and shock should have paralyzed me, but the miracle of survival makes a person strong.

That strength might have given me the courage to have a change of heart, but I also had a persistent feeling. Perhaps Doug's spirit lingered at the site and could only be released if I returned there at the exact time of the crash.

People often ask me if my pain lessens with each passing year. I tell them that pain has intensified. Not only do I continue to feel the loss of Doug, but now I feel the pain of the other victims and their families. They have become more than names or numbers, they now have shape. They are living and breathing mothers, fathers, sisters, brothers, husbands, wives, sons, and daughters.

Yet as the fifth anniversary of the crash approached, I felt the need to join those who would gather to remember that tragic night of February 12, 2009. Kim and Jill did not feel ready to revisit the site on the exact time and date. I understood, and actually felt it would be better for me not to have them there. I would be so concerned with their reaction that I would not be open to my own. My friend Sue would accompany me.

As the day drew near, anticipation chipped away at my resolve that going to the memorial was the right thing to do. Sleep did not come easily to me the night before, and physical fatigue added to mental exhaustion as I attempted to get through the work day. Nothing else mattered. I just wanted to see what emotions would be unleashed.

I visited Doug's gravesite a few hours before the remembrance ceremony. The cemetery looked more desolate since my last visit. The lush bushes around the tombstones had been trimmed. Except for an occasional splash of color created by a flower lovingly placed on a grave, the vista was a sea of white and grey. I could have remained in the road next to Doug's grave but I needed to touch the stone. Kim must have had a similar thought. Earlier in the day she had visited and her footsteps had left deep furrows in the high snow. I followed, carefully retracing her steps, and felt compelled to speak out loud to Doug. "Thank you for all those wonderful years, and thank you for all the inspiration you give me to write."

As Sue and I walked into the Zion Lutheran Church in Clarence Center, where a memorial service would precede the vigil on Long Street, we were met by 3407 family members. We exchanged updates on weddings and births. Kathy Johnston, Justine Krasuski, and I discussed the recent interview we did with Channel 2's Scott Brown. We had two things in common: 3407 had made us widows, and we remained in the limbo of litigation. Scott's segment was sensitive to the gag order that hindered us from discussing our lawsuits, and it also captured the pain that we continue to carry with us every day.

Sharon Green, another 3407 widow, joined Sue and me as we entered the church. At the first 5k run in June of 2009 we were asked to speak about our loved ones. I did not trust myself to speak without breaking down, so I had asked my future son-in-law to say a few words. At that time I was impressed with Sharon's courage to speak lovingly of her husband, Brad. I remember thinking that yes, that was exactly how I felt. I wished I could express myself that well.

Sharon and I had seen each other at different events. She was at the 3407 ladies weekend retreat I had attended in the summer of 2013. She had left the retreat on Saturday because it was her wedding anniversary, and she needed time on her own to reflect. She commented that she realized she shouldn't, but she still counts the years they would have been together. Again, I do exactly the same thing. A few weeks before the fifth anniversary Sharon and I met for dinner. She has experienced the bittersweet joy of three grandchildren arriving since the crash. We seem to share so many experiences. I wonder, though, if my grandchildren might someday share the story Sharon's twin grandsons told her. Born after their grandfather's death, these little guys separately, on two different occasions, pointed to Brad in a picture and said, "He tickles me."

The fifth anniversary remembrance provided an opportunity for the families to thank the community for all their help, support, and kindness. I assumed that the speakers would include family members detailing the support of the community. I soon discovered this would not totally be the case, and received some emotional surprises.

I was stunned to see my Long Street neighbors Michele and Paul Beiter walk to the podium. Few people know that Paul Beiter was the first neighbor Jill and I had met as we fled from the destruction of our home. That memory is forever etched in my mind. Amid a sea of strangers, Paul's astonished face was before me: "What are you doing here?" he had asked. Considering the roaring flames that were consuming our home it seemed inconceivable that Jill and I should be standing there. Paul and Michele had sheltered us in the immediate aftermath of the crash.

Now at the remembrance, I listened as they recalled how their initial intention had been to move as far away from Long Street as they possibly could. Then, much to her surprise, Michele became immersed in the lives of those lost that night, and felt the desire to help the family members left behind in any way she could. The entire Beiter family became the protectors of the site. When Paul and Michele walked back to their seats, I stumbled out of my pew and embraced them. Tears mingled with my thank you while we stood in the aisle locked in a group hug.

Some New York State Troopers took the podium. John Kausner, who had lost his daughter Elly, introduced them as "guardian angels," who had protected the Long Street site in the days after the crash. The troopers had insisted that the remains of those lost be respected and not left alone. One trooper spoke for the group, and toward the end of his speech recalled how one of his vivid memories was "escorting the Wielinski family to the site a few days after the crash." There was one thing that stuck out in his mind: "Despite the pain she was dealing with, Karen Wielinski was concerned about our men standing in the rain." I was amazed he would remember that. I recall all work ceasing when we arrived, the troopers lining up on the perimeter of the land at attention, and me shaking some hands and offering thanks to those "guardian angels" as we left the scene. I was touched by his acknowledgement.

At this service the organizers played a song "For Good" from the musical *Wicked*. That brought not only memories of Doug but of special people I have met since the crash who have left their "handprint on my heart." They also played Josh Groban's "To Where You Are." The lyrics no doubt summed up the feelings of all those who had lost someone in the tragedy, and how we feel they are watching over us.

Jerry Zremski of *The Buffalo News* would aptly write that the remembrance turned "pain into poetry." Not only was that reflected in the lyrics of these songs, but the poem, "Sisters" was read, written by Eva Friedner and Dana Wehle in honor of their sister Susan Wehle. I also considered it an honor to have my poem "Just Because" included on the back cover of the program. One by one family members placed red roses near the poster displaying the smiling faces of those lost February 12, 2009, and a slide show reminded us how much life was extinguished that night. Sharon Green and I held hands. I heard a small cry escape from her when a family photo, taken at her daughter's wedding, flashed on the church wall. I draped my arm over her shoulders, not only as support but to let her know I understood her pain. I mourned not only for Doug, but for the people I have come to know through the recollections of their loved ones left behind. The photos that filled a stark, white wall reminded us what we had lost.Then the images were suddenly gone—reminding us of the void in our lives.

I shared hugs, encouragement, and thanks with family members, my attorney, the Beiters, and state troopers. Those hugs kept me warm as we walked the two short blocks in the crisp night air to Long Street. Memories of walks in the past came into my mind.

When we first moved to Long Street, Williams Hall stood stoically next to the Clarence Center Fire Station. Built in 1911, its walls resonated with history and the stories of neighbors who had spent their entire lives in the community during the hall's days as a community gathering place. By the time we arrived the building had outlived its usefulness and was in a state of ruin. The slow removal of the building seemed like such an undignified end considering its past importance. Doug and I were sad to see the old building torn down. Concealed in the darkness of night, we ran down Long Street and plucked several bricks from the rubble. We wanted a piece of history.

I am not overly proud of my other remembrance, as it caused Jill pain. Reading the real estate listings one night Doug saw that a couple we knew from soccer had purchased a home in Clarence Center. Curiosity got the better of us, and we dashed out the door into the night to see what home they bought. We laughed at how silly we were for being nosy, but that laughter turned to remorse as we came home to find Jill in tears. She had been upstairs when we left, and when she came downstairs to find no trace of Doug and me—lights still ablaze and door open—she could only think that someone had abducted her parents. We felt terrible for not letting her know where we were going.

Remorse seemed a fitting word as I turned the corner and approached 6038 Long Street. This was the part of the evening

I had dreaded most. What would I encounter? It was not what I expected.

The scene looked like a carnival to me: news trucks lined the street, motors running as they prepared to record; a light perched at the top of a tall crane illuminating the site; a large crowd assembled. Sue and I worked our way through the crowd and looked for Doug's name on one of the luminaries that lined the walk. Doug's light had been placed by the tree that marked the location of the house we were told. We paused on the knoll in front of the tree behind the plaque commemorating the Wielinski home and "endurance of Long Street."

"It feels like we're on a stage," I said to Sue. I had to shield my eyes to make out those in front of us. Silence fell at last and then fifty-one names were read. A bell tolled. I closed my eyes and tried to block out the present. Flashes from that night five years ago replayed in my mind—vivid reminders of how a routine evening at home had disintegrated into chaos.

We had been watching a video of *American Idol*. Around ten, Doug left the family room. A few minutes later he returned and sat on the couch. I asked if he wanted to keep watching the video. I didn't tell him that I was thinking of watching something else. I was interested in a special edition of *Ace of Cakes*. It was celebrating some sort of an anniversary at Macy's. I can't even remember why I thought that was important.

How trivial and unimportant these details seem now I'm forced to think about all the "what ifs." Would Doug have survived if he had stayed in the family room?

But he didn't stay. He asked how much longer American Idol would last.

"About an hour," I said.

Then he made me laugh with teasing so typical of him. "I don't have time for that!" he said as he hopped off the couch.

That was the last thing he said to me and the last time I saw him.

I picked up the remote and flipped on *Ace of Cakes*. I glanced at the clock on the VCR. 10:15.

An unusual noise intruded on the quiet night. It didn't sound like the planes that often flew over our house. We had become immune to those sounds.

This was different. More rumbling and deep. What is that? I thought. If that's a plane, it could hit something.

How can I describe what happened next? The sound changed from a rumble to an explosion. Then came a cascade of plaster, wood, and roofing crashing all around me.

*It hit us!*

In the moments that followed I wondered if this was what death felt like. It was so quiet.

Wait, I am still alive.

I had watched a segment on *20/20* a few weeks before that discussed how many people in disasters do not survive because of panic. I had not watched *20/20* in years. Why had I watched it then?

I thought about my high blood pressure. I was alive. Why panic and end up suffering a stroke or heart attack?

I stayed on the loveseat. What was on top of me? I could not allow myself to think about how much rubble was above.

I tried to push some of the debris off. No success.

I noticed a small opening above me to the right. Maybe someone was out there.

I called several times. No reply.

It was up to me to free myself. I pushed again, and this time there was movement, enough so I could stand on the arm of the loveseat, squeeze through the opening, and pull myself out.

As I emerged from the debris, I heard the crying of a woman. Until that moment, I had not thought about Doug and Jill.

I prayed it was Jill crying. Miraculously it was.

Later she would tell me that I had risen out of that hole "like a flower popping up."

How can I describe what I saw? I faced my neighbor's yard where my van and Doug's car were parked, now windowless. I turned to face the back of the house. In disbelief, I saw that the back and side walls, and everything that had been within them were completely gone.

The cabin of a huge plane filled the dining room. The tail, with the emblem of a globe seemed to be resting where the kitchen had been.

There were no flames at the back of the house but I could see flames in the front.

I am sure I stood for a moment and just shook my head. I could hardly comprehend what I saw. Why didn't I scream?

I turned to my right. Jill was standing there.

Thank God! Jill and I walked toward each other.

As I walked, two sad thoughts popped into my mind. I was going to find out what it was like to be alone and Doug was going to miss our daughters' weddings. I couldn't believe I was having such thoughts at that moment.

Jill approached. "A plane hit the house."

"Yes," I said.

She was sobbing. "Where's Dad?"

"I don't know."

"We have to find him!" She started to walk toward the house.

"No!"

I grabbed her arm.

We had to get out of there. There could be additional explosions. I held her tightly. I was afraid she would get away from me and run toward deadly danger. Later, I learned Jill had bruises on her arm. I may have caused them from the pressure of my hold on her.

As I forced myself back into the present an image of what Doug must have experienced entered my mind, but I cannot say that I felt the reunion with his spirit that I longed for.

After the final name was spoken and the bell tolled for the last time the crowd began to disburse. There was one more thing I needed to experience again. I wanted to retrace my steps and Jill's as we had fled the destruction of that night.

Only a thin layer of ice and snow had covered the ground in 2009 as we ran behind the houses on Long Street toward Clarence

Center Road. Now there were mounds of accumulated snow. As Sue and I trudged through it, Clarence Center Road seemed so much closer than it had the night of the crash. My eagerness to reach it was somehow as real as it had been that night.

How absurd was my compelling need to retrace our steps? How disrespectful it seemed when I found myself laughing, as one step into the crunchy snow thrust my leg unexpectedly deep. Maybe it was not so wrong, though. This laughter—verging on hysteria—symbolized the relief that Jill and I had survived, and I had faced this return visit head-on.

In *that* moment I felt Doug's spirit. He was there with me, sharing my laughter and disbelief.

"Can you believe this? Can you believe how I died?"

It was craziness, utter craziness. We laugh because otherwise we would cry.

2/17/14

# Just Because

*by Karen Wielinski*

Just because
we laugh and smile
does not mean
we forget a while.

Just because
we hide the pain
it lingers still
and will remain.

Just because
some take
offense
reconsider for our sake.

Recall the joy
they always found
in simply living—
enjoying sight and sound.

They would frown
and shake their head
if we constantly
were filled with dread.

Embrace each moment
though changed by fate
Bittersweet,
yet celebrate.

Life goes on,
memory lingers,
warms the heart
like burning embers.

Their life still glows
in what comes after
we should shout it
from a rafter.

Just because
we laugh and smile
we still love
them all the while.

1/7/14

# PART FOUR

## THE TRIAL

# EIGHT DAYS

3407 was a cruel taskmaster right from the start, arriving without warning at our doorstep—totally unwanted. It brought chaos and destruction, and continues to arrive unannounced bringing unhappiness. This time it lingered relentlessly for eight long days.

The shadow of 3407 reared its ugly head at what my lawyers called a pre-trial conference on a Monday. The day dawned with the hope that meetings with attorneys and a judge could hasten an end to legal proceedings. How silly I was to expect such a reasonable result. Possible court dates were once again set back, and more information was demanded of me. There would be still more probing into our lives. The "Big Brother" defense was definitely watching us, keeping an eye on us, and looking—looking for what—the hint that our lives were wrought with discontent, conceit, and unhappiness?

Were they looking for proof that Doug was not important to us, that he had sat idly by and had done nothing for his family? They will not find it. The judge denied our protests against continued inquisitions. My attorney was told that once I had signed the complaint I had opened up my life for investigation. That was true, but the remark seemed cold and unfeeling. The legal process appears to be so one-sided. I hate it, but it has gone on too long to give up.

What am I supposed to say? "Excuse me for wasting your time. You win. I will placidly accept whatever you offer." I cannot do that. The longer the proceedings go on, the angrier I become. Besides, Doug would want me to continue. I know he would.

The shadow continued to hover on Tuesday, but this time the memory of 3407 resulted in good news. There was an announcement from Washington that important changes in pilot training and qualification provided for in the 2010 law would finally be implemented. I gathered with other 3407 family members at the Clarence Town Hall for a press conference. Joy and relief showed on the faces of people who had fought so long and hard to make flying safer—to help prevent tragedies like the one that had changed our lives. We hugged and talked about recent milestones—another son married, a new baby's arrival, a child's birthday. Yet, the pain of 3407 could not be denied. One couple thanked those who continue to remember their unborn grandson among those lost that night; and a seven-year old girl, dressed head-to-toe in pink, told reporters she had lost her daddy.

Wednesday 3407 interrupted my life again and I was back at the Town Hall. My attorney, my brother-in-law, and the president of the 3407 Foundation—my "Three Musketeers"—joined me as we presented our case as to why the property on Long Street should be transferred to the town. Along with bringing me some closure, I wanted the weight of owning the site to be lifted from my shoulders. The town probably did not want the responsibility either so what could I say to urge them to take on the obligation? As I drove to the hall a logical explanation burst through the fog in my mind. I told them how, a few short days after the crash, my daughter Lori mentioned: "Since dad always loved history, it seems fitting that he is now part of history."

My voice cracking, I spoke to the members of the Clarence Town Board. "The tragedy that night transformed 6038 Long Street from a family home to an important part of the community's history. By accepting ownership, the town would acknowledge that history." I left the meeting that day not knowing if my statement had convinced them.

Another day dawned and with it the reality that my life was not my own—3407 threatens to control my actions. I had written about being unsure about Doug's opinion of my writing endeavors in Loveland. If the defense lawyers got wind of my fleeting doubt, they could say: "Ah, there was a lack of communication in this marriage." That particular piece of writing ended on a happy note—I cited two beautiful pieces of correspondence that proved

Doug's love. But those defense lawyers could take my words out of context and twist them against me. "Tread carefully," I was constantly reminded.

On Friday, it appeared 3407 had taken a day off from casting its shadow, but it was not meant to be. My attorney called that evening to tell me that the judge in the outstanding federal cases (we were in state court) might rule against a plaintiff attorney's request to depose an airline official about the lack of training. It would be irrelevant to the case. Irrelevant? Really? Lack of training was a major cause of the crash. How could that be irrelevant?

That weekend, a friend asked if we could visit the Long Street site where 3407's reign of terror had begun. I was pleased that my friend considered the site to be a moving tribute. I was glad that she thought it was respectful of those who had died and of the many lives changed that night, and that it was also respectful of the neighborhood. She had never been to Clarence Center, so we enjoyed lunch in a cozy restaurant and visited local shops. Several times throughout the afternoon I saw people I knew. They hugged me and continued to express their concern for the girls and for me. That support continues to be so important to me—I still need it.

Monday, I met my brother-in-law Billy for lunch. It had been some time since we could sit and catch-up. Our conversation turned to the last time Billy had seen Doug. It was in January of 2009. Doug and I had gone to Toronto, where the UB Bulls football team was playing Connecticut in the International Bowl at the Rogers Centre. Doug had the opportunity to go with Billy and his son Brian, but had instead invited me. Billy had kidded Doug about bringing me to the game instead of going with the guys. I was one lucky lady to have a husband who still wanted to share such experiences with me, and I had fond memories of that trip.

The night before the game, Doug and I explored the area around the hotel and stopped for a drink in the pub in Toronto's Flat Iron Building. After our drink we left and tried to find a restaurant. Nothing caught our eye, so we decided to head back to the pub. Our route took us through a small park. The trees were still lit by strings of tiny white Christmas lights. Doug stopped and kissed me. "I love you," he said. After almost thirty years, he could still make me feel young and romantic. My memory of that kiss took on more significance after the crash.

Later at dinner, sitting in an intimate booth in the friendly pub, we discussed coming changes in our lives. Our girls would be getting married and starting new lives. How would we handle the empty nest? Retirement wasn't too far in the future.

That was a happy night. Doug and I were ready to begin a new phase of our lives. 3407 would change that.

Those memories swirled through my head after my lunch with Billy. I finally released the emotion that had built up over the last few days when I sent an email to my psychologist:

> I decided to go to bed early...put on some nice soft music...bad idea. The last week was just one 3407 thing after another thrown at me....now I am thinking about that night in Toronto when Doug stopped and kissed me and said he loved me surrounded by Christmas lights. It doesn't get much better than that. As if recalling that wasn't enough emotion for one day, I decided to go thru another box of retrieved items...mostly unimportant paper items, although it reminded me how Doug pulled articles out of magazines and papers since he might want to read them again...amid all that were some pictures of him from a few of the marathons—he looked great. There was a scrap of paper that he had written comments on about one marathon—how he felt at certain points—and then he had written, "saw Karen at 22". That was nice to see. More emotion was yet to come...there was a card his parents gave him when he graduated from Niagara with his Masters. Still inside was the twenty dollar bill they gave him for "something special." Made me laugh to think it was still in there (a bit of a miracle actually considering what those retrieved items have gone through), but made me cry too. I think the mood music needs to be turned off.

Eight days—you would think that after almost five years the shadow of 3407 would not linger so tenaciously. I should know better. Even on those days when the shadow is not right by my side, I know it is hovering close. 3407 came with a life sentence, although I get time off for good behavior. I have the ability to break through its grasp and find freedom. When I am surrounded by my daughters and grandchildren it fades somewhat, but then 3407 comes out of hiding and reminds me again that Doug is not here to share these moments. I must resign myself to the fact that the shadow of 3407 will be the visitor who never knows when to leave. I have news for it though—it will never break my spirit. Each new day brings hope and promise, despite its heavy presence.

11/20/13

# ANTIDOTES

It had been an emotional week—a week where we once more had to re-visit horrific events. Our depositions in preparation for trial had begun. The terror of one night continued to weave its way into our lives, but we now had to delve into every detail. We were expected to justify all the emotional pain that defines who we are. We told our story to opposing legal forces. Our words, though, did not seem to generate sympathy from them. In my mind, they were not moved by destruction and loss.

I stood at my husband's grave with those thoughts swirling through my mind. The timing of the recent inquisition was ironic. Today would have been our thirty-fifth wedding anniversary. My thoughts did not seem to be enough. I needed to speak to him.

*Happy anniversary, I miss you. We have another grandchild. Can you believe it, two boys and a girl, and another boy on the way? Boys! I am still not sure what to do with these little guys, but I am having a wonderful time figuring it out. And Lydia? What a sparkling personality she has. You would have happily embraced the role of Grandpa.*

*It has been quite a week. I hope you think I am handling this legal situation OK. I think you would want me to fight for the security of your girls. I think you would want me to validate your life. I should not have to defend you—a good man, but yet I must.*

*You changed my life. You fulfilled me. That really defines what you did for me: made me happy and content, satisfied my needs, let me reap the benefits of loving someone, completed me.*
*Thank you for loving me.*

I left the cemetery, and stopped at the town park before returning to work. Spring continued to work its way back into our lives after a long winter. I felt relief from my emotions as I stood under blossoming trees and gazed over the sparkling pond and its fountain. I watched plumes of water continually interrupting the pond's smooth surface and couldn't help comparing it with the way my ordinary life had been interrupted. Yet, as plumes of water shot high then crashed into the water below the flow calmed me as it rejoined the pond.

The water sustained the life at its edge. A family of geese nibbled grass on the slope above the pond. As I approached, Mom and Dad slipped into the safety of the water followed by their six little ones. The goslings naturally formed a straight line between their protective parents. Such simple sights can warm a heart and refresh a troubled spirit.

That evening I babysat for Lydia. What an antidote that was for the sadness of a wedding anniversary without the one you love. She greeted me with her smile, although she still clung to the safety of her mom and dad. Once they were gone she decided to accept my presence. She was delighted that bath time allowed her the opportunity to wallow and splash in water. Was that water on the floor from her splashing, or had she seized a moment of freedom from her diaper before being lifted up into the waiting tub?

Later she brought me books to read. Elmo, one of her favorites, taught her about numbers, colors, and shapes. We then searched for a smile, along with other hidden items, in a different book, one with a mirror on its back cover where she and I could see our own smiles. Is there any other feeling that matches the warmth that creeps through while reading to a small child snuggled on your lap?

Lydia loved when I recited "This Little Piggy." I pulled on each little toe and ended with my fingers dancing up her leg straight to her chin. "And this little piggy cried 'weeee' all the way home." She insisted that I do this over and over on each foot.

I am filled with peace when I watch her suddenly plop on the floor to explore the possibilities of some toy, or to test the patience of Leo, the cat. Suddenly, she raised her arms to me requesting to be held.

"May I have a kiss? I asked.

"Yeah," she replied as she pursed her lips.

Sadness is often my companion, but on this day I found a few small ways to ease the ache. The beauty of nature can brighten a day, and the sweet innocence of a child reminds me what wonders can result from two people falling in love.

*Happy Anniversary, Doug.*

5/20/14

# GUILT

*"As the rain and the snow come down from heaven, and do not
return to it without watering the earth and making it bud and
flourish so that it yields seed for the sower and bread for the eater,
so is my word that goes out from my mouth: It will not return
to me empty, but will accomplish what I desire and achieve
the purpose for which I sent it."*

*~ Isaiah 55:10-11*

Usually it is the music that makes my eyes well with tears in
church, but on this Sunday Isaiah's verse was the trigger.

I have been told that emotional tears are part of having Post
Traumatic Stress Disorder (PTSD). Those tears threaten often
these days. We are in the midst of a legal battle and, surprisingly,
we continually find ourselves having to prove our "alleged" psy-
chological scars. It amazes me that the defense attorneys seem
unable to comprehend that someone who is sitting in her home
one night, has a plane fall on that house, crawls out of the rubble
to find total destruction, realizes that her husband is more than
likely dead under the tangled mess before her, is reunited with
her hysterical daughter who has just slid down to the ground
from a second floor bedroom on part of a plane, could possibly
have PTSD. So experts must analyze us.

The analyzing psychologists/psychiatrists usually come
around to one question: "Do you have survivor's guilt?" Do I feel
guilty that I lived and others died? One psychiatrist suggested
another view of that guilt—the guilt associated with being happy.
That struck a chord with me. How could I step away from the
pain and destruction and eventually be happy?

The survival of my daughters that horrific night is a source of great happiness. It is unbelievable that Jill escaped from that second floor and reached the back of the house just as I emerged from the rubble. What would either of us have done if we had not found each other so quickly?

Imagine the shock that Kim experienced as she drove toward billowing smoke, abandoned her car, ran to Long Street, and realized it came from her home. Luckily people at the site helped her as she stood perilously close to the house—paralyzed with fear that she had lost her family, and realizing that if she had arrived home five or ten minutes sooner she could have died.

What mother would not feel happiness at the survival of her daughters?

Some happiness, despite the circumstances, is acceptable in the eyes of others. Being surrounded by four daughters and now grandchildren certainly grants me a right as a survivor to experience happiness. They are a constant reminder of what Doug's love gave me. They are an extension of his love.

Survival is an amazing feeling. It is a second chance to share the essence of your life, to watch the growth of what you have to give, maybe even see it affect the lives of others. That realization does bring happiness, as well as guilt. How do I justify the joy writing brings? Writing has become a lifesaver for me. It keeps me afloat. The gift of being able to express myself was present before the crash of Flight 3407, but found a true voice when I chronicled the unbelievable tragedy and its aftermath. My survival has made me more aware of what I had, what I still have, and what I can still obtain from life, which brings me back to Isaiah.

Perhaps I survived so that my words could "yield seed for the sower and bread for the eater." Perhaps my words can offer me comfort, but can also touch others and encourage them to appreciate and savor the simple treasures of life. Survivors are blessed with an opportunity to reap more from life. Survivors can strive to prevent their gifts from returning empty. Such prospects ease my guilt. Thanks, Isaiah, for reminding me that guilt really doesn't accomplish much. Like worry it wastes precious time that could be used simply enjoying life. Lesson learned.

7/29/14

# TEARS

At first they came like droplets barely brushing my cheeks, but quickly they escalated into a steady, pounding force.

I miss my Sunday morning walks. I like the solitude that enables me to enjoy the sights and sounds of the quaint little village I chose to make my home four years ago. Settling here provided me with an escape from painful memories—reminders of a love and life lost. That is what I originally thought, but I keep those memories embedded in me. It remains an emotional balancing act.

The events of the last six months have filled my days. While her husband stayed in Japan, my daughter Lori and her son, Caden, lived with me for three months while we waited for the new addition to our family tree. Rowan arrived on August sixth. Before his arrival we faced Lori's bouts with food poisoning and false labor. I discovered the art of juggling the challenges presented by a pregnant daughter and my delightful, almost two-year-old grandson. I rediscovered the simple joys of life through his eyes. There were a few family walks, but my Sunday morning leisurely strolls through the village somehow vanished.

During this time of lawsuits, depositions, motions, and Frey hearings sapping my energy, I often debated whether to get up early or stay in bed. Hiding under the covers always seemed like the better choice.

Chris returned from Japan a day before Rowan's arrival. Lori and her young family moved back to their Kentucky home in September. A week later the lawsuit we had filed over five years before finally brought us into the courtroom.

All the planning in the world had not prepared us for the bizarre procedures to come. There was surely enough evidence to convince a jury about the liability of Continental Airlines. But Continental and Colgan had denied any responsibility, placing all the blame on the pilots. I wanted the opportunity to prove that lack of training and airline policies had been an important cause of the crash. I considered the judge's ruling that a jury could hear the evidence to be a victory not only for us but for all the families who had lost loved ones in the crash of Flight 3407.

We had looked forward to our day in court but suddenly Continental was "vicariously liable" which meant somehow that evidence could not be presented. The liability part of our lawsuits vanished. It was a defeat for us in many ways. We headed to court engaged in a battle involving a wrongful death suit for Doug and damage suits for Jill and me. It was disturbing to me that Kim's lawsuit had been dismissed due to a legal technicality stemming from the fact that she was not at home at the time of the crash.

Now, only a few short days into the trial, I was beginning to question our decision to take on a major airline. Why was I subjecting myself, my family, and my friends to the painful words and visions that would intensify memories of such a horrific event? We had reached a point of no return.

Jess came to stay with me for a while during the trial. She would join Kim, Jill, and me to represent our family in the surreal world of state court.

The week before her arrival for the trial, Jess had run her first mini-marathon in Washington D. C. Jess ran in memory of her dad. And she had found the perfect shirt for the occasion imprinted with an adaptation of an old poem by an unknown author:

> Those we love don't go away
> They run beside us every day...
> Unseen, unheard, but always near
> Still loved, still missed
> And held so dear

How Doug would have loved to see one of his girls following in his running footsteps.

Still in her preparation mode for that race, Jess was out early on this Sunday for a morning run. She inspired me to get my lazy butt out of bed and get walking. The sky was filled with clouds, and forewarned that rain would follow shortly so I grabbed an umbrella.

Those first drops of rain on my face seemed to provide some cleansing of my doubts and lessened the uncertainly I felt about this trial. I had just lifted my umbrella to shield myself from a good drenching when I noticed a white car driving down the street toward me.

Jess yelled out the window: "Thought you might need an umbrella."

A simple act of kindness, unsolicited, took me back to country roads, miles away from our Long Street home. On a bleak rainy day, punctuated with thunder and lightning, I hopped in a car in search of Doug, who despite threatening weather just had to get a training run in before an upcoming race. I tracked him down, cringing through every flash of lightening. Slowing down I urged him to hop into the safety of the car.

"It's not that bad," he proclaimed. "Go ahead, I want to finish. I'll be home soon."

Just another example of my complete confusion over why people think running is fun, but I know that Jess understands such dedication and would love to discuss it with her dad. Memories you think are long forgotten can reappear in an instant, bathing you with the warmth of good times. These are memories of a man whose worth to his family was priceless. I now find myself in court trying to prove that fact. Why is such justification even needed?

Doug's words echoed in my mind offering encouragement and strength. "It's not that bad. Go ahead. I want you to finish."

It seems funny to me that despite an umbrella to shield me those pounding drops of water continued to fall silently down my face.

10/14/14

# RELENTLESS

C2030000 Wielinski, D. $36. 0025

It is one bag of many that sat in a plastic bin in my basement for over five years. The contents of the bin were collected from the crash site, mainly loose change but there is also one bag of burnt one dollar bills. My intention has always been to sort the money and donate it to charity. How could I possibly spend it?

True, Doug kept cans of pennies waiting to be checked for the possibility of being more valuable "wheat pennies," and there were bags of quarters handy to take when a vehicle needed to be vacuumed or emergency trips to the laundromat were necessary, but all that money could not have been just ours.

A women's club I belong to was collecting for UNICEF. My piggy banks were suffering from malnutrition so I decided to find the bin for some change. I picked up that bag and could not stop crying.

The trial lasted seven weeks. During that time, for one reason or the other, there was an occasion for me to cry almost every day.

A defense attorney claimed I could not count the pain of the 3407 families as a contributor to my post-traumatic stress disorder. "The pain of those families has nothing to do with the Wielinski damage suits. Those families have settled their cases."

Several of the family members were in the courtroom that day, and I wanted to assure them that their pain did haunt me and was most certainly part of the distress I will always carry with me. Jess, Jill, and I fled from the courtroom and rushed to a room reserved for plaintiffs. We stormed through the door, dissolving in tears, much to the surprise of a former Clarence Center fire chief who was waiting to testify.

"I'll give you ladies some privacy," he quickly said before leaving the room.

We were emotional wrecks, and it was only the second day of the trial.

Even before my daughters spoke one word on the witness stand my eyes welled with tears. Their faces reflected the sadness they have dealt with since the crash. Not only did their memories of their dad cause pain, but my frustration with defense attorneys limiting what the girls could say about their emotions on February 12, 2009, often resulted in tears.

It was not just the events unfolding in the courtroom that would make me cry. Weekends were not exempt.

One Sunday, I spent most of the day at the home of my attorneys in preparation for testifying. Those preparation sessions could be grueling. From there I headed to the office to retrieve calendars from my desk that could identify any days I had missed work since the crash. Not only did I have to document my absentee record, I also had to look for more information about my finances, which had been demanded by the defense. I frantically flipped through an abundance of unfiled papers and eventually found what my lawyers needed. As far as the calendars were concerned, I was successful in securing most years but could not locate 2009 and 2010. I tried praying to St. Anthony, the patron saint responsible for helping people find lost items. "I am a good person. Help me."

My patience and endurance were stretched to the max, evident in a text I sent to my attorneys:

> Will email you what I have on the attendance records in a few minutes. I have been trying to find my calendars for 2009 and 2010…they are not where I thought they were. I am sending what I have and if I get a burst of energy perhaps I will look for those two calendars again. You really have asked far too much of me today. Between doing that, looking for that financial information and also dealing with the pretrial prep, it really has been too much. I am losing it. It is time for

```
me to forget about this for the rest of the night
or I will be in no condition to testify tomorrow.
Again, I do not think that doing all this today
is helping me prepare for tomorrow. Enough for
one day.
```

Shortly after detailing my emotional stress I glanced in my work bag and found the two missing calendars. St. Anthony had answered my prayers. I cried again.

I cried as witnesses shared their memories of Doug. I cried as I heard a detailed description of what filled forty-five boxes of destroyed sports collectibles retrieved from the crash site. I heard Doug's good friend Jim, and fellow flea market acquaintance Alan, describe items they knew Doug had purchased over the years, had not sold, and were now missing—pages and pages of collectibles. I cried because I knew what collecting had meant to Doug. I knew the love and pride he felt in maintaining his collection. I cried because I mourned the loss of my husband's encyclopedia-like knowledge of collectibles and history.

I had explained to the jury the comfort I derived from writing, the therapeutic benefits I obtained from it, and the feeling that it provided a legacy for my family. It was not totally unexpected but yet when the defense attorney tried to use passages from those writings negatively, I sobbed. "I can't believe you are now using these writings, which are so important to me, against me." The judge told me I could not "spar" with the defense attorney and could only answer his direct questions.

With settlement reached, I hoped this daily stream of emotion expressed by tears flowing down my cheeks would somehow be depleted. For two weeks tears would still well in my eyes, but the outbursts seemed to have subsided.

Then I went looking for change and picked up a small bag of quarters. I had visions of Flight 3407, passengers with wallets in pockets or handbags, plummeting from the sky and slicing into our home. On impact, coins rained down upon burning embers and broken dreams. The dam broke once more.

Apparently these emotions are relentless and will never

completely slacken. I never know what will trigger a reaction. Tears come persistently and without mercy. Perhaps they are a necessary aspect of healing broken hearts—they release some of the sorrow and pain that remains bottled up inside me. Perhaps crying is one of the compromises I must face as a survivor of death, destruction, heartache—and law suits.

11/16/14

Author's Note: In December of 2015, I sent a check for $310.68 to Habitat for Humanity Buffalo. It only seemed fitting that money retrieved from the destruction of one home should be used toward the construction of another.

# WORDS

*"First they ignore you, then they laugh at you, then they fight you, then you win."*

~ *Mahatma Gandhi*

I turned away from the celebrative mood that echoed through the hall and walked over to the courtroom doorway. Just a few short hours earlier, strong feelings had filled the room as seven grueling weeks reliving the events of February 12, 2009, were finished. An enormous sense of relief washed over me when I realized I would never have to enter that room again.

My girls and I had begun this journey into the legal jungle on September 18, 2014. It had taken over five years to reach that point. It had taken that long for the airlines to recognize us. Remember us? You killed a wonderful husband and father, destroyed our home, and left behind women who must live with memories of crawling through debris in order to survive.

Mahatma Gandhi's words above perfectly fit our battle with the airlines. They would become my mantra during the trial.

It seemed ridiculous that we had come to the point of having to prove the worth of one man's life, the happiness of a family, and the devastation that followed one horrific night.

From the very first day, I disliked the tension that permeated the room. How dare the defense attorney in his opening statement discuss our experiences from that night? I remembered my attorney saying what an impact our telling of those events would have on a jury, and here the defense attorney was detailing actions and emotions that he had no way of knowing about. Wasn't that hearsay? That would become a word I would come to detest.

There were other words that made me cringe.

Kim was the first in our family to take the witness stand. I was so proud of the strength she displayed, as she looked the jury straight in the eye and tried to tell her story. I say tried because the word *irrelevant* kept popping up. Even though she experienced the terror of coming home to discover a ball of fire and black smoke consuming her home; even though she stood amidst the chaos, close enough to have the smell of smoke taint her hair, skin, and clothing into the next day; and even though not knowing the fate of her family filled her with terror, her testimony was irrelevant. Why? Because she was not at the site at the time of the crash and that limited what she could say.

We would also be introduced to the word *repetitive* during Kim's testimony. The defense attorney interrupted the questioning with "Objection…We have already heard from several people regarding the scene of the crash. This testimony is repetitive."

It was true. Several first responders, along with residents who had videotaped the frenzied scene after the crash, had taken the witness stand before Kim, but shouldn't a family member who stood in front of her burning home be able to tell what she saw, heard, smelled, and felt that night? Where is there repetition in that?

The word irrelevant would haunt us throughout the trial. Every time I heard irrelevant, I could feel my blood pressure rising, and many times I wanted to spring out of my seat and scream "how can you even say that." This was especially true when it came to the testimony of the girls.

I should point out that this trial brought together three separate lawsuits: a wrongful death suit filed by the girls and me as a result of Doug's death, and suits by Jill and me for our pain and suffering.

My out-of-town daughters, Lori and Jessica, experienced their own brand of terror the night of the crash, as they frantically tried to learn the fate of their family. In the end, our lawsuits were settled before Jess could testify. The defense attorneys had limited much of what Lori could say about the night of the crash. They claimed, especially in Jill and my lawsuits, that Lori's testimony was irrelevant.

Excuse me, but the terror all my daughters experienced that night is relevant to me, and still contributes to the stress and pain I live with every day.

Part of the defense's case involved trying to negate Doug's value as a father. Even if he did provide financial support and guidance to his daughters while they were growing up, defense reasoning was that the girls' husbands certainly would assume that responsibility once they were married.

Lori may not have been able to divulge her feelings about the night of the crash, but she delivered the greatest answer when questioned about that continued guidance. "My husband is my peer," she said. "But my father was my mentor."

Well done, Lori!

Let us get back to that word *hearsay*.

Jill's husband, Dan was in North Carolina at the time of the crash and her good friend, Annmarie called Dan that night. When Annmarie testified, she was not allowed to discuss that phone call. Hearsay, they said.

Hearsay can be considered information that someone did not directly hear or witness, isn't it? Therefore, how can information from the person who spoke it be called hearsay? It is hard to figure out why she was denied the right to tell that part of her story.

Another group of words strung together, which I might add were used repetitively, annoyed me. *"Does this refresh your memory?"* The defense kept trying to prove that Doug habitually spent money for his collection, at the expense of his neglected family. We never lacked for food, clothing, and attention because of Doug's love of collecting. If anything, he purchased items that he knew could be of value to his family in the future. To refresh my memory, I was shown list after list of withdrawals Doug made from our bank account—from 2005 to shortly before his death. Over and over I was asked if I knew why this money had been withdrawn. It is hard enough to remember what I spent last year-let alone what Doug spent years ago. So, I repeatedly would have to say, "No, it does not refresh my memory." Why wasn't that badgering repetitive?

I was grateful that my attorneys later supplied the answers to explain those withdrawals, and produced proof of deposits in a checking account in addition to cancelled checks Doug wrote for college, cars, insurance, mortgage, and an array of other payments to insure the support and comfort of his family.

At one point in the trial I was asked whether I remembered what we paid for or sold our various homes for over the years. When I could not, I would be shown documents to refresh my memory. I endured this repetitious ritual several times.

"Do you recall what you paid for the house?" the defense attorney asked.

"No," I said.

He picked up a piece of paper from his podium but before he could speak I jumped in.

"But I am sure you are going to show me something that will refresh my memory."

Laughter erupted in the courtroom from the jury, my attorneys, and even the team of defense attorneys. It was a great moment.

Many of the questions would begin with: *"Did there come a time?"* I realized attorneys must carefully word their questions for legal reasons but this phrase often seemed to just prolong testimony.

I can think of other questions where those words could have been used more effectively.

"Did there come a time you questioned this court action?"

Yes, from the very first day, but it was necessary.

"Did there come a time you began to wonder how you would be able to sit through the defense's closing statement?" I did not think I could endure that narrative, but I knew I would have to be in the courtroom when that time came.

Luckily, I did not have to be tested on my ability to listen to those closing statements. A word we had longed to hear finally was spoken. Settlement.

When we walked out of that courtroom for the final time, there were still those who wanted to hear our words. A gag order imposed by the judge had denied us the right to speak with the media during the trial as it could be *prejudicial* (another of those overused words) to the defense. The settlement lifted that ban.

Several members of the jury also wanted to meet us. Their support of our family was apparent when they spoke with us, and their comments that they had personally gotten to know Doug warmed my heart. That realization was a win in itself.

The flurry of words that had swirled throughout the courtroom unleashed memories and uncovered images that we at times wished had not been brought to light, and fueled the still

*Jill, Jess, Kim and Karen share an embrace at the conclusion of the trial.*
Photographer Derek Gee/*The Buffalo News*

smoldering pain associated with that night in 2009. That fire will never be totally extinguished.

It is true that we were not able to explore airline practices that contributed to the crash of Flight 3407 during the trial but we made the most of the opportunity to use our words to describe the terror of that night, the devastation of a family in the years after the crash, and, most important, we defended a good man who certainly did not deserve to be attacked in the first place.

Our words became declarations of love.

3/3/15

# PART FIVE

## AFTERMATH

# 24 MORE HOURS

Recently, I was informed that a documentary film, *The Truth of the Sky*, by Jim McSherry recounted a tragic Air Inter crash in France twenty years ago. The filmmaker's brother was lost on that flight. McSherry asked family members what they would do if they were granted twenty-four more hours with their loved ones. It has me thinking—what would I do if I had twenty-four more hours with Doug?

My question: would we know it was his last twenty-four hours? If we didn't it would probably be an ordinary day, just like February 12, 2009. Doug would head off to work. He enjoyed his job and the people he worked with, so hopefully there wouldn't be much stress.

He'd return home and I'd heat up leftovers for dinner. "Some food tastes better when heated the second time," Doug would often say. During the evening hours he'd work on various projects—maybe on his collection or a home improvement. He'd watch a bit of TV. No marital or parental arguments, no hassles. A good night.

But, if we knew it would be his last twenty-four hours? I'd tell him to take the day off and do some of the things he loved. Hit a few antique stores and find a treasure or two. Sort through some of his collectibles and reminisce about how he acquired them. Call the girls and see what they were up to. Share his own experiences with them and see if he could give them any guidance. Forget about hip pain and grab the old hockey gear, find a pick-up game, and skate like the wind!

In the evening, we'd check out some little tavern and share a few beers. He'd probably find a sports or historical topic to chat about with the bartender, and I'd smile at the pleasure that would bring him. I'd be amazed at all the facts he stored in his head.

Most of all, I would want to hold him. I would listen to his breathing and his heartbeat. I'd let my fingers comb through the curls that caressed his neck. I'd tell him that I loved him. I'd let him know that he was the best thing that ever happened to me.

4/20/11

# SIX YEARS LATER

**2/11/15**

I came to dislike this photo. It surfaced following the crash of Flight 3407 and it was everywhere, a constant reminder of a happy family torn apart.

I have learned to cherish it again. It was taken on Thanksgiving Day 2008. It is the last picture we have of the entire family; even old Spots consented to be held by Lori. The picture was taken in the living room of 6038 Long Street. I get a chill when I see my hands on Doug's and Jill's shoulders. Three people in the house six years ago tomorrow connected by a touch of hands. That really is remarkable.

*Counterclockwise from left: Kim, Lori, Spots, Jess, Jill, Karen and Doug – Nov. 2008.*

This year's anniversary cuts deeper. Like February 12, 2009, the date falls on a Thursday. The recent trial magnified not only the events of that night, but also unleashed new facts that intensified our pain and suffering. I now know that the nose of Flight 3407 rested in that living room where we posed for our picture.

My sadness remains but I like to reflect on memories of my thirty years with Doug, and I am thankful for the greatest gifts he gave me: Kim, Lori, Jessica, Jill, and the four beautiful grandchildren who will definitely know their Papa. Doug's spirit remains in them and there are many other people who know him even if they never met him. They know him because we keep him alive with our words.

Tomorrow I will remember the happiness he brought, and continues to bring, to my heart. I will remember all those lost on Flight 3407, their wonderful families, the Long Street neighborhood, and a community that came together in a time of tragedy. I will also be thankful for all those who continue to support and extend kindness to our family.

### 2/12/15

The tick, tick, tick of the clock drummed continually in my head during the day, as it had during the entire week. Or perhaps it had begun its countdown on January 1. The pattern of unease and watchfulness seems to begin building right after the holidays. Prepare yourself, it is coming again. Despite the passing years, I try to relive the moments leading up to the crash of Flight 3407. What did we do? What did we say? No matter how much I beg my mind to dig deep and remember every detail only bits and pieces surface.

On this six-year anniversary my friend Zoe and I met early in the evening for drinks and appetizers. We sat at the bar, and I cringed when the local news flashed on the television that it was the sixth anniversary of Flight 3407. Please do not show our family picture, I thought. Please do not let the other patrons, lifting their wine and beer glasses, question the woman at the bar who looks like one of the victims of 3407.

I was thankful that the news clip only showed the Long Street memorial and a couple visiting the site in memory of their loved one.

I arrived back home by eight and began my vigil, waiting for 10:17. Two drinks had reduced the tick, tick, tick in my mind to a murmur. I contacted my girls to let them know I was thinking of them and loved them. I felt like it was very important to tell them I loved them. I wrapped a quilt around me, the work of art stitched together from pieces of uniforms, shirts, a family photo, and other memorabilia symbolizing Doug's life and mine. Its warmth penetrated my loneliness, and made me thankful for the comfort it provided and for the life I had with Doug.

I was lulled into a state of soothing calm. The dreaded 10:17 slipped by while I drifted contentedly, allowing me to be spared the emotional jolt that has often pierced my heart. Doug led me safely through the storm of emotion.

**2/14/15**

Another difficult thing about the tragedy of 3407 is that it shattered our lives two days before Valentine's Day. My friend Tammy, who is experiencing her first Valentine's Day since the sudden death of her husband, posted an article from the *New York Times* by Patrick O'Malley about grief. The last paragraph of that article speaks loudly to me, and sums up the comfort I receive from writing.

> "All sorrows can be borne if you put them in a story or tell a story about them," said the writer Isak Dinesen. "When loss is a story, there is no right or wrong way to grieve. There is no pressure to move on. There is no shame in intensity or duration. Sadness, regret, confusion, yearning and all the experiences of grief become part of the narrative of love for the one who died."

It works for me, and helps me celebrate my Valentine. He was lost, but remains an important part of my life.

In the evening, I babysat my granddaughter Lydia and

grandson Curtis. Their laughter and love are extensions of Doug's spirit and love. Now that was a Valentine's Day gift to cherish.

2/17/15

# FEBRUARY 2016

I find little rest in February. Random thoughts prod and poke, each urging me to pay attention to it. It is a month where my mind is filled with thoughts—bits and pieces of scenes from other years that dart in and out, trying to fit into the reality of the here and now.

The countdown towards the seventh anniversary of the crash of Flight 3407 into our home on Long Street has begun. Seven years? It seems impossible.

As I tossed and turned in my bed after a restless night, one such random thought entered my mind: if you add the individual digits in 2-12-09 and 3407, the answer is 14 for both. To me, that seems ironic and somewhat crazy, but it adds to the unbelievable significance of those numbers in my life. I can take this equation even further, divide fourteen by two and you arrive at the seventh anniversary. I am sure a mathematician could expound on this phenomenon.

Instead of wondering why such thoughts enter my mind, I should concentrate on what February has brought me so far this year.

Last week, I once again joined a group of 3407 family members in Washington D.C. to continue a fight for airline safety. Much has been accomplished during the last seven years as the group strives for one level of safety including:

- Regional carrier ticket disclosure which now requires travel agents and internet air ticketing sites to disclose if there are regional carrier legs of a trip.

- Safety Inspections of regional carriers now require the FAA to conduct yearly, random, onsite inspections of regional carriers.

329

- Task Force on Air Carrier Safety/Training requires that Congress be updated on industry best practices regarding training, professional standards, mentoring, and information sharing.

- New requirements on flight and duty times, and fatigue risk management plan for each carrier. Congress must receive updates on each carrier's participation in voluntary safety programs, industry best practices regarding pilot pairing, crew resource management techniques, and commuting.

- Implementation of NTSB Training Recommendations on stall and upset training, as well as for carrier pilot remedial training programs, and updates on stick pusher/weather event training.

- Enhancing the screening and qualification requirements of crew members; mandating Airline Transport Pilot certification.

- Revamping training programs, and enhancing the FAA's ATP certification program.

Our goal on this trip was primarily to remind those on Capitol Hill about the importance of maintaining the requirement that all regional airline entry-level first officers have an airline transport pilot license (ATP) prior to being hired. This license requires 1500 hours of flight time as well as additional training experience. The airlines had begun an aggressive lobbying push in an attempt to water down these requirements.

It was only my fifth time in D.C. to advocate for our position, but many of the family members have been there 80 times. We continue to make our presence known; we are relentless and determined in our quest for safer air travel to honor the loved ones we lost.

Joining our group on this visit was thirteen-year-old Alex Safran, who lost her mother on Flight 3407. At a press conference, she courageously reminded a group of Western New York representatives and senators that she was only six when the crash occurred. She has few memories of her mother, and her younger sister Sydney, less than a year old in 2009, has no recollection of the woman she never had the chance to call Mom.

Two fathers recalled the last time they saw their daughters. John Kausner, on a busy vacation time table, almost bypassed the opportunity to make a side trip to have lunch with his daughter Elly, on Groundhog Day 2009. Any inconvenience this may have caused him was forgotten when, on parting, she kissed him and said, "I love you Daddy."

Scott Maurer and his wife Terry never saw their daughter Lorin look happier than when she introduced them to her new boyfriend Kevin in February 2009. Two weeks later, Lorin was on Flight 3407 heading to Buffalo for Kevin's brother's wedding, where she would meet his parents.

These last moments together with loved ones bring solace to the families, especially as they were filled with happiness. Doug's last words as he bounced off the couch proclaiming he didn't have time to watch a television show were a simple proclamation, but he said it in a manner that he knew would make me laugh. Except for the fact that I wish I had given him a kiss as he left the room, I could not ask for better parting words.

This February, one of my daughters is dealing with an impending divorce. She has learned that there is no guarantee for happily-ever-after. Life is not a fairy tale, and often results in heartbreak. We once again face grief, as we experience feelings of shock, pain, anger and reflect on how unexpected sadness has once again entered our lives.

I was also reminded of how 3407 continues to affect our lives when another daughter texted me.

```
I have been working with my therapist the past two
days on processing anything that still bothers me
with the crash. Definitely feeling off because of
it but pushing through.
```

As a mother I want to wave a magic wand and remove sadness from my daughters' lives. Again, we are dealing with real life here and not fairy tales. All I can do is boost their morale and offer love and support.

February does have some saving grace, though.

Thankfully, it is a short month. It paves the way toward spring. Rebirth.

And Jess' birthday is February 26. That brings happy thoughts.

I shake my head, put random thoughts in their place, and eagerly wait for March.

2/7/16

# COMPARISONS

I kept debating what I should do. Should I go, or stay home? Should I call a friend for support, or go alone? In the end, I went alone.

The lights dimmed, and I took a deep breath as *Sully*, a movie about the "Miracle on the Hudson," January 15, 2009, burst on to the screen.

I remembered Doug and me standing in our family room on Long Street as we watched an account of the miraculous Hudson landing on the evening news. Who could forget the image of the passengers of U. S. Airlines Flight 1549 standing on the plane's wings after an emergency water landing on the Hudson River. Doug and I both marveled at the miracle. How amazing it was that all aboard had survived.

Now, watching the movie, I could not help but compare that miracle to our tragedy. Colgan/Continental Flight 3407 crashed into our home and our lives less than a month later. Few people remember the proximity of those two events. The movie reinforces the importance of training, airline policy, and experience in the cockpit, qualities that enabled Captain Chesley Sullenberger and First Officer Jeff Skiles to make a successful water landing.

I wondered what if more experienced pilots had been at the controls of Flight 3407. From all indications, the 3407 pilots panicked and improperly responded to "stick shaker" and "stick pusher" warnings. The shaker activates and shakes to get the pilot's attention that the plane is slowing down. The right response from a pilot should be to give the plane more power to speed it up. The pusher activates to signal that the plane is getting dangerously slow, so it forces the stick in the pilot's hand to push forward. This drops the nose of the plane and causes it to dive and recover speed to prevent it from stalling. Unfortunately, the pilots were startled by both warnings. They fought the pusher by pulling back on the stick and raising the nose. This slowed the plane down even more and basically doomed the flight. Their action guaranteed that the plane would stall and they would lose control.

What if the flight had been scheduled for daytime arrival and not late at night? When I see aerial views of the landscape surrounding 6038 Long Street I see open fields which would have been visible during the day. Would the pilots have been able to change their course and avoid the plummet into our home?

I was thankful for the dark theater, and that I was alone. I cried throughout the movie. I shed tears of regret and loss, but they were mixed with tears of joy for Flight 1549's happy ending.

Both Captain Sullenberger and First Officer Skiles have joined the 3407 family members in Washington, and it has been an honor for me to meet them. Tom Hanks and Aaron Eckhart's portrayals were spot on. They took on the mannerisms of Sully and Skiles.

It seemed crazy to me that I actually had met the people portrayed in this movie.

My meetings with First Officer Skiles have been brief—a quick introduction and a hand shake. But many of the 3407 family members have worked closely with him. They know his dedication to air safety, and they have also witnessed his subtle wit that came through in the movie.

I first met Captain Sullenberger in February of 2015. He was to meet 3407 family members and Senator Chuck Schumer at the Long Street Memorial. He intended to lend his support to the families' continuing efforts to enforce a law enacted in 2010. That law required one level of safety for all airlines. At the time of the Sullenberger visit, Buffalo had been hit with a lake effect storm, and it looked like the gathering on Long street might be called off. Before the decision had been made I was able to attend a private breakfast before the scheduled news conference. I was introduced to both the Captain and his wife Lorrie. As I shook their hands, I was impressed by their genuine concern for the 3407 families. They were soft-spoken and gracious.

The news conference went on, although it was moved to the town hall. Despite the swirling winds and snow there was a large contingent of 3407 families and local reporters. Senator Schumer even managed to arrive in Buffalo despite the storm. As promised, Captain Sullenberger vowed to join the efforts of the families to secure enforcement of the safety law.

John Kausner, who lost his daughter Ellyse in the crash, saw things in a different light. "He didn't join our effort, we joined his," he said. "Captain Sullenberger has been safety conscious long before we ever knew there was an issue. We're joining his lifelong efforts to make sure that the pilots in the sky are safe, trained, and as reliable as he was that day."

When Captain Sullenberger enters a room the atmosphere changes. You can feel the electricity. He deserves respect, and automatically receives it. I felt that respect at both the news conference and on the occasions he gathered with us in D.C.

At the movie I noticed that the theater was filled with people of all ages, including families. That was refreshing to see. The world needs more heroes like Sully and Skiles, and those who came together in rescue efforts. People stepping up to help others—that is one thing Flight 1549 and Flight 3407 have in common.

No doubt their hearts were beating rapidly that January day, but Sully and Skiles kept their minds sharp and were able to use their training and experience to prevent tragedy. They became heroes.

I continue to make comparisons—different circumstances, different levels of training and experience. I posted my thoughts about my reaction to Sully on Facebook and some comments to that post brought additional "what ifs" to my mind.

One friend asked if I knew how much time the 3407 pilots had between realizing that there was a problem and the crash. Her question prompted me to sit in front of my computer, in the wee hours of the morning, scrolling through the NTSB's official report, which included the cockpit recordings. It was too painful and I had to stop before finding an answer.

Why do I do such things? I've discussed this many times with my psychologist. I call it my masochistic tendencies—feeling like I have to delve deeper into 3407, even if I know it will hurt me. There is that saying "if you feel pain, you at least know you are alive." Perhaps, as a survivor, that is why I keep searching for explanations and insights.

In the end, I contacted Kevin Kuwik, a 3407 family member and leader in the fight for airline safety. His reply confirmed that answers could be found in the NTSB report, but he kindly summarized their findings for me. There was only a 27 second interval from when the first warning occurred to when the plane started to wobble and veer, and finally crashed.

In the movie the NTSB recreated, via a simulation with real pilots, what would have happened if Sully and Skiles had tried to take the plane back to an airport. I asked Kevin if the NTSB had done such a simulation for 3407's crash. "The simulation that the NTSB did share at the hearing was basically a 27 second video recreation of how the plane twisted and turned in the last 27 seconds," he said. "Very chilling."

Yes, chilling is the perfect description. I have seen that re-creation, and although it was hard to watch I cannot imagine what it was like for the family members, knowing that their loved ones were on that plane.

Who thought that going to a movie and munching on popcorn could bring additional havoc into your life. Well, in honesty, I figured it would.

I know you cannot change what has happened, but the comparisons I have made more than justify the efforts of the 3407 families, and those who support them in their fight for airline safety. We cannot drop our guard, and we must continue to reach for those happy endings.

9/17/16

# THE WEB

It would be so much easier for me if I could put 3407 behind me. I should move on, forget about that night, forget about the many lives affected, forget about the pain and emptiness. I should keep those memories in a faraway haze, and concentrate on the present and what lies ahead.

But I am like a spider on its web, lurking in wait for potential information, lunging forward to wrap myself around what it has to offer, and using it to strengthen the fiber of life the tragedy left behind. So I seize any opportunity that comes my way, and surprisingly there never seems to be a lack of occasions to expose myself to new avenues of knowledge.

I eagerly will talk with anyone who wishes to share their experiences of February 12, 2009. I am touched by how that tragedy, Doug, or we as a family have impacted the lives of others.

I think back to hundreds of boxes stacked in an airport hangar filled with thousands of recovered items. Considering the flames that consumed our home, how could that number have been so large? I have been reminded that many pieces of our household goods were thrown outside by the plane's initial impact. I picture that awful scene in my imagination.

Neighbors told me about how dedicated crews in hazmat suits had worked for days gathering shovels of ashes and charcoal-like debris from the site—how they had sifted the debris through large screens in pursuit of any small item that could bring comfort to the families left behind. The work was done with the upmost respect, and was performed tirelessly by people who considered it an honor to help in any way they could. I would like to tell all of them how even the smallest scraps of paper they retrieved for us brought comfort and restored memories.

3407 has a strong emotional pull on people, and they can easily become enmeshed in my web. Some I can keep securely close, but, despite my desire, I must release my grasp and set some of them free. Regardless, they all contribute to my strength and security.

After telling my friend Sheila about my web, she shared an interesting experience of hers. Her furnace had not been working properly and the repair man had come upstairs to report his findings—a spider web in one of the pipes would not allow the furnace to stay on. "Spider webs are much stronger than people realize," the repairman explained. "Sometimes they have to be cut to get through them. I had to cut yours. It was unbelievably strong. After a cold winter, the spiders simply want to be inside in a warm area."

"Your web is just another part of your strength, with you looking to be wrapped in its cocooning warmth," Shelia said. "And that, my friend, is absolutely OK." I often question my strength, but I would agree that I do need the warmth provided by others.

I have read that the word "cobweb" sometimes refers to abandoned spider webs. I do not see any possibility that I will ever abandon my web. It is true that there is danger in being caught in a web, but have you ever seen one glistening with morning dew or droplets of rain following a storm? There is beauty in that vision. There is peace.

Traditional European medical practice uses cobwebs on wounds to help healing. Perhaps that is why I continually seek to strengthen my web. I may be trapped in it, but it offers another form of personal healing and, if I look closely enough, I may capture the beauty of all the facets that came together to form it.

February 12, 2009, changed many lives, but for one man, one home, and one family on the ground, one plane could not destroy the bond that continues to unite them. It is the bond of love that provides the strength of my web.

3/15/15 (2 a.m.)

*Photo by Kateri Ewing*

# ACKNOWLEDGEMENTS

*"In friendship or in love, the two side-by-side raise hands
together to find what one cannot reach alone."*

~ *Kahlil Gibran*

So many people have extended their love and kindness to our
family since the crash of Flight 3407, and others have helped me
reach the seemingly impossible goal of writing this book.

I would be lost without my daughters, Kim, Lori, Jessica and Jill.
I am blessed to have them in my life. Thanks also to their husbands, especially at those times when they must contend with all
five Wielinski women at one time!

Thanks to my Schoenwetter and Schwab family members for
their support and love. Special thanks go to my sister Barbara
Fox and her husband, Bill. My cousin Janet Frappier has become
one of my staunch writing critics, and her comments always give
me more insight into what I write.

Thanks to the Wielinski and Schork families, who put aside their
own sorrow from the loss of a dear brother and uncle, to comfort
us. Special thanks and gratitude must go to my brother-in-law,
Billy Wielinski, who is definitely my protector.

The Clarence Central School District immediately stepped
up following the crash. They were inundated with phone calls
in those first few days, and continually provided us with support. Protecting our family's privacy was always upmost in their
minds. Special thanks go to Dr. Thomas Coseo, Dr. John Ptak,
Shelia Rivera, Laura Kelly, Rae Ann Nugent, Chris DiGadio, and
Janet Ramsey.

The Paul William Beltz law firm spent countless hours researching and presenting a successful case for us against Continental Airlines. Thanks to Phil and Anne Rimmler, and everyone at the firm who put so much time and effort into this undertaking.

My association with the Flight 3407 Foundation and Memorial Committee has allowed me to work with so many dedicated people. Special recognition goes to Lori Adams, John Leamer, Mike Powers, and Joe D'Angelo, who designed a thoughtful and fitting Long Street Memorial.

I have found an ally in *The Buffalo News*. They have supported my family and the 3407 families in the fight for airline safety. They have also provided encouragement to me in my writing endeavors. Special thanks go to Bruce Andriatch, Jerry Zremski, Joe Popiolkowski, Donn Esmonde, and James Staas.

The list of friends who are always ready to lend a helping hand, or a shoulder to cry on, is endless, but some special thanks go to Zoe May, Deb Sullivan, Sue Muchow, and Jim Maceijewski.

Dr. Lisa Keenan is my ultimate sounding board. I am thankful for her counsel, understanding, and kindness in helping me continue a healing process that will never be completely reached.

Thanks to my 3407 Family. They reached out to my family following the crash, and waited patiently for me to accept their invitation of support. I thank them for including my family in their numbers, and for introducing me to their amazing loved ones who were lost that night. Their strength and courage sustains me.

As previously mentioned, without Rick Ohler and his creative writing classes, and *USA Today*'s Erik Brady's desire to make Doug more than "one on the ground," I would never have begun the quest to write this book. I am so grateful to them.

Finally, Sallie and John Randolph, and Cathy Carey who provided the answer to my question, "How do I publish this book?" Their acceptance of me as a writer, and their guidance and support deserve immense thanks. Thanks to Leslie Taylor for her creative talents, which transformed a manuscript into a book.

My list of thanks could go on and on, and I apologize for any omissions. I have put my heart and soul into this book, and I hope my thanks have been conveyed in its pages. But please know that any act of kindness or support was, and continues to be, appreciated and etched in my heart.

# ABOUT THE AUTHOR

*The bond of love unites us, and we celebrate life surrounded by Doug's spirit.*

Karen Wielinski is a freelance writer who has lived in East Aurora, New York since 2010. Along with the love of her daughters and grandchildren, her involvement in a local writing group continues to be a source of inspiration and strength to her.

# THE DOUGLAS C. WIELINSKI
# MEMORIAL SCHOLARSHIP FUND

Doug loved to delve into history. Collecting allowed him to preserve the past, and he always loved the opportunity to share what he learned with others. He especially enjoyed bringing history to life for high school students by sharing his Viet Nam War experiences with them.

After the crash my daughter Lori said that since her dad had always loved history, it seemed only fitting that he was now a part of history.

The Douglas C. Wielinski Memorial Scholarship Fund was established in 2009 to provide assistance to students who have a genuine love of history. It is my hope that profits from the sale of *One on the Ground* will enable more students to benefit from this fund.

If you are so inclined to help in this effort, donations can also be sent to:

> The Douglas C. Wielinski Memorial Scholarship Fund
> P.O. Box 241
> East Aurora, NY 14052

Thank you for considering to honor Doug in this way.

~ Karen Wielinski

CPSIA information can be obtained
at www.ICGtesting.com
Printed in the USA
LVHW09*0537051018
592509LV00005B/16/P